How to Solve
Word Problems in Chemistry

How to Solve
Word Problems in Chemistry

David E. Goldberg

McGraw-Hill

New York   Chicago   San Francisco   Lisbon   London
Madrid   Mexico City   Milan   New Delhi
San Juan   Seoul   Singapore
Sydney   Toronto

McGraw-Hill

A Division of The McGraw·Hill Companies

1 2 3 4 5 6 7 8 9 0   DOC/DOC   0 9 8 7 6 5 4 3 2 1

ISBN 0-07-136302-5

This book was set in ITC Stone Serif by TechBooks.

Printed and bound by R. R. Donnelley & Sons Company.

This publication is designed to provide accurate and authoritative information
in regard to the subject matter covered. It is sold with the understanding that the
publisher is not engaged in rendering legal, accounting, or other professional
service. If legal advice or other expert assistance is required, the services of a
competent professional person should be sought.

> *—From a declaration of principles jointly adopted by a committee of the
> American Bar Association and a committee of publishers.*

 This book is printed on recycled, acid-free paper containing
a minimum of 50% recycled de-inked fiber.

Contents

To the Student

There may be more material presented in this book than is required in your course. Look for the material in your text to make sure that you are responsible for each subject. If necessary, ask your instructor what to concentrate on.

Cover the solutions to the Examples and try to solve them yourself. Then look at the answer given to see if you are correct. Do not merely read the solutions; you must *do* the problems to really understand the principles. Do not try to memorize chemistry. A given problem can be asked in many different ways, and you must *understand* what you are doing in order to succeed.

Key terms are presented in **boldface** type. These terms are defined in the Glossary.

Some of the Supplementary Problems are presented more than once, in slightly different forms. For example, a problem may be presented in parts, then the same problem (perhaps with different numbers) is presented as a single problem such as might be asked on an examination. These are designed to get you to be able to do complicated problems (you have already done them) one step at a time without being coached in what to do next.

Chapter 1

Introduction

1.1 Scientific Calculations

One of the principal ways science courses are distinguished from other courses is that scientists use quantitative results—the results of measurements. The results are presented with a *number* and a *unit* or combination of units. The unit is as important as the number. For example, it is very important to the mail carrier to know whether a new customer has a dog that is 5 *inches* tall or 5 *feet* tall! Always use units. Moreover, as we will see in Section 1.2, the units actually help us figure out how to solve many problems.

Chemistry involves many symbols—for elements, for variables, for constants, for units. We try to have a different symbol for each one of these, but there are more things to represent than different letters. It is extremely important to use the standard symbol for each of the items to be represented. For example, the symbol Co represents cobalt, but CO represents carbon monoxide. The capitalization is critical. As another example, 1 mg (milligram) is 1-billionth the mass of 1 Mg (megagram), as introduced in Section 2.1. Do not get confused; we must take the tiny amount of extra time to do things correctly from the beginning of our study of chemistry.

Chemists (and chemistry teachers) did not invent new ways to do calculations to make their lives more difficult. When we learn a new subject, it might seem hard at first, but remember that it is presented to enable us to do more things or to do the things we already know more easily.

Don't make the mistake of falling behind. Keep up with the work if at all possible. Science builds on itself. Missing the background material makes it more difficult to understand the present material, especially to learn without an instructor. Try to attend every class, and before class skim the material to be covered to get an idea what it is about. Use this book and other study aids to learn missing material without a teacher.

When a new principle is taught, be sure to understand where it applies. There is no use knowing something and applying it to the wrong thing. For example, we will learn that seven elements are diatomic *when they are uncombined* with other elements. It is a mistake to think that hydrogen must be written H_2 in all of its *compounds*. The equation $M_1V_1 = M_2V_2$ is perfectly fine for dilution problems, but don't use it for titration problems with a balanced equation for reagents not in a 1:1 mole ratio (Chapter 6).

How to Approach a Word Problem

Working word problems requires understanding the principles involved and being able to apply them to the case at hand. The best way to ensure success is to practice, practice, practice.

To do a word problem, follow these steps:

1. Read the problem carefully.
2. List all the values given, complete with units. Some problems have values to be determined elsewhere, as from tables of data or the periodic table (which is always supplied when needed). Make a note that these values have to be obtained, or actually write down these values.
3. Look for implied relationships. For example, if a binary compound of A and B is 25% by mass element A, there is (25 g A)/(100 g total) by definition. In addition, there is (75 g B)/(100 g total) and also there is (25 g A)/(75 g B).
4. Write down the quantity to be found, complete with units.
5. Think of the relationships (equations, rules, etc.) that we know which might connect the values given and desired. Think how the data can be manipulated so that the proper units result for the answer.
6. Solve the problem using the correct relationship. (If one equation won't work, try a different equation.)
7. Check the answer to see that it is reasonable. Some problems have reasonable checks built in, like the percent composition problems in Section 4.3. If the percentages don't add up to 100%, there is a mistake somewhere. For others, we can use the answer to calculate one of the original values, as in empirical formula problems (Section 4.4). Still others require that we know the range of possibilities for our answer. For example, if we get a molarity of 10,000 M (Section 6.1) we know there is a mistake, because 10,000 moles of anything cannot fit into a liter. We cannot get an atomic mass of less than 1 amu or more than a couple of hundred

amu; they don't come that way. For most problems, just consider if the answer is about the right size.

How to Approach a Complicated-Looking Problem

If a problem seems too difficult to see how to do the whole thing, do as much as possible. Perhaps the partial answer will lead to further steps that will end in a complete solution. Consider the following fable: A boy scout troop went on an all-day excursion. The bus stopped at the parking lot, and the troop marched up the "mountain" past the rock that looked like a lion, down the other side, waded across the shallow stream, and walked up the next hill past the broken-off tree. They ran down the other side to the play area and picnic grounds. They spent the morning playing, had lunch, took a swim in the pond, and undertook numerous other activities. When it was time to head back, the troop leader did not remember how to get back. What to do? He did not panic, especially where the boys could see him. He knew that he could see the bus from the top of some peak, but where was it? He looked around and saw the broken-off tree. He marched his troop up the hill, from where he saw the small stream and the "lion" rock. Down the hill and up the "mountain" and from there he saw the bus in the parking lot. *No one knew that he had not known all along how to get back.* What is the moral to this fable? If we can't see our way through to the end of a chemistry problem, at least we will do as much as we can. The answer to the first part might suggest what to do next. Also, we can think about what we need for the final answer. If we know what we need, that might give us a clue as to what to calculate next. (At least, a partial answer might get some credit and some feeling of accomplishment.)

Here is a problem from the world outside chemistry: "A hunter aims his rifle due south directly at a bear. The bear moves 30 feet due east. The hunter fires his rifle due south and kills the bear. What color is the bear?" Don't assume that this puzzle cannot be logically solved. Let's do what we can do. The original direction of aim and the final direction are both due south, but the bear moved. The hunter may be standing directly on the north pole, so *every* horizontal direction is due south. Therefore, the bear is a polar bear, and is white. (The hunter may also be standing very near the south pole, so that the bear's path took it in a complete circle, and the hunter fired without moving his rifle. In this case also, the bear must be a polar bear.)

We must try to *understand* the material as we progress. Memorizing specifics instead of understanding principles might enable us to pass one exam, but it won't get us to the point to be able to understand the next course. There are enough details in chemistry that we must memorize. Besides, there are many problems that sound alike but are completely different, and many that sound different but are really the same.

Sometimes it helps to assume a value to work with, especially with intensive properties such as concentrations. We will encounter problems of this type later, for example in molality to mole fraction conversions (Section 6.4).

To remember the value of a constant in an equation, we often can use the equation with known values and solve for the constant. [For example, to get the value for the ideal gas law constant (Section 7.2), put the values 1.00 mol sample of gas at STP with a volume of 22.4 L into the ideal gas law equation.] We can then use that constant in the problem we are trying to solve.

Designation of Variables

In algebra, unknowns are represented by letters such as x, y, and z. In science we could also use such variables, but we find it much easier to use letters that remind us what the letter stands for. For example, we use V for an unknown volume and m for an unknown mass. We then can write an equation for density, d, in terms of mass and volume as $d = m/V$. We could have written $x = y/z$ to represent the relationship among mass, volume, and density, but then we would have to remember what x stands for, and so on. We solve these equations in the same way that we solve algebraic equations (and we don't often use more than simple algebra). One problem with the use of letters to identify the type of unknown that our variable represents is that we have more types of unknowns than letters. We attempt to expand our list of symbols in the following ways:

Method	**Example**
1. By using capital letters for one purpose and lowercase letters for another.	T for absolute temperature and t for Celsius temperature
2. By using *italic* symbols for one purpose and Roman symbols for another.	m for mass and m for meter
3. By using different subscripts to distinguish between variables of the same kind.	V_1 for one volume and V_2 for a second
4. By using combinations of letters.	MM for molar mass
5. By using Greek letters for some variables.	μ (Greek mu) for micro-

Each such symbol may be treated like an ordinary algebraic variable.

1.2 Dimensional Analysis

An extremely useful tool for scientific calculations (for everyday calculations too) is **dimensional analysis**, also called the **factor label method**. This system enables us to convert from a quantity in one set of units to the same quantity in another set, or from a quantity of one thing to an equivalent quantity of another. For example, if we have $2.00 or 200 cents, we have the same amount of money. We can change from one of these to the other with a factor—a ratio—of 100 cents divided by 1.00 dollar, or the reciprocal of that ratio.

EXAMPLE 1   Convert 2.25 dollars to cents using dimensional analysis.

Solution

$$2.25 \; \text{dollars} \left(\frac{100 \text{ cents}}{1 \text{ dollar}} \right) = 225 \text{ cents}$$

The method starts by putting down the quantity given, *complete with its unit*, and multiplying it by a ratio (the factor) that has *the given unit in its denominator and the unit desired in its numerator*. We multiply all the numbers in the numerator and divide by each of the numbers in the denominator. In this example, the given quantity was 2.25 dollars, and the ratio had dollars in the denominator. In this method, it does not matter if the unit is singular (dollar) or plural (dollars)—they cancel anyway. (In fact, we use the same abbreviations for singular and plural, and often do not know whether our answer will be greater than one or not.) The units are treated like algebraic variables (x, y, and so forth); a unit divided by the same unit cancels out. This method tells us to multiply dollars by 100 to convert to cents. The method is presented here with dollars and cents to get us familiar with the system using conversions we already know.   □

We can use the reciprocal of that factor to convert cents to dollars.

EXAMPLE 2   Convert 1535 cents to dollars.

Solution   Again we put down the quantity given, and this time multiply it by a ratio with cents in the denominator:

$$1535 \; \text{cents} \left(\frac{1 \text{ dollar}}{100 \text{ cents}} \right) = 15.35 \text{ dollars}$$

We see that the conversion factor used here is the inverse of the one used in Example 1. In each case, we used the one we needed to convert from the unit that we *had* to the one that we *wanted*. □

We can use more than one factor to do conversions that are a little more complicated.

EXAMPLE 3   Change 1.660 hours to seconds.

Solution   We know that there are exactly 60 minutes in an hour, and exactly 60 seconds in each minute:

$$1.660 \text{ hours} \left(\frac{60 \text{ minutes}}{1 \text{ hour}} \right) = 99.60 \text{ minutes}$$

$$99.60 \text{ minutes} \left(\frac{60 \text{ seconds}}{1 \text{ minute}} \right) = 5976 \text{ seconds}$$

Alternatively, we can do both operations without solving for the intermediate answer in minutes:

$$1.660 \text{ hours} \left(\frac{60 \text{ minutes}}{1 \text{ hour}} \right) \left(\frac{60 \text{ seconds}}{1 \text{ minute}} \right) = 5976 \text{ seconds}$$

(If we know that there are 3600 seconds in an hour, we do not need two factors, but there will be many problems in chemistry later in this book in which more than one factor is needed, so it is well that we learned how to handle more than one factor here.)   □

Working dimensional analysis problems with familiar problems will enable us to use the methods with the less familiar problems still to come. We can't make the mistake of not learning the method here because we don't need it yet.

We can use percentages as factors in working with dimensional analysis. For example if an elementary school class is 40% girls and 60% boys, we can tell how many children are in a class with 48 boys:

$$48 \text{ boys} \left(\frac{100 \text{ children}}{60 \text{ boys}} \right) = 80 \text{ children}$$

In chemistry, if a compound of elements A and B is 25% by mass element A, there is (25 g A)/(100 g total) by definition. But also, there is (75 g B)/(100 g total) and also there is (25 g A)/(75 g B).

EXAMPLE 4   Calculate the number of people in an audience if 45 people vote. The percentage of voters is 75%.

Solution

$$45 \text{ voters} \left(\frac{100 \text{ people total}}{75 \text{ voters}} \right) = 60 \text{ people} \qquad \square$$

It is also possible to use the factor label method to convert from one ratio to an equivalent ratio, using one factor at a time.

EXAMPLE 5   Convert the speed of a car going 45.0 miles per hour into its speed in feet per second.

Solution   The word *per* means *divided by.* Thus 45.0 miles per hour is 45.0 miles divided by 1 hour.

$$\frac{45.0 \text{ miles}}{1 \text{ hour}} \left(\frac{5280 \text{ feet}}{1 \text{ mile}} \right) \left(\frac{1 \text{ hour}}{60 \text{ minutes}} \right) \left(\frac{1 \text{ minute}}{60 \text{ seconds}} \right)$$

$$= \frac{66.0 \text{ feet}}{1 \text{ second}} = 66.0 \text{ feet/second}$$

Here we needed three factors to convert our ratio to an equivalent ratio with different units. (Don't worry about not remembering that there are 5280 feet in 1 mile. We don't use English system measurements much at all in science, although they are used some in engineering.) $\square$

We will use dimensional analysis throughout this book, and indeed we will use it throughout our chemistry careers.

1.3 The Scientific Calculator

A scientific calculator can save countless hours of calculation time, and (if it is permitted) valuable minutes on examinations. However, it is critical that we know how to use the calculator without thinking about it too much while we are thinking about the chemistry problems! Read the instruction booklet about how the calculator works. We don't have to read about every function; we will learn about those that we will use first, delay those that we will use only later, and ignore those that we will never use. Chemistry requires principally the arithmetic operations keys ($\boxed{+}$, $\boxed{-}$, $\boxed{\times}$, $\boxed{\div}$), $\boxed{\text{EE}}$ or $\boxed{\text{EXP}}$, $\boxed{\text{FLO}}$, $\boxed{\text{SCI}}$, the reciprocal key $\boxed{1/x}$, $\boxed{x^2}$, $\boxed{\sqrt{x}}$, $\boxed{x^3}$, $\boxed{\sqrt[3]{x}}$, $\boxed{\text{LOG}}$, the natural logarithm key $\boxed{\text{LN}}$, the antilogarithm key $\boxed{10^x}$, the natural antilogarithm key $\boxed{e^x}$, and perhaps $\boxed{y^x}$. Begin with the first of these and add the others later (but before we use them in chemistry class). We must practice with each operation using simple numbers until we are sure that we know how the calculator works. For example, we know that $\frac{12}{12} = 1$, so enter the following calculation on the calculator to see what it gives:

$$\frac{4 \times 3}{6 \times 2}$$

If the calculator displays 1, the problem has been done correctly and the calculator is suitable for this course. If it displays 4, read the subsection on precedence rules below.

In general, there are more functions on the calculator than keys. There is a special key, called variously $\boxed{2^{nd}}$, $\boxed{2^{nd} F}$, $\boxed{SHIFT}$, or $\boxed{ALT}$ depending on the model calculator. In addition on some calculators, there is a key labeled $\boxed{MODE}$ that acts similarly. Somewhat like the SHIFT key on a typewriter, pressing this key first makes the next key pressed perform a different operation than it normally would. (Some do exactly the opposite operation—antilogarithm instead of logarithm, for example.)

The following keys are among those that operate immediately on whatever value is displayed: $\boxed{FLO}$, $\boxed{SCI}$, $\boxed{1/x}$, $\boxed{x^2}$, $\boxed{\sqrt{x}}$, $\boxed{x^3}$, $\boxed{\sqrt[3]{x}}$, $\boxed{LOG}$, $\boxed{LN}$, $\boxed{10^x}$, and $\boxed{e^x}$. We do not need to press the $\boxed{=}$ key to get the desired value. For example, if 2 is in the display and we push the $\boxed{x^2}$ key *twice*, we get 16 as an answer. The first press yielded 4, and the second squared that value.

Precedence Rules

In calculations that involve more than one operation to be performed, we must know which one to do first. The order is called the order of **precedence**. For example, in algebra, in the absence of any other indication, we always multiply or divide before we add or subtract. [An exception states that in a division using a *built-up fraction*, whatever operation(s) is(are) in the numerator and/or in the denominator is(are) done *before* the division. Thus

$$\frac{2+3}{1+9}$$

has a value of 0.5, because both additions are done before the division. (Note the difference from $2 + 3/1 + 9$, which follows the normal precedence rules.) Multiplication and division have higher

Table 1-1   Order of Precedence

Highest
Parentheses
Exponentiation or unary minus
Multiplication or division
Addition or subtraction
Lowest

precedence than do addition or subtraction. The orders of precedence are presented in Table 1-1.

Operations of equal precedence are done from left to right except for exponentiation and unary minus, which are done from right to left. (Unary minus is a minus sign that denotes a negative number rather than a subtraction.)

EXAMPLE 6   Calculate each answer on the calculator:

(a) $2 + 3 \times 4 - 5$
(b) ab/cd, where $a = 6$, $b = 3$, $c = 2$, and $d = 4$
(c) 2^{x^2} with $x = 3$
(d) -3^2
(e) $(-3)^2$

   Solution

(a) The answer displayed is 9, corresponding to $2 + 12 - 5$. (The multiplication is done first.)
(b) The answer displayed is 2.25, corresponding to $\frac{18}{8}$. If the answer displayed was 36, the 9 in the display was *multiplied* by the 4. Because the calculator has a different precedence rule for division and multiplication than we follow in the algebraic expression ab/cd, where both multiplications are done first, we must divide the 18 by 2 and then *divide* that answer by 4. Alternatively, we may place parentheses around the (2×4).

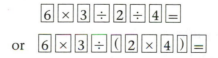

(c) 512. This answer is equivalent to 2^9 rather than 8^2 since exponentiation is done right to left.
(d) -9. The squaring is done on the 3, not on -3, because exponentiation and unary minus are done right to left.

(*e*) +9. The parentheses instruct the calculator to square the negative number. □

The EE or EXP Key

To enter an exponential number (see Section 2.3) into the calculator, enter the coefficient and then press the EE or EXP key (whichever is on the calculator) followed by the exponent. The EE or EXP key represents "times 10 to the power." *Do not press the multiply key or the* 1 *and* 0 *keys!* The display of exponential numbers on the calculator reserves the last three columns for the exponent—a space or a minus sign followed by two digits. (Some calculators have the exponent raised and in smaller numbers.) Thus the following exponential numbers are shown in the display as follows:

Number	Display
4×10^3	4 03
4×10^{-3}	4 − 03
-4×10^3	−4 03
-4×10^{-3}	−4 − 03

EXAMPLE 7 (*a*) How do we enter 1.66×10^5 into the calculator? (*b*) What does the display show?

Solution

(*a*) Enter 1 . 6 6 EE or EXP 5. If we mistakenly enter 1 . 6 6 × 1 0 EE or EXP 5 we will get the equivalent of $1.66 \times 10 \times 10^5$.

(*b*) 1.66   05 □

The Change Sign Key

The change sign key +/− is used to convert a positive number to a negative number or vice versa. Do not use the subtract key to try to change the sign of a value in the display! For exponential numbers, to change the sign of the coefficient, press the change sign key *before* the EE or EXP key. To change the sign of the exponent, press the change sign key *after* the EE or EXP key.

The Reciprocal Key

This key takes the reciprocal of whatever is in the display. It is not absolutely essential, but it can save storing a value in memory. For example, to solve $a/(b+c)$, if we have the value for $b+c$ in the display, we merely press the $\boxed{1/x}$ key and then *multiply* the result by a. [The reciprocal of $(b + c)$ is $1/(b + c)$, which then is multiplied by a.]

The Logarithm Keys

Four functions are available on scientific calculators to take common logarithms $\boxed{\text{LOG}}$, natural logarithms $\boxed{\text{LN}}$, common antilogarithms $\boxed{10^x}$, and natural antilogarithms $\boxed{e^x}$. Each key operates immediately on the value on display. The common logarithm is the exponent of the power of 10 that is equal to a number. For example, the logarithm of 2 is 0.30103 because $10^{0.30103}$ is equal to 2. The natural logarithm is the exponent of the power of e that is equal to a number: $\ln 2 = 0.69317$. (The number e is the base of natural growth.) The antilogarithms reverse the process; they give the value of 10 or e raised to that power. For example, antilogarithm $2 = 100$ because $10^2 = 100$. Natural logarithms are as easy to use on the calculator as common logarithms, and are often more intimately connected to a chemistry problem.

Supplementary Problems

1. There were 20.0% boys and 27.5% girls in a certain class. The rest of the class was made up of adults. One day, 6 boys and 2 adults were absent, and only 2 boys attended. How many adults attended?

2. Calculate the number of hours in 7992 seconds.

3. If we spent $1000 per day, how many years would it take us to spend (a) 1.00 million dollars? (b) 1.00 billion dollars?

4. If a bank advertises a special discount of 25% on their regular 16% rate for a personal loan, what is the rate that they will actually charge?

5. Use the calculator to compute the value of each of the following expressions:

    (a) $5 \times 7 - 7 \times 6$ (b) $\dfrac{6 \times 7}{4 \times 14}$ (c) $3x^2$ where $x = 5$

    (d) $5.11 \times 7.20 - 7.13 \times 6.00$ (e) $\dfrac{6.52 \times 7.11}{4.92 \times 14.1}$

    (f) $3.02x^2$ where $x = 5.15$

6. Use the calculator to compute the value of each of the following expressions:

    (a) $5.00 \times 10^{14} - 4.30 \times 10^{15}$ (b) $5.00 \times 10^{14} \div 4.30 \times 10^{15}$
    (c) $5.00 \times 10^{-14} - 4.30 \times 10^{-15}$ (d) $(96,500)/(6.02 \times 10^{23})$

7. Determine the value of x in each of the following:
   (a) $\log x = 2.0000$ (b) $x = \log(2.95 \times 10^4)$
   (c) $\ln x = 2.0000$ (d) $x = \ln(2.95 \times 10^4)$
8. Determine the value of (a) $1/2.65$ (b) $(7.43)^2$ (c) $10^{0.699}$
   (d) antilogarithm of 3.09
9. Show the calculator display in floating-point format for the logarithm of each of the following numbers and state which digits in the answers are the significant digits:
   (a) 2.59×10^{-1} (b) 2.59×10^{-4}
   (c) 2.59×10^{-10} (d) 2.59×10^{-14}

Solutions to Supplementary Problems

1. In a complicated problem, be sure to label the work to know exactly what each term means. In this problem, it is straightforward to determine that 52.5% of the class were adults and 8 class members were boys. Therefore the number of adults enrolled was

   $$8 \text{ boys} \left(\frac{100 \text{ people}}{20.0 \text{ boys}} \right) \left(\frac{52.5 \text{ adults enrolled}}{100 \text{ people}} \right) = 21 \text{ adults enrolled}$$

   Since 2 adults were absent, 19 attended.
   Alternatively, we could have determined:

   $$8 \text{ boys enrolled} \left(\frac{52.5 \text{ adults enrolled (per hundred)}}{20.0 \text{ boys enrolled (per hundred)}} \right)$$
   $$= 21 \text{ adults enrolled}$$

   Probably, few of us knew how to do this entire problem before starting any calculations at all.

2. $7992 \text{ seconds} \left(\frac{1 \text{ minute}}{60 \text{ seconds}} \right) \left(\frac{1 \text{ hour}}{60 \text{ minutes}} \right) = 2.220 \text{ hours}$

3. (a) $1,000,000 \text{ dollars} \left(\frac{1 \text{ day}}{1000 \text{ dollars}} \right) \left(\frac{1 \text{ year}}{365 \text{ days}} \right) = 2.74 \text{ years}$

   (b) $1,000,000,000 \text{ dollars} \left(\frac{1 \text{ day}}{1000 \text{ dollars}} \right) \left(\frac{1 \text{ year}}{365 \text{ days}} \right)$
   $$= 2740 \text{ years} = 2.74 \times 10^3 \text{ years}$$

4. The 16% is 16% of the amount of the *loan*; the 25% is 25% of the amount of the *interest*. (We must be sure to label the work so that we know exactly what each term means.)

12

Thus they will be charging 75% of their regular rate:

$$\frac{16 \text{ dollars (regular)}}{100 \text{ dollars of loan}} \left(\frac{75 \text{ dollars (special)}}{100 \text{ dollars (regular)}} \right)$$

$$= \frac{12 \text{ dollars (special)}}{100 \text{ dollars of loan}} = 12\%$$

5. (a) -7 (b) 0.75   (c) 75
   (d) -6.0 (The subtraction left only two significant digits.)
   (e) 0.668 [Not too different from answer (b) because the values were not too different.]
   (f) 80.1 [Not too different from answer (c) because the values were not too different.]
6. (a) -3.80×10^{15} (Watch the minus sign and the significant digits.)
   (b) 0.116   (c) 4.57×10^{-14} (Note that -14 is larger than -15.)
   (d) 1.60×10^{-19} (We never touched the multiply key!)
7. (a) 100.0   (b) 4.470   (c) 7.389   (d) 10.292
8. Each model calculator is different, so read the instruction booklet if the instructions here are not applicable.
   (a) 0.377 (Use the $\boxed{1/x}$ key.)
   (b) 55.2 (Use the $\boxed{x^2}$ key or another method on a more powerful calculator.)
   (c) 5.00 (Use the $\boxed{2^{nd} \text{ F}}$ and $\boxed{\text{LOG}}$ keys.)
   (d) 1.2×10^3 (Use the $\boxed{2^{nd} \text{ F}}$ and $\boxed{\text{LOG}}$ keys; use only two significant digits, since the 3 shows the magnitude of this number.)
9. Each model calculator is different, so the results may be slightly different from these.
   (a) -0.586700236 (b) -3.586700236 (c) -9.586700236
   (d) -13.58670024
   The only difference among the numbers given are the powers of 10. The only difference in the logarithms are the integer portions [except for a round-off in part (d)]. The *characteristic* (integer portion) of the logarithm shows only the magnitude of the original number, and the first three digits of the *mantissa* (the decimal fractional part) are the significant digits (reflecting the three significant digits in the numbers given). We should report the values
   (a) -0.587 (b) -3.587 (c) -9.587 (d) -13.587

Chapter 2

Measurement

2.1 Metric System Calculations

The **metric system** along with its newer counterpart, the **SI (system internationale)** system of measurement, was designed to make our measurements and our calculations as easy as possible. Once we have learned it, it is much easier to use than the English system, as we will see later. It is possible to learn more than 90% of the metric system needed in a beginning chemistry course using only the seven terms and their abbreviations in Table 2-1. The units will be introduced in the three following subsections. The prefixes will also be introduced there, but will be intensively used in the metric conversion subsection. Please note carefully the abbreviations, and use the proper one for each term. Note that the abbreviation for meter and for milli- are both the same—m. It is easy to tell the difference because milli- is a prefix, so an m before another letter means milli-. If the m is not before another letter, it means meter. Please note that of the abbreviations in Table 2-1, only the L for liter is capitalized. We must use the proper capitalization from the start or we will mix ourselves up. For example, capital M stands for another quantity (molarity) or another prefix (mega-).

Length or Distance

The unit of length or distance in the metric system is the **meter**. The meter was originally defined as 1 ten-millionth of the distance from the north pole to the equator through Paris, France. That is a rather difficult measurement to make, so later the meter was defined as the distance between two scratches in a special bar kept in a vault in Sevres, France. There is an even later definition, but we will be satisfied that it is the distance between those two

Table 2-1 Most Important Metric Terms and Abbreviations

Unit	Abbreviation	Prefix	Abbreviation
meter	m	kilo-	k
gram	g	deci-	d
liter	L	centi-	c
		milli-	m

scratches. The symbol for the meter is m. The meter is about 10% longer than a yard, but that statement is merely to give us some idea of its length. It is not too important to convert from meters to yards (unless instructed otherwise).

The meter can be divided into subunits (Fig. 2-1), and multiples of the meter can be defined. The metric system uses the same prefixes to define the subunits and multiples for the meter as it does for all its other units, which is a great advantage. The most important prefixes for us to learn in the metric system are presented in Table 2-2, along with their meanings.

The only real use that we will make of the prefix deci- is with volume measurements, where a cubic decimeter is a useful sized volume. We rarely use the prefix centi- except with meters.

Mass

The *unit* of mass is the **gram**. However, the gram is such a small unit, about the mass of a paper clip, that both SI and the United States Congress have designated as the **standard** of mass the

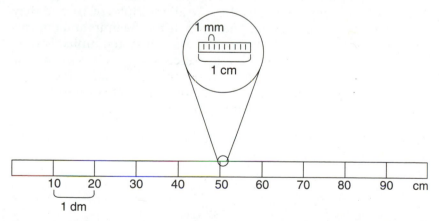

Fig. 2-1 The meter is divided into 10 dm, each of which is divided into 10 cm, each of which is divided into 10 mm.

Table 2-2 Metric Prefixes*

Prefix	Symbol	Meaning	Example
mega-	M-	1,000,000	$1\,Mg = 1 \times 10^{6}\,g$
kilo-	k-	1000	$1\,km = 1000\,m$
deci-	d-	0.1	$1\,dm = 0.1\,m$
centi-	c-	0.01	$1\,cm = 0.01\,m$
milli-	m-	0.001	$1\,mm = 0.001\,m$
micro-	μ-	0.000001	$1\,\mu m = 0.000001\,m$
nano-	n-	0.000000001	$1\,ng = 1 \times 10^{-9}\,g$
pico-	p-	1×10^{-12}	$1\,pm = 1 \times 10^{-12}\,m$

*The prefixes in **boldfaced** type are the most important for us to learn first.

kilogram—1000 grams. The gram is the unit—the name that the prefixes are added to—and the kilogram is the mass against which all other masses are compared. (A certain metal bar in Sevres, France, is the worldwide standard of mass.)

The same prefixes are used with mass as with distance, and they have the same meanings. That is one facet that makes the metric system so easy. In the English system, the subdivisions of a yard are a foot—one-third of a yard—and an inch—one-thirty-sixth of a yard. The subdivision of an Avoirdupois pound is an ounce, one-sixteenth of a pound. The subdivision of a Troy pound is an ounce, one-twelfth of that pound. (Gold and silver are measured in Troy ounces.) Each type of measurement has a different subdivision, and none is a multiple of 10. The metric system uses the same prefixes for all types of measurements, they are all multiples of 10, and they always mean the same thing. The symbols for the units and prefixes are easier to learn than those for the English system units. For example, pound is abbreviated lb and ounce is oz, whereas the metric prefixes are almost always closely related to their names. It is easier to convert metric measurements because the prefixes mean some multiple of 10 times the fundamental unit.

EXAMPLE I   (*a*) Convert 1.275 miles to feet. (*b*) Convert 1.275 km to meters.

Solution

(*a*) 1.275 miles $\left(\dfrac{5280\,feet}{1\,mile} \right) = 6732$ feet

(*b*) 1.275 km $\left(\dfrac{1000\,m}{1\,km} \right) = 1275$ m

The first calculation requires pencil and paper or a calculator; the second can be done in our heads by moving the decimal point three places to the right. □

Volume

The metric unit of volume is the **liter**, abbreviated L, originally defined as the volume of a cube 1 dm on each edge. The SI unit of volume is the **cubic meter**, m^3. That volume is too large for ordinary laboratory work, so smaller related units are used—the cubic decimeter (equal to a liter), or the cubic centimeter (equal to a milliliter). A comparison of these units is presented in Table 2-3.

Some textbooks use the classical metric unit, the liter, and its related volumes; others use the SI unit, cubic meters, and its related volumes. We must know both. For simplicity, after this chapter, we will use liters (L) in this book rather than cubic decimeters, because almost everyone is familiar with liters and its subdivisions from everyday use. (How much does a 2-liter bottle of cola cost?)

Figure 2-2 shows the relationships among the various units of volume. Please note that to convert from *cubic* meters to *cubic* centimeters does not involve a factor of 100, but $(100)^3$.

Metric Conversions

We can use dimensional analysis to convert a measurement from one metric unit to another. We recognize that by definition 1 dollar = 100 cents, and also that 1 cent = 0.01 dollar. We can use a factor corresponding to either of those equalities. Note that *cent* is related to *centi-*, the metric prefix for 0.01. We can simply substitute 0.01 for the c of cm, 0.001 for the m of mm, and 1000 for the k of km.

EXAMPLE 2   Convert 1.49 m to (*a*) km. (*b*) cm. (*c*) mm.

Solution

(*a*) $1.49 \, \text{m} \left(\dfrac{1 \, \text{km}}{1000 \, \text{m}} \right) = 0.00149 \, \text{km}$ (substitute 1000 for the k)

Table 2-3   **Comparison of Classical Metric and SI Units of Volume**

SI	Metric	Equivalent
$1 \, m^3$	1 kL	1000 L
$1 \, dm^3$	1 L	1 L
$1 \, cm^3$	1 mL	0.001 L
$1 \, mm^3$	$1 \, \mu L$	0.000001 L

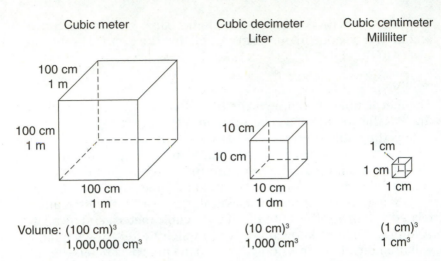

Cubic meter   Cubic decimeter   Cubic centimeter
Liter   Milliliter

100 cm
1 m

100 cm
1 m

100 cm
1 m

10 cm

10 cm

10 cm
1 dm

1 cm

1 cm
1 cm

Volume: $(100\text{ cm})^3$ $(10\text{ cm})^3$ $(1\text{ cm})^3$
1,000,000 cm³   1,000 cm³   1 cm³

Fig. 2-2 Relationships of SI and Metric Units of Volume. (Not drawn to scale.)

(b) $1.49\text{ m}\left(\dfrac{1\text{ cm}}{0.01\text{ m}}\right) = 149\text{ cm}$ (substitute 0.01 for the c)

(c) $1.49\text{ m}\left(\dfrac{1\text{ mm}}{0.001\text{ m}}\right) = 1490\text{ mm}$ (substitute 0.001 for the first m) □

EXAMPLE 3   Convert 2.50 m^3 to cubic centimeters.

Solution

$$2.50\text{ m}^3\left(\frac{1,000,000\text{ cm}^3}{1\text{ m}^3}\right) = 2,500,000\text{ cm}^3 = 2.50 \times 10^6\text{ cm}^3$$

Note that 1 cubic meter is equal to 1 million cubic centimeters! (See Fig. 2-2.) □

EXAMPLE 4   Convert 2.50 m^3 to liters.

Solution   We know that 1 cubic meter is equal to 1000 cubic decimeters (Fig. 2-2) and that it is also 1000 L.

$$2.50\text{ m}^3\left(\frac{1000\text{ L}}{1\text{ m}^3}\right) = 2500\text{ L}$$ □

Units in Scientific Calculations

When arithmetic operations are done with measurements, some-times the units must be adjusted. (1) In addition or subtraction problems, the units of the measurements must be the same. For example, to add 2.00 m and 10.0 cm, we must change one of the values to the units of the other: 200 cm + 10.0 cm, is one possibility. (2) In multiplication or division of lengths, the square of lengths, and/or the cube of lengths, the length units must be the same. For example, to divide $2 \, cm^3$ by a length, the length must be in cen-timeters. To multiply 2.00 m and 10.0 cm, again we should change one to the units of the other: 200 cm $\times$ 10.0 cm, is one possibility. (3) Otherwise, in multiplication or division, the units do not have to be the same. To divide 40.0 g by $23.0 \, cm^3$, we do not have to change any units because grams is not a unit of length.

2.2 Significant Digits

No measurement can be made perfectly. Every measuring instru-ment has a limit as to how precisely it can be read. For example, we would never try to measure the length of our shadow with an automobile odometer (mileage indicator). Scientists attempt to read every instrument to one-tenth the smallest scale division. Thus a meter stick with 1000 division marks (that is, 100 centimeters, with each centimeter divided into 10 parts) can be estimated to 0.1 mm. When a scientist reports the results of the measurement, the scien-tist uses as many digits as necessary to indicate how precisely the measurement was made. The scientist might report 0.0531 m to re-port a length. We have to recognize which of these digits record the precision of the measurement, which are present *only to specify the magnitude of the answer*, and which do both. If the digit helps report the precision, it is called a **significant digit** or a **significant figure**. The word *significant* in this sense does not mean *important*; it means *having to do with precision*! Every digit serves to report either the magnitude or the precision of the measurement, or both. If the digit reports the magnitude only, it is nonsignificant.

Significant Digits in Reported Values

First we must learn to recognize which digits in a properly reported number are significant. They include all nonzero digits. Zeros are determined to be significant or not according to the following rules:

1. All zeros to the right of all other digits *and* to the right of the decimal point are significant. For example, in 1.200 cm, the zeros are significant.

2. All zeros between significant digits are significant. For example, in 1.003 cm, the zeros are significant.
3. All zeros to the left of *all* other digits are not significant. For example, in 0.022 cm, the zeros are not significant.
4. All zeros to the right of all other digits *in an integer* cannot be determined merely by inspection to be significant or not. For example, in 1200 cm, the zeros are undetermined without further information. (Some texts assume that these zeros are not significant, and they add a decimal point at the end to signify that *all* the trailing zeros are significant.)

EXAMPLE 5   Underline the significant digits in each of the following measurements, and place a question mark below each digit that is undetermined.

    (*a*) 0.0220 m   (*b*) 10.4 kg   (*c*) 12.0 L   (*d*) 100 cm

    Solution   (*a*) 0.0<u>220</u> m   (*b*) <u>10.4</u> kg   (*c*) <u>12.0</u> L
(*d*) <u>100</u> cm
In (*a*), the zero to the right of the second 2 is right of all other digits and the decimal point, and is significant (rule 1), but the zeros to the left of the first 2 are not (rule 3). In (*b*), the zero between the 1 and 4 is significant (rule 2). In (*c*), the zero to the right of the 2 and the decimal point is significant (rule 1). In (*d*), the zeros to the right of the other digits in an integer cannot be determined to be significant or not. See Example 7 in the next subsection. ☐

Significant Digits in Calculations

Warning: Electronic calculators do not consider the rules of significant digits. If they give the proper numbers of significant digits, it is just by chance.

    There are two different rules for significant digits in an answer determined by calculation. In multiplication and/or division, the *number* of significant digits in the answer is the number of significant digits in the least precise measurement in the calculation (the measurement with the fewest significant digits). In addition and/or subtraction, the *number* of significant digits in the measurements is not the deciding factor but their *positions* are critical. We cannot keep any digit in the final answer that is farther to the right than the digit least far to the right in any of the values added or subtracted.

EXAMPLE 6 Determine the answer in each of the following to the proper number of significant digits: (*a*) 1.20 cm × 3.52 cm (*b*) 5.92 cm + 13.921 cm (*c*) (12.95 g − 11.42 g)/(1.866 mL)

Solution

(*a*) The calculator gives the answer 4.224 cm², but because there are only three significant digits in each factor, we must limit the answer to three significant digits: 4.22 cm².

(*b*)   5.92 cm
     + 13.921 cm
       19.841 cm → 19.84 cm

The 2 in 5.92 was an estimated value, and the 4 in the answer thus is an estimated value. The digit after that represents an estimated 1 in the second measurement added to a completely unknown value in the first, and thus is completely unknown.

(*c*) (12.95 g − 11.42 g)/(1.866 mL) = 0.820 g/mL

Subtracting the values in the numerator of this fraction yields an answer of 1.53 g, a value with three significant digits. Dividing this value by the measurement in the denominator yields an answer with only three significant digits: 0.820 g/mL. Despite the fact that each measurement was done to four significant digits, the difference between two almost equal values has fewer significant digits, and thus so does our answer.   □

The number of significant digits in the answer is determined by the numbers in our *measurements*, not in *defined values* like the number of millimeters in a meter.

EXAMPLE 7   (*a*) How many significant digits are present in each of the following measurements? 1.2 m, 1.20 m, 1.200 m. (*b*) Convert each of those measurements to millimeters, and determine the number of significant digits in each answer. Can we tell the number of significant digits in each answer just by looking at the result or from the value from which it was calculated?

Solution

(*a*) Two, three, and four, respectively.

(*b*) $1.2 \, \text{m} \left(\dfrac{1 \, \text{mm}}{0.001 \, \text{m}} \right) = 1200 \, \text{mm}$ $1.20 \, \text{m} \left(\dfrac{1 \, \text{mm}}{0.001 \, \text{m}} \right) = 1200 \, \text{mm}$

$1.200 \, \text{m} \left(\dfrac{1 \, \text{mm}}{0.001 \, \text{m}} \right) = 1200 \, \text{mm}$

Multiplying measurements by defined conversion factors does not change the precision with which they were made. The values still have two, three, and four significant digits, respectively, *but they all look the same*. The only way we can tell is by knowing where they came from. Just by looking at these values we cannot tell if the zeros are significant or not; they are undetermined. The problem of undetermined numbers of significant digits can be overcome by use of scientific notation (Section 2.3). □

Rounding Off

When we do calculations that give us too many digits to be kept, we must reduce the number to reflect only the significant digits. We do that by rounding off. We drop any extra decimal place digits and convert any extra integral digits to nonsignificant zeros. If the first digit that we drop is 5 or greater, we increase the last digit retained by 1. If the first digit dropped is less than 5, we do not change the last digit retained.

A more elegant method of rounding involves only the case in which the digit 5 only or a 5 with only zeros is dropped. In this method, we do not change the last digit retained if it initially is even, but round it up if initially it is odd. For example, if we are rounding to one decimal place:

14.05, 14.050, 14.0500, ... would all round to 14.0.
14.15, 14.150, 14.1500, ... would all round to 14.2.
14.25, 14.250, 14.2500, ... would all round to 14.2.

Note that 14.050000001 would round to 14.1, because it is not covered by this rule. (It has a digit other than zero after the 5 to be dropped.) Most courses do not use this rule, and if the first digit to be dropped is 5, they merely round the last retained digit to the next higher digit whether it is even or odd. In this book, we will follow that general practice.

EXAMPLE 8 Round off the following numbers to three significant digits each: (*a*) 12.34 g   (*b*) 1234 g   (*c*) 12.39 g
(*d*) 0.02233 g   (*e*) 0.24648 g

Solution   (*a*) 12.3 g   (*b*) 1230 g   (*c*) 12.4 g
(*d*) 0.0223 g   (*e*) 0.246 g
(*a*) The 4 is merely dropped. (*b*) The 4 must be changed to a nonsignificant 0 so that we don't change the magnitude of the number very much. The incorrect answer 123 g, resulting from merely dropping the 4, would be very far from the measured value. (*c*) We drop the 9, but since it is greater than 5, we increase the 3 to 4.

(*d*) We merely drop the last 3, leaving us three significant digits. Do not confuse the number of significant digits with the number of decimal place digits. (*e*) We drop the 48, since the 4 is less than 5. We do *not* drop one digit at a time. We do not round the 4 to 5 by dropping the last digit and then change the 6 to 7 by dropping that 5. The 48 is less than 50, so we do not round up the last remaining digit. □

Sometimes it is necessary to *add* digits to obtain the proper number of significant digits in our answer.

EXAMPLE 9 Divide $7.86 \, cm^2$ by $3.93 \, cm$.

Solution The answer on our calculator is 2 (cm), but the answer must contain three significant digits, so we add two zeros to the calculator's result to get $2.00 \, cm$. □

The question is often asked "How many significant digits should we use?" The answer is that we determine how many by using the measurements given in the problem. For example, if the products in a multiplication all have four significant digits, then we use four in the final answer. If a quantitative problem has no numeric data in its statement, as in a percent composition problem (Section 4.3), then we use at least three significant digits in its solution so that rounding errors don't give incorrect results.

2.3 Scientific Notation

Scientists report numbers from literally astronomical to almost infinitesimal. In order to do so conveniently, we use **scientific notation**, also known as **standard exponential notation**. Scientific notation is a form of a number with a decimal coefficient times a power of 10. The following number is in scientific notation, with its parts identified:

$$\underset{\text{coefficient}}{1.246} \times \underset{\text{exponential part}}{\overset{\overset{\text{base} \quad \text{exponent}}{}}{10^3}}$$

A number in scientific notation has a coefficient that is 1 or more but less than 10, and it has an integral exponent, which may be positive, zero, or negative.

EXAMPLE 10 Which one(s) of the following numbers are in scientific notation?

(a) 1.246×10^3 (b) 0.246×10^3 (c) 10.246×10^3
(d) $1.246 \times 10^{3.5}$ (e) 1.246×10^0 (f) 10.0×10^{-3}
(g) 1.00×10^{-3}

Solution   The numbers in (a), (e), and (g) are in scientific notation; (b) is not because its coefficient is not as great as 1; (c) and (f) are not because their coefficients have two integral digits each; (d) is not because it has a fractional exponent.   □

All digits in the coefficient of a properly reported value in scientific notation are significant, because the exponential part of the number gives the magnitude. The electronic calculator will do the arithmetic with numbers in scientific notation, but we still have to know how the process works because the calculator does not consider significant digits. See Section 1.3 for a discussion of calculator processing of numbers in exponential form.

EXAMPLE 11   Perform the following arithmetic operations with exponential numbers, giving the answers in scientific notation and with the proper number of significant digits:
(a) 2.67×10^2 cm $+ 2.29 \times 10^1$ cm
(b) 2.67×10^{-2} cm $+ 2.29 \times 10^{-1}$ cm
(c) $(2.67 \times 10^2$ cm$)(2.29 \times 10^1$ cm$)$
(d) $(2.67 \times 10^2$ cm$^2)/(2.29 \times 10^1$ cm$)$

Solution

(a) 2.90×10^2 cm. We change 2.29×10^1 to 0.229×10^2 before adding. If we are not convinced, we can change each number to a decimal number and add:

$$
\begin{array}{r}
267 \ \text{cm} \\
\underline{22.9 \ \text{cm}} \\
290 \ \text{cm}
\end{array}
$$

(b) 0.256 cm $= 2.56 \times 10^{-1}$ cm. Again watch the significant digits.
(c) 6.11×10^3 cm^2. Three significant digits are required because there are three in each measurement. Caution: We must watch out for the units even while considering a completely different part of the problem.
(d) 11.7 cm. See the comments in part (c).   □

2.4 Density

The **density** of a sample is defined as its mass per unit volume $d = m/V$. To get density, we merely divide the mass by the volume. Density is an intensive property of matter (it doesn't matter how much sample is present), so density is useful to identify substances. The subject is used here to review all the material covered in Sections 2.1 though 2.3.

EXAMPLE 12 A prospector in the old west brought a sample of shiny metal into the assayer's office to see if the sample was gold (which has a density of 19.3 g/cm^3). The assayer found the mass to be 256 g and the volume to be 51 cm^3. Was the sample gold?

Solution The density of the sample was $(256 \text{ g})/(51 \text{ cm}^3) = 5.0 \text{ g/cm}^3$. The sample was not gold. (It was iron pyrite, known as "fool's gold.") $\square$

Because density is a ratio, it can be used as a factor in dimensional analysis problems.

EXAMPLE 13 (*a*) Calculate the volume of 255 g of gold (density $= 19.3 \text{ g/mL}$). (*b*) Calculate the mass of 153 mL of mercury (density $= 13.6 \text{ g/mL}$).

Solution

(*a*) $255 \text{ g} \left(\dfrac{1 \text{ mL}}{19.3 \text{ g}} \right) = 13.2 \text{ mL}$

(*b*) $153 \text{ mL} \left(\dfrac{13.6 \text{ g}}{1 \text{ mL}} \right) = 2080 \text{ g} = 2.08 \text{ kg}$ $\square$

2.5 Time, Temperature, and Energy

Time

The basic unit of time is the second. Longer periods of time are measured in minutes and hours (instead of kiloseconds, etc.), but shorter periods use the regular metric prefixes. Thus a millisecond is 0.001 second. We should not have any trouble with time because we are so familiar with the longer periods and now have become familiar with the subunits. However, watch out for times stated in two units, such as "an hour and 15 minutes."

EXAMPLE 14 How many seconds are there in exactly 1 hour and 15 minutes?

Solution   Note that an hour and 15 minutes is *not* 1.15 hours. We need to convert each part of the time separately.

$$1\,\text{hour}\left(\frac{60\,\text{minutes}}{1\,\text{hour}}\right)\left(\frac{60\,\text{seconds}}{1\,\text{minute}}\right) = 3600\,\text{seconds}$$

$$15\,\text{minutes}\left(\frac{60\,\text{seconds}}{1\,\text{minute}}\right) = 900\,\text{seconds}$$

The total time is exactly 4500 seconds.   □

Temperature and Energy

Temperature and energy are not the same. We can prove this to ourselves by heating a pan with 1 inch of water in it on a burner at home for 2.00 minutes. With a thermometer, we measure the rise in temperature. We discard that water, cool the pan, and fill it almost full with water at the same original temperature and heat it on the same burner at the same setting for an equal 2.00 minutes. Again we measure the temperature before and after. The pan with less water was warmed to a higher temperature by the same quantity of heat.

There are three temperature scales in use in the world (Table 2-4). The Fahrenheit scale is in common use in the United States. The freezing point of water on this scale is 32°F and its normal boiling point is 212°F. The metric system scale is the Celsius scale, on which the freezing point of water is 0°C and its normal boiling point is 100°C. The SI scale is the Kelvin scale, on which these same two points are 273.15 K and 373.15 K, respectively. These latter temperatures are often rounded to three significant digits for ease of use. We must remember the values 273 K and 373 K. On the Kelvin scale, the "degree" sign is not used, and the units are called kelvins. Chemists use t to represent Celsius temperature and T to represent Kelvin temperature.

Table 2-4   Temperature Scales

	Freezing Point of Water	Normal Boiling Point of Water
Fahrenheit (F)	32°F	212°F
Celsius (t)	0°C	100°C
Kelvin (T)	273 K	373 K

To convert from Fahrenheit to Celsius or back, use the following equation, where F stands for the Fahrenheit temperature:

$$t = (F - 32°)/(1.8)$$

Although the Fahrenheit scale is in common everyday use in the United States, it is not used often by scientists. Ask the instructor if the conversions between Fahrenheit and Celsius are necessary to learn.

To convert from the Celsius scale to the Kelvin scale or back, use the following simple equation:

$$T = t + 273°$$

Energy is measured in **joules** (J). A joule is the energy required to move a force of 1 Newton through a distance of 1 meter, and a Newton is the force required to accelerate a 1 kg mass 1 meter per second every second. The important part of these definitions for us is the units that result by multiplying 1 Newton by a meter:

$$1\,J = 1\,kg \cdot m^2/s^2$$

It takes 4.184 J to heat 1.000 g of water 1.000°C.

Kinetic energy (KE) is the energy of motion. The kinetic energy of a body is

$$KE = \tfrac{1}{2}mv^2$$

These energy and temperature relationships will be developed more fully in later chapters, where they are used.

Leading Questions

1. What is the SI equivalent of (a) 1 L? (b) 1 mL? (c) 1000 L?
2. How many significant digits and how many decimal place digits are present in each of the following measurements? Is there any apparent relationship between the two? (a) 0.0987 g (b) 1.100 g (c) 9.1 g (d) 0.991 g
3. Calculate the sum of exactly 1 m + 2 dm + 3 cm + 4 mm.
4. What is the difference between 2 mg and 2 Mg?

5. Units of what variable are obtained when a mass is divided by a length times a width times a depth?

6. Which ones of the following sets of units are the dimensions of density?

$$g/cm^3 \quad g/mL \quad mg/mL \quad kg/m^3 \quad kg/L \quad kg/dm^3 \quad g/cm$$

Answers to Leading Questions

1. (a) $1\,dm^3$ (b) $1\,cm^3$ (c) $1\,m^3$

2. (a) 3 significant digits, 4 decimal place digits
    (b) 4 significant digits, 3 decimal place digits
    (c) 2 significant digits, 1 decimal place digit
    (d) 3 each. As we can see, there is no apparent relationship.

3. The answer is any of the following:
    $1.234\,m = 12.34\,dm = 123.4\,cm = 1234\,mm$

4. $2\,mg = 0.002\,g$; $2\,Mg = 2{,}000{,}000\,g = 2$ metric tons

5. Density

6. All but g/cm (which might be the basis for pricing a gold chain for a necklace).

Supplementary Problems

1. Convert (a) 2.44 m to centimeters. (b) $2.44\ m^3$ to cubic centimeters.

2. Convert (a) 4.852 km to meters. (b) 6.66 mm to meters (c) 10.3 cm to meters.

3. Convert (a) 4.852 kilowatts to watts (W). (b) 4.2 megahertz to hertz (Hz).

4. Convert 3.50 L (a) to cubic meters. (b) to cubic decimeters. (c) to cubic centimeters.

5. Convert 331 cm^3 to liters.

6. Convert 4.68 km to (a) centimeters. (b) millimeters.

7. Multiply 3.55 cm^2 times 2.22 cm.

8. Divide 117.0 g by 23.5 cm^3.

9. Calculate the volume in cubic centimeters of a rectangular solid 0.200 cm by 8.20 cm by 11.5 mm. (Be sure to convert the millimeters to centimeters before multiplying.)

10. Calculate the volume of a rectangular solid 0.200 cm by 8.20 cm by 11.5 mm.

11. Underline the significant digits in each of the following. If a digit is uncertain, place a question mark below it. (a) 2.400 kg
    (b) 0.721 cm   (c) 22.402 m   (d) 300 L   (e) 0.0°C

12. How many significant digits are present in the Kelvin scale equivalent of 0°C?

13. What is the sum, to the proper number of significant digits, of 1.83×10^{11} m and 6.74×10^9 m?

14. What is the sum, to the proper number of significant digits, of 1.83×10^{11} cm and 6.74×10^9 m?

15. Calculate the density of a rectangular solid that is 40.0 cm by 10.0 cm by 5.00 cm and has a mass of 4.50 kg.

16. Which has a greater density, a sample of oxygen gas at 2.00 g/dm^3 or a sample of water at 1.00 g/cm^3? Explain.

17. A rectangular drinking trough for animals is 2.10 m long, 43.1 cm wide, and 21.7 cm deep. A 2.60×10^5 g sample of liquid with density 1.73 kg/dm^3 is placed in it. (a) To find the depth of the liquid, what should we do to the measurements with regard to their units? (b) How can we calculate the volume of the trough? (c) What can we calculate from the density and the mass of liquid? (d) Do we expect the volumes of the trough and the liquid to be the same? (e) How can we calculate the height of the liquid from its volume, length, and width?

18. If light travels 3.00×10^8 m/s, what distance can light travel in 1.00 year?

19. If light travels 3.00×10^8 m/s and it takes light about 500 s to get from the sun to the earth, how far away is the sun?

20. It takes light about 4 years to get from the nearest big star to the earth, and light travels 3.00×10^8 m/s. How far away is the star?

21. A rectangular drinking trough for animals is 2.10 m long, 43.1 cm wide, and 21.7 cm deep. A 2.60×10^5 g sample of liquid with density 1.73 kg/dm^3 is placed in it. (a) Convert the length to centimeters and the density to grams per cubic centimeter. (b) Calculate the volume of the trough. (c) Calculate the volume of the liquid. (d) Are the volumes of the trough and the liquid the same? (e) Calculate the height of the liquid.

22. Calculate the volume of 2.50 kg of mercury (density 13.6 g/mL).

23. Calculate the mass of 1.75 L of iron (density 7.86 g/mL).

24. A sample of a pure substance has a mass of 329 g and a volume of 41.9 mL. Use a table of densities to determine the identity of the substance.

25. Convert 35°C to the Kelvin scale.

26. Convert 422 K to Celsius.

27. Convert the density 5.94 kg/m^3 (a) to g/cm^3. (b) to kg/dm^3.

28. Under certain conditions, air has a density of about 1.3 kg/m^3.

Calculate the mass of air in a lecture room 10.0 m by 15.0 m by 3.0 m.

29. A rectangular drinking trough for animals is 1.90 m long, 53.1 cm wide, and 30.7 cm deep. A 1.95×10^5 g sample of liquid with density 1.55 kg/dm³ is placed in it. Calculate the height of the liquid in the trough.

30. A certain ore is made up of 17.5% by mass of an iron compound, and the compound contains 69.9% iron. Calculate the percentage of iron in the ore.

Solutions to Supplementary Problems

1. (a) $2.44 \, \text{m} \left(\dfrac{1 \, \text{cm}}{0.01 \, \text{m}} \right) = 244 \, \text{cm}$

   (b) $2.44 \, \text{m}^3 \left(\dfrac{1,000,000 \, \text{cm}^3}{1 \, \text{m}^3} \right) = 2,440,000 \, \text{cm}^3 = 2.44 \times 10^6 \, \text{cm}^3$

2. (a) $4.852 \, \text{km} \left(\dfrac{1000 \, \text{m}}{1 \, \text{km}} \right) = 4852 \, \text{m}$

   (b) $6.66 \, \text{mm} \left(\dfrac{0.001 \, \text{m}}{1 \, \text{mm}} \right) = 0.00666 \, \text{m}$

   (c) $10.3 \, \text{cm} \left(\dfrac{0.01 \, \text{m}}{1 \, \text{cm}} \right) = 0.103 \, \text{m}$

3. The metric prefixes mean the same thing no matter what unit they are attached to.

   (a) $4.852 \, \text{kW} \left(\dfrac{1000 \, \text{W}}{1 \, \text{kW}} \right) = 4852 \, \text{W}$ [Compare to Problem 2(a).]

   (b) $4.2 \, \text{MHz} \left(\dfrac{1,000,000 \, \text{Hz}}{1 \, \text{MHz}} \right) = 4.2 \times 10^6 \, \text{Hz}$

4. (a) $3.50 \, \text{L} \left(\dfrac{1 \, \text{m}^3}{1000 \, \text{L}} \right) = 0.00350 \, \text{m}^3$

   (b) $3.50 \, \text{L} \left(\dfrac{1 \, \text{dm}^3}{1 \, \text{L}} \right) = 3.50 \, \text{dm}^3$

   (c) $3.50 \, \text{L} \left(\dfrac{1000 \, \text{cm}^3}{1 \, \text{L}} \right) = 3500 \, \text{cm}^3 = 3.50 \times 10^3 \, \text{cm}^3$

5. $331 \, \text{cm}^3 \left(\dfrac{1 \, \text{L}}{1000 \, \text{cm}^3} \right) = 0.331 \, \text{L}$

6. (a) $4.68 \, \text{km} \left(\dfrac{1000 \, \text{m}}{1 \, \text{km}} \right) \left(\dfrac{1 \, \text{cm}}{0.01 \, \text{m}} \right) = 468{,}000 \, \text{cm} = 4.68 \times 10^5 \, \text{cm}$

(b) $4.68 \, \text{km} \left(\dfrac{1000 \, \text{m}}{1 \, \text{km}} \right) \left(\dfrac{1 \, \text{mm}}{0.001 \, \text{m}} \right) = 4{,}680{,}000 \, \text{mm}$

$$= 4.68 \times 10^6 \, \text{mm}$$

7. $(3.55 \, \text{cm}^2)(2.22 \, \text{cm}) = 7.88 \, \text{cm}^3$ (Watch out for units and significant digits.)

8. $(117.0 \, \text{g})/(23.5 \, \text{cm}^3) = 4.98 \, \text{g/cm}^3$ (Watch out for units and significant digits.)

9. $(0.200 \, \text{cm})(8.20 \, \text{cm})(1.15 \, \text{cm}) = 1.89 \, \text{cm}^3$

10. This is the same problem as Problem 9, but without a hint about the units.

11. (a) 2.400 kg   (b) 0.721 cm   (c) 22.402 m   (d) 300 L
(e) 0.0°C

12. Three $(0°\text{C} + 273.15 \, \text{K} = 273 \, \text{K})$

13. $1.83 \times 10^{11} \, \text{m} + 0.0674 \times 10^{11} \, \text{m} = 1.90 \times 10^{11} \, \text{m}$

14. $1.83 \times 10^{11} \, \text{cm} + 6.74 \times 10^9 \, \text{m} = 1.83 \times 10^9 \, \text{m} + 6.74 \times 10^9 \, \text{m}$
$$= 8.57 \times 10^9 \, \text{m}$$

15. The volume is $(40.0 \, \text{cm})(10.0 \, \text{cm})(5.00 \, \text{cm}) = 2000 \, \text{cm}^3 = 2.00 \, \text{dm}^3$
The density is the mass divided by the volume:

$$(4.50 \, \text{kg})/(2.00 \, \text{dm}^3) = 2.25 \, \text{kg/dm}^3$$

(We changed to cubic decimeters to show the number of significant digits explicitly, not because the density had to be in these units.)

16. Watch out for the units! The oxygen is in grams per cubic decimeter; its density in grams per cubic centimeter is given by

$$\frac{2.00 \, \text{g}}{1 \, \text{dm}^3} \left(\frac{1 \, \text{dm}^3}{1000 \, \text{cm}^3} \right) = 0.00200 \, \text{g/cm}^3$$

The oxygen is less dense.

17. (a) Having the units of all the measurements comparable is necessary to solve the problem. Because the lengths are given in different units, we must convert them to comparable units.
(b) Multiply the length times the width times the height (all in centimeters). (c) The volume of the *liquid*. (d) There is no reason to expect the trough to be full, so they could very well have different volumes. (e) Solve the equation $V = lwh$ for h.

18. $1.00 \, \text{year} \left(\dfrac{365 \, \text{days}}{1 \, \text{year}} \right) \left(\dfrac{24 \, \text{hours}}{1 \, \text{day}} \right) \left(\dfrac{3600 \, \text{s}}{1 \, \text{hour}} \right) \left(\dfrac{3.00 \times 10^8 \, \text{m}}{1 \, \text{s}} \right)$
$$= 9.46 \times 10^{15} \, \text{m}$$

19. $500 \, s \left(\dfrac{3.00 \times 10^8 \, m}{1 \, s} \right) = 2 \times 10^{11} \, m$

("About" indicates 1 significant digit.)

20. $4 \, years \left(\dfrac{365 \, days}{1 \, year} \right) \left(\dfrac{24 \, hours}{1 \, day} \right) \left(\dfrac{3600 \, s}{1 \, hour} \right) \left(\dfrac{3.00 \times 10^8 \, m}{1 \, s} \right)$

$= 4 \times 10^{16} \, m$ (about 25 thousand billion miles)

21. (a) $2.10 \, m \left(\dfrac{1 \, cm}{0.01 \, m} \right) = 2.10 \times 10^2 \, cm$

$\dfrac{1.73 \, kg}{1 \, dm^3} \left(\dfrac{1000 \, g}{1 \, kg} \right) \left(\dfrac{1 \, dm^3}{1000 \, cm^3} \right) = 1.73 \, g/cm^3$

(b) $V_{trough} = (2.10 \times 10^2 \, cm)(43.1 \, cm)(21.7 \, cm) = 1.96 \times 10^5 \, cm^3$

(c) $V_{liquid} = 2.60 \times 10^5 \, g \left(\dfrac{1 \, cm^3}{1.73 \, g} \right) = 1.50 \times 10^5 \, cm^3$

(d) The volumes are not the same.

(e) $h = V/lw = (1.50 \times 10^5 \, cm^3)/(2.10 \times 10^2 \, cm)(43.1 \, cm)$

$= 16.6 \, cm$

22. $2.50 \, kg \left(\dfrac{1000 \, g}{1 \, kg} \right) \left(\dfrac{1 \, mL}{13.6 \, g} \right) = 184 \, mL$

23. $1.75 \, L \left(\dfrac{1000 \, mL}{1 \, L} \right) \left(\dfrac{7.86 \, g}{1 \, mL} \right) = 13{,}800 \, g = 13.8 \, kg$

24. $d = (329 \, g)/(41.9 \, mL) = 7.85 \, g/mL$ (The substance is iron.)

25. $35°C + 273° = 308 \, K$

26. $422 \, K - 273° = 149°C$

27. (a) $\dfrac{5.94 \, kg}{1 \, m^3} \left(\dfrac{1000 \, g}{1 \, kg} \right) \left(\dfrac{1 \, m^3}{1 \times 10^6 \, cm^3} \right) = 5.94 \times 10^{-3} \, g/cm^3$

(b) $\dfrac{5.94 \, kg}{1 \, m^3} \left(\dfrac{1 \, m^3}{1 \times 10^3 \, dm^3} \right) = 5.94 \times 10^{-3} \, kg/dm^3$

28. $V = (10.0 \, m)(15.0 \, m)(3.0 \, m) = 450 \, m^3$ (two significant digits)

$450 \, m^3 \left(\dfrac{1.3 \, kg}{1 \, m^3} \right) = 590 \, kg$ (over half a metric ton)

29. $1.90 \, m \left(\dfrac{1 \, cm}{0.01 \, m} \right) = 1.90 \times 10^2 \, cm$

$\dfrac{1.55 \, kg}{1 \, dm^3} \left(\dfrac{1000 \, g}{1 \, kg} \right) \left(\dfrac{1 \, dm^3}{1000 \, cm^3} \right) = 1.55 \, g/cm^3$

$$V_{\text{liquid}} = 1.95 \times 10^5 \, g \left(\frac{1 \, cm^3}{1.55 \, g} \right) = 1.26 \times 10^5 \, cm^3$$

$h = V/lw = (1.26 \times 10^5 \, cm^3)/(1.90 \times 10^2 \, cm)(53.1 \, cm) = 12.5 \, cm$

The steps of Supplementary Problem 21 are followed, except that the volume of the trough need not be calculated because it is not equal to the volume of the liquid.

30. $\dfrac{17.5 \, g \ compound}{100 \, g \ ore} \left(\dfrac{69.9 \, g \ iron}{100 \, g \ compound} \right) = \dfrac{12.2 \, g \ iron}{100 \, g \ ore} = 12.2\% \ iron$

Chapter 3

Classical Laws of Chemical Combination

3.1 The Law of Conservation of Mass

The **law of conservation of mass** states that in any chemical reaction, mass is neither gained nor lost. That means that the total mass of the reactants is equal to the total mass of the products.

EXAMPLE 1 Calculate the mass of the product of reaction of 6.54 g of zinc with 3.21 g of sulfur.

Solution The compound produced has a mass equal to the total mass of the reactants:

$$6.54\,g + 3.21\,g = 9.75\,g \qquad \square$$

The law of conservation of mass is important especially for reactants or products that are hard to weigh. Also, this law can be used to solve for the masses of reactants as well as those of products, just as the algebraic equation $x = a + b$ can be solved for x if a and b are given as well as it can be solved for b if a and x are given.

EXAMPLE 2 Calculate the mass of the oxygen that reacts with 1.24 g of methane (natural gas) to form 3.41 g of carbon dioxide and 2.79 g of water. (The mass of each product was also determined using the law of conservation of mass. See Supplementary Problem 2.)

Solution The total mass of the products is $3.41\,g + 2.79\,g = 6.20\,g$. The total mass of the reactants must also be 6.20 g, so the oxygen has a mass of $6.20\,g - 1.24\,g = 4.96\,g$. $\square$

EXAMPLE 3 What mass of aluminum oxide must be electrolyzed with carbon electrodes to yield 1.59×10^6 g of aluminum and 2.48×10^6 g of carbon monoxide in the Hall process for the industrial production of aluminum. The carbon electrodes lost a total of 1.06×10^6 g of mass.

Solution

$$(1.59 \times 10^6 \text{ g}) + (2.48 \times 10^6 \text{ g}) - (1.06 \times 10^6 \text{ g})$$
$$= 3.01 \times 10^6 \text{ g aluminum oxide} \quad \square$$

3.2 The Law of Definite Proportions

The **law of definite proportions** states that the elements in any given compound are in definite proportions by mass. That is, the ratio of mass of each element to that of every other element in the compound is a constant.

EXAMPLE 4 If 6.537 g of zinc reacts with exactly 7.0906 g of chlorine to form the only compound of chlorine and zinc, how much zinc will react with (a) 14.18 g of chlorine? (b) with 28.36 g of chlorine? (c) with 100.0 g of chlorine?

Solution

(a) With twice the mass of chlorine, twice the mass of zinc must react: 13.07 g.
(b) With four times the mass of chlorine, four times the mass of zinc must react: 26.15 g.
(c) With $(100.0)/(7.0906)$ times the mass of chlorine, $(100.0)/(7.0906)$ times the mass of zinc must react:

$$6.537 \text{ g} \left(\frac{100.0}{7.0906} \right) = 92.19 \text{ g zinc}$$

In each case, the ratio of mass of zinc to mass of chlorine is the same!

$$\frac{7.0906 \text{ g}}{6.537 \text{ g}} = \frac{14.18 \text{ g}}{13.07 \text{ g}} = \frac{28.36 \text{ g}}{26.15 \text{ g}} = \frac{100.0 \text{ g}}{92.19 \text{ g}} = 1.085 \quad \square$$

EXAMPLE 5 The reaction of 6.54 g of zinc and 3.20 g of oxygen produces 9.74 g of zinc oxide, the only compound of these elements. (a) How much zinc oxide would be produced if 6.54 g of zinc and

5.00 g of oxygen were mixed and allowed to react? (*b*) What law enables us to answer this question?

Solution (*a*) 9.74 g. (Zinc and oxygen react in a ratio of 6.54 g to 3.20 g, no matter how much extra oxygen is present.) (*b*) The law of definite proportions. □

EXAMPLE 6 (*a*) In the experiment of Example 5, how much oxygen did not react? (*b*) What law enables us to answer this question?

Solution (*a*) Since 3.20 g of the 5.00 g reacted, 1.80 g did not react. (*b*) The law of conservation of mass. □

EXAMPLE 7 From the data of Example 5, calculate the mass of zinc that would react with 1.00 g of oxygen.

Solution

$$1.00 \text{ g oxygen} \left(\frac{6.54 \text{ g zinc}}{3.20 \text{ g oxygen}} \right) = 2.04 \text{ g zinc} \qquad □$$

3.3 The Law of Multiple Proportions

The **law of multiple proportions** states that when two or more compounds consist of the same elements, for a given mass of one of the elements, the masses of the other elements are in small, whole number ratios. For example, carbon monoxide and carbon dioxide both consist of carbon and oxygen only. In a certain sample of carbon monoxide, 1.00 g of carbon is combined with 1.33 g of oxygen. In a sample of carbon dioxide containing 1.00 g of carbon, there is 2.66 g of oxygen. Thus, for a given mass of carbon (1.00 g), there is a ratio of oxygen equal to (1.33 g) : (2.66 g) = 1 : 2. That is a small, whole number ratio. *Note well*, it is not the ratio of mass of carbon to mass of oxygen that is a small whole number according to the law of multiple proportions, but the masses of oxygen in the two compounds.

EXAMPLE 8 A sample of a compound of sodium, chlorine, and oxygen contains 2.00 g of sodium, 3.08 g of chlorine, and 1.39 g of oxygen. A second compound made with these same elements contains 1.00 g of sodium, 1.54 g of chlorine, and 2.78 g of oxygen. Show that these data support the law of multiple proportions.

Solution First we must get a fixed mass of one of the elements. (Any one will do.) It might be easiest to take half the masses of each element in the first compound, to get 1.00 g of sodium in each.

1.00 g sodium, 1.54 g of chlorine, and 0.695 g of oxygen

For the fixed mass (1.00 g) of sodium, there are

$$\frac{\text{Compound 1}}{\text{Compound 2}} \quad \overset{\text{Chlorine}}{\frac{1.54\,g}{1.54\,g}} = \frac{1\,g}{1\,g} \quad \overset{\text{Oxygen}}{\frac{0.695\,g}{2.78\,g}} = \frac{1\,g}{4\,g}$$

The ratios of masses are small whole number ratios, as required by the law of multiple proportions. □

EXAMPLE 9 Show that the following data are in accord with the law of multiple proportions:

	Element 1	Element 2	Element 3
Compound 1	29.1%	40.5%	30.4%
Compound 2	32.4%	22.6%	45.0%

Solution Assume that we have 100.0 g of compound, in which case each percentage is equal to the number of grams of that element in our sample. To get a fixed mass of one of the elements, it is easiest to divide each mass in each compound by the magnitude of the mass of one of the elements in that compound. Use the same element in each compound as the divisor! Taking the element with the smallest percentage in one or both compounds is perhaps best.

	Element 1	Element 2	Element 3
Compound 1	29.1 g/29.1 = 1.00 g	40.5 g/29.1 = 1.39 g	30.4 g/29.1 = 1.04 g
Compound 2	32.4 g/32.4 = 1.00 g	22.6 g/32.4 = 0.698 g	45.0 g/32.4 = 1.39 g

The ratio of masses of element 2 in the two compounds is 1.39 g : 0.698 g = 2 : 1. (Never round off more than 1% or 2%.) The ratio of masses of element 3 in the two compounds is 1.04 g : 1.39 g = 0.75 : 1.0. This is not a whole number ratio, but it can be made into a whole number ratio of equal value by multiplying both numerator and denominator by 4:

$$\frac{0.75}{1.0} = \frac{3}{4}$$

Thus, for a given mass of the first element, the ratios of the other two elements are whole number ratios, in accord with the law of multiple proportions. □

To convert ratios containing decimal fractions to whole number ratios, convert them to common fractions and multiply the numerator and denominator by the *denominator* of the common fraction. For example, 0.75 is $\frac{3}{4}$, so we can multiply the 0.75 and the 1 in the ratio $\frac{0.75}{1}$ by 4 (the denominator of the common fraction) to

Table 3-1   Some Common Fraction Equivalents to Decimal Fractions

0.5	$\frac{1}{2}$	0.2	$\frac{1}{5}$
0.250	$\frac{1}{4}$	0.4	$\frac{2}{5}$
0.333	$\frac{1}{3}$	0.6	$\frac{3}{5}$
0.667	$\frac{2}{3}$	0.8	$\frac{4}{5}$
0.750	$\frac{3}{4}$		

get the ratio $3:4$. (We also in simple cases merely use the common fraction, $\frac{3}{4}$.) A set of some common fraction equivalents is given in Table 3-1.

EXAMPLE 10   Convert each of the following ratios to an integral ratio: (*a*) $(0.50\,\text{g})/(1\,\text{g})$; (*b*) $(1.50\,\text{g})/(1\,\text{g})$; (*c*) $(2.667\,\text{g})/(1\,\text{g})$.

Solution

(*a*) $(0.50\,\text{g})/(1\,\text{g}) = \frac{1}{2}$

(*b*) $(1.50\,\text{g})/(1\,\text{g}) = \frac{3}{2}$ (The fractional part is $\frac{1}{2}$, so multiply by 2.)

(*c*) $(2.667\,\text{g})/(1\,\text{g}) = 2\frac{2}{3} = \frac{8}{3}$ (The fractional part is $\frac{2}{3}$ or $\frac{8}{3}$, so multiply by 3.)   □

Leading Questions

1. What mass of an element is present in a 100.0-g sample if the element is 29.1% of the compound?
2. In Example 9, when we divide the mass of each element of compound 2 by 32.4, what happens to our 100.0-g sample of the compound?

Answers to Leading Questions

1. $100.0\,\text{g}\left(\dfrac{29.1\,\text{g}}{100\,\text{g}}\right) = 29.1\,\text{g}$.   (The number of grams is equal in magnitude to the percentage.)

2. We have reduced the 100.0-g mass to $(100.0\,\text{g})/(32.4) = 3.09\,\text{g}$. Note that after the divisions, the sum of the masses of all the elements is 3.09 g.

Supplementary Problems

1. How much oxygen is required to convert 11.24 g of cadmium to 12.84 g of cadmium oxide?

2. In a certain experiment, when 0.547 g of methane is burned in excess oxygen, carbon dioxide and water vapor are formed. The water is absorbed by phosphorus pentoxide, and the carbon dioxide is absorbed by slaked lime. The tube containing the phosphorus pentoxide increases in mass by 1.23 g and the tube containing the slaked lime increases 1.50 g. How much oxygen reacted?

3. A 10.0-g sample of sodium chloride consists of 39.3% sodium and the rest chlorine. (a) What is the percentage of sodium in a 4.00-g sample? (b) What is the mass of sodium in a 4.00-g sample?

4. Show that the following data support the law of multiple proportions:

	Compound 1	Compound 2
Element 1	1.00 g	4.88 g
Element 2	2.00 g	7.32 g
Element 3	4.00 g	9.76 g

5. Show that the following data support the law of multiple proportions:

	Compound 1	Compound 2	Compound 3
Element 1	15.8%	18.4%	13.8%
Element 2	28.1%	32.7%	49.3%
Element 3	56.1%	48.9%	36.9%

6. When 5.40 g of aluminum reacts with 9.62 g of sulfur, it forms 15.02 g of the only compound of just these two elements. In a second experiment, if the mass of aluminum is increased, what will happen to it? How can we tell?

7. Convert each of the following ratios to integral ratios: (a) (1.50 g A)/ (1.00 g B); (b) (2.50 g A)/(1.00 g B); (c) (3.50 g A)/(1.00 g B).

8. Convert each of the following ratios to integral ratios: (a) (2.67 g A)/ (1.00 g B); (b) (4.75 g A)/(1.00 g B); (c) (1.60 g A)/(1.00 g B).

9. (a) Would a set of mixtures of carbon monoxide (42.9% carbon, 57.1% oxygen) and carbon dioxide (27.3% carbon, 72.7% oxygen) be expected to have a definite composition? (b) What are the extreme limits on the percentage of carbon in such a set of mixtures?

10. Show that the compounds in the prior problem obey the law of multiple proportions.

11. Consider the following data about two compounds consisting of the same three elements:

	Element 1	Element 2	Element 3
Compound 1	7.53 g	627 mg	1.67 g
Compound 2	50.0%	5.56%	44.4%

(a) What should we do about the units in the data of compound 1 to simplify any calculations to be done? (b) How can we get mass ratios from percentages? (c) How can we get a fixed mass of one element in the two compounds? (d) Do we consider the mass ratio of element 1 to element 2 in each compound to establish the law of multiple proportions? (e) What ratios do we consider?

12. Consider the following data about two compounds consisting of the same three elements:

	Element 1	Element 2	Element 3
Compound 1	7.53 g	627 mg	1.67 g
Compound 2	50.0%	5.56%	44.4%

(a) Calculate the mass in grams of element 2 in compound 1.
(b) Convert the percentages in compound 2 to masses.
(c) Calculate the mass of elements 1 and 3 in each compound per gram of element 2. (d) Show that these data support the law of multiple proportions.

13. Consider the following data about three compounds consisting of the same three elements:

	Element 1	Element 2	Element 3
Compound 1	0.1279 kg	10.66 g	28.43 g
Compound 2	62.07%	10.34%	27.59%
Compound 3	10.68 g	1.334 g	7.117 g

Show that these data support the law of multiple proportions.

Solutions to Supplementary Problems

1. The law of conservation of mass requires that
   $12.84\,g - 11.24\,g = 1.60\,g$ of oxygen has reacted.
2. The law of conservation of mass requires that
   $1.23\,g + 1.50\,g - 0.547\,g = 2.18\,g$ of oxygen reacted.

3. (a) 39.3%. (All samples contain this percentage, according to the law of definite proportions.)

(b) $4.00 \text{ g NaCl} \left(\dfrac{39.3 \text{ g Na}}{100 \text{ g NaCl}} \right) = 1.57 \text{ g Na}$

4. Dividing each element in compound 2 by 4.88 to get a fixed (1.00 g) mass of element 1 in the two compounds yields

	Compound 1	Compound 2
Element 1	1.00 g	1.00 g
Element 2	2.00 g	1.50 g
Element 3	4.00 g	2.00 g

The ratio of element 2 in the two compounds is $2.00 \text{ g} : 1.50 \text{ g} = 4 \text{ g} : 3 \text{ g}$, an integral ratio. The ratio of element 3 is $4.00 \text{ g} : 2.00 \text{ g} = 2 \text{ g} : 1 \text{ g}$, again an integral ratio.

5. First we change each percentage to a mass in grams. Then we divide each element in each compound by the magnitude of the mass of element 1 in the compound to get a fixed (1.00 g) mass of element 1 in the three compounds:

	Compound 1	Compound 2	Compound 3
Element 1	1.00 g	1.00 g	1.00 g
Element 2	1.78 g	1.78 g	3.57 g
Element 3	3.55 g	2.66 g	2.67 g

For the fixed mass (1.00 g) of element 1, there is a ratio of $1 \text{ g} : 1 \text{ g} : 2 \text{ g}$ of element 2 and $1.33 \text{ g} : 1.00 \text{ g} : 1.00 \text{ g}$ of element 3 in the compounds. That last ratio can be made integral merely by multiplying by 3, to get $4 : 3 : 3$.

6. The extra aluminum will not react, because the law of definite proportions states that the elements in a given compound have definite proportions by mass (in this case, 5.40 g of aluminum to 9.62 g of sulfur).

7. Because 0.5 is equal to $\frac{1}{2}$, multiply each ratio by 2, to get
(a) $(3 \text{ g A}) / (2 \text{ g B})$; (b) $(5 \text{ g A})/(2 \text{ g B})$;
(c) $(7 \text{ g A})/(2 \text{ g B})$.

8. (a) $(2.67 \text{ g A})/(1.00 \text{ g B})$
0.67 is equivalent to $\frac{2}{3}$ so multiply numerator and denominator by 3:

$$(8.01 \text{ g A})/(3.00 \text{ g B}) = (8 \text{ g A})/(3 \text{ g B})$$

(b) $(4.75 \text{ g A})/(1.00 \text{ g B})$
0.75 is equivalent to $\frac{3}{4}$ so multiply numerator and denominator by 4:

$$(19.0 \text{ g A})/(4.00 \text{ g B})$$

(c) $(1.60 \text{ g A})/(1.00 \text{ g B})$
0.60 is equivalent to $\frac{3}{5}$ so multiply numerator and denominator by 5:

$$(8.00 \text{ g A})/(5.00 \text{ g B})$$

9. (a) No, mixtures do not obey the law of definite proportions.
(b) A given mixture might be anywhere from 99.99% carbon monoxide, with 42.9% carbon, to 99.99% carbon dioxide, with 27.3% carbon.

10.

	Carbon monoxide	Carbon dioxide
Carbon	42.9 g	27.3 g
Oxygen	57.1 g	72.7 g

Per gram of carbon in each compound:

	Carbon monoxide	Carbon dioxide
Carbon	1.00 g	1.00 g
Oxygen	1.33 g	2.66 g

Per gram of carbon, the ratio of masses of oxygen in the two compounds is an integral ratio: $(2.66 \text{ g}) : (1.33 \text{ g}) = 2 \text{ g} : 1 \text{ g}$

11. (a) We should convert the mass of element 2 in compound 1 to grams. (b) Assuming that we have 100.0 g of compound, we merely change the percent signs to grams. (c) We divide each mass by the mass of element 2, the smallest mass in each compound. (d) No. (e) With a fixed mass of element 2, the mass ratios of element 1 in one compound to element 1 in the other compound and of element 3 in one compound to element 3 in the other compound are used to establish the law of multiple proportions.

12. (a) $627 \text{ mg} \left(\dfrac{0.001 \text{ g}}{1 \text{ mg}} \right) = 0.627 \text{ g}$

(b) Assuming a 100-g sample, we merely change the percent signs to g for grams. These conversions yield:

HARRISON COLLEGE
Indianapolis Downtown

	Element 1	**Element 2**	**Element 3**
Compound 1	7.53 g	0.627 g	1.67 g
Compound 2	50.0 g	5.56 g	44.4 g

(c)

	Element 1	**Element 2**	**Element 3**
Compound 1	12.0 g	1.00 g	2.66 g
Compound 2	8.99 g	1.00 g	7.99 g

(d) For a fixed (1.00 g) mass of element 2, the mass ratio of element 1 in the two compounds is $12.0\,g : 8.99\,g = 4\,g : 3\,g$, and that of element 3 in the two compounds is $2.66\,g : 7.99\,g = 1\,g : 3\,g$.

13. This problem is the similar to the prior problem, except that it is not presented in parts.

$$0.1279\,kg \left(\frac{1000\,g}{1\,kg}\right) = 127.9\,g$$

	Element 1	**Element 2**	**Element 3**
Compound 1	127.9 g	10.66 g	28.43 g
Compound 2	62.07 g	10.34 g	27.59 g
Compound 3	10.68 g	1.334 g	7.117 g

	Element 1	**Element 2**	**Element 3**
Compound 1	12.00 g	1.000 g	2.667 g
Compound 2	6.003 g	1.000 g	2.668 g
Compound 3	8.006 g	1.000 g	5.335 g

For a fixed (1.000 g) mass of element 2, the mass ratio of element 1 in the three compounds is

$$12.00\,g : 6.003\,g : 8.006\,g = 2\,g : 1\,g : 1.334\,g$$

which is equal to $6 : 3 : 4$. That of element 3 in the three compounds is

$$2.667\,g : 2.668\,g : 5.335\,g = 1\,g : 1\,g : 2\,g.$$

Chapter 4

Formula Calculations

4.1 Atomic and Formula Masses

Atomic Mass

The **atomic mass** of an element is the weighted average of the masses of its atoms. The unit of atomic mass is called, fittingly enough, the **atomic mass unit**. It is defined as one-twelfth the mass of the ^{12}C atom, and it is abbreviated **amu** in most books but **u** in some. (A few chemists use the *dalton* as the unit of atomic mass, in honor of John Dalton.) Although John Dalton in his atomic theory postulated that all atoms of the same element had the same mass, we now know that the different isotopes of an element have different masses. For example, ^{12}C atoms have a mass of exactly 12 amu each, whereas ^{13}C atoms have a mass of 13.00335 amu each. It turns out that the ratio of isotopes of each of the elements in all naturally occurring samples is very constant (to three or more significant digits), so the weighted average of the masses of the atoms of an element is constant, which is why Dalton's hypotheses worked.

Please note that atomic mass, called **atomic weight** in some texts, is different from mass number. The mass number refers to a specific isotope, and is an integer—the number of protons plus neutrons in each atom. The atomic mass is based on the naturally occurring mixture of isotopes, and is not an integer. Atomic masses for almost all the elements are presented in the periodic table; mass numbers are presented there only for elements that do not occur naturally. Note that atomic masses vary from about 1 for hydrogen to a little over 250 for the largest elements. If we ever solve a problem and get an atomic mass outside this range, we know we have likely made a mistake. Also note that no atom has an atomic mass in the range of 1 to 250 *grams*. That might be the mass of a mole of atoms (Section 4.2).

The **weighted average** of several sets of items is the average with regard to the number in each set. For example, if the Jones family has triplet boys, each weighing 90 pounds, and one girl, who weighs 50 pounds, the average of one boy and the girl is 70 pounds, but the weighted average of all the children is 80 pounds:

90 pounds

90 pounds   or 3(90 pounds) + 50 pounds = 320 pounds

90 pounds

50 pounds

320 pounds

Weighted average = (320 pounds)/(4 children) = 80 pounds

The atomic mass of each element can be determined in two different ways: (1) as was done historically, by comparing the naturally occurring mixture versus a standard (now ^{12}C), or (2) as presently done with the modern *mass spectrometer*, by measuring the mass of each isotope and the percentage abundance of each.

EXAMPLE 1   (a) The atoms of a certain element have a mass 2.026 times the mass of an equal number of ^{12}C atoms. What is the atomic mass of the element? (b) Which element is it? (c) What is the best way to make sure that we get equal numbers of atoms of two elements to compare total masses?

Solution

(a) The mass of the average atom is 2.026 times that of a ^{12}C atom:

$$2.026(12.00\,amu) = 24.31\,amu$$

(b) Magnesium (see the periodic table).
(c) The best way to get equal numbers of atoms is to make a compound of the two elements that has them in a $1:1$ ratio.   □

EXAMPLE 2   Naturally occurring magnesium consists 78.70% of ^{24}Mg, with atoms of mass 23.98504 amu, 10.13% of ^{25}Mg, with atoms of mass 24.98584 amu, and 11.17% ^{26}Mg, with atoms of mass 25.98259 amu. Calculate the atomic mass of magnesium.

Table 4-1 Types of Formula Masses

Formula Unit	Name	Example	
Atom	Atomic mass	Hg	200.6 amu
Molecule	Molecular mass	NH_3	17.0 amu
Molecule	Molecular mass	H_2	2.0 amu (a diatomic element)
Formula unit of an ionic compound	Formula mass	$MgCl_2$	95.2 amu

Solution

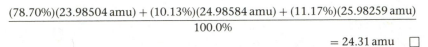

$$\frac{(78.70\%)(23.98504 \text{ amu}) + (10.13\%)(24.98584 \text{ amu}) + (11.17\%)(25.98259 \text{ amu})}{100.0\%}$$

$$= 24.31 \text{ amu} \quad \square$$

Atomic masses are used to describe combined as well as uncombined atoms.

Formula Masses

The subscripts in the formula of a compound give the ratio of the number of atoms of each element to the number of atoms of each other element in the formula. The collection of atoms written to represent the compound is defined as one **formula unit**. That is, the formula unit of ammonium sulfide, $(NH_4)_2S$, contains two atoms of nitrogen, eight atoms of hydrogen, and one atom of sulfur. The term **formula mass** (sometimes called *formula weight*) refers to the sum of the atomic masses of every atom (not merely every element) in a formula unit. There are several names for formula masses corresponding to different kinds of formulas. For uncombined atoms, the formula mass is the atomic mass. For covalent compounds, which consist of molecules, the formula mass can be called the **molecular mass**. For ionic compounds, there is no special name for formula mass. These terms are summarized in Table 4-1.

It turns out that determining formula masses does not depend on the nature of the formula unit; merely add the atomic masses of each atom present no matter what the nature of the formula unit.

EXAMPLE 3 Determine the formula mass for each of the following: (*a*) $AlCl_3$ (*b*) U (*c*) H_2O (*d*) Br_2 (*e*) U in UF_6

Solution (*a*) 26.98 amu + 3(35.453 amu) = 133.34 amu
(*b*) 238.0 amu   (*c*) 18.02 amu   (*d*) 159.8 amu
(*e*) 238.0 amu

Calculations for (c) and (d) are done the same way that the calculation for (a) is done. The values for (b) and (e) show that the *atomic mass does not depend on whether the atom is in a compound or not.* ☐

4.2 The Mole

Atoms, most molecules, and formula units of ionic compounds are extremely tiny. Their formula masses are measured in atomic mass units, which are useful for comparison purposes only. In order to get weighable quantities of matter, a huge collection of formula units is required. The **mole** is defined as the number of ^{12}C atoms in exactly 12 *grams* of ^{12}C. A **millimole** is 0.001 mol, and is useful for calculations with small quantities of substances. The mole is abbreviated mol, not m or M, which are used for related quantities, and millimole is abbreviated mmol.

That is, *one* ^{12}C atom has a mass of 12 **amu**;
one mole of ^{12}C atoms has a mass of 12 *grams*;
one millimole of ^{12}C atoms has a mass of 12 *mg*.

The number of ^{12}C atoms in 12.0 g is 6.02×10^{23}; this number is called **Avogadro's number**, and must be memorized. It turns out that this number is the number of atomic mass units in 1.00 gram:

$$\frac{6.02 \times 10^{23}\ ^{12}C\ \text{atoms}}{1\ \text{mol}\ ^{12}C} \left(\frac{1\ \text{mol}\ ^{12}C}{12.0\ \text{g}}\right) \left(\frac{12.000\ \text{amu}}{1\ ^{12}C\ \text{atom}}\right)$$

$$= 6.02 \times 10^{23}\ \text{amu/g}$$

Avogadro's number may be used in chemistry problems the way a dozen is used in everyday problems, to convert back and forth between the number of individual items and the number of moles of those items.

EXAMPLE 4 Calculate the number of (a) lemons in 3.50 dozen lemons. (b) atoms in 3.50 mol of atoms.

Solution

(a) $3.50\ \text{dozen} \left(\dfrac{12\ \text{lemons}}{1\ \text{dozen}}\right) = 42\ \text{lemons}$

(b) $3.50\ \text{mol} \left(\dfrac{6.02 \times 10^{23}\ \text{atoms}}{1\ \text{mol}}\right) = 2.11 \times 10^{24}\ \text{atoms}$ ☐

Just as with dozens, the *mass* of a mole of atoms depends on which atoms are specified.

EXAMPLE 5 (*a*) Which is heavier, two dozen lemons or two dozen watermelons? (*b*) Which has a greater mass, 2 mol of uranium atoms or 2 mol of lithium atoms?

Solution (*a*) The watermelons weigh more, despite there being an equal number, because each watermelon weighs more than each lemon. (*b*) The mole of uranium has a greater mass despite there being equal numbers of atoms, because each uranium atom has a greater mass than each lithium atom. □

To convert masses to moles or vice versa, we use the molar mass of the substance. **Molar mass** has the same numeric value as the number of atomic mass units in a formula unit, but it is expressed in units of *grams per mole*. For example, the molar mass of water is 18.0 g/mol because the formula mass of water is 18.0 amu/molecule. Because molar mass is a ratio, it can be used as a factor in problem solving.

EXAMPLE 6 Calculate (*a*) the weight of 3.50 dozen lemons, assuming that the average weight is 3.00 pounds per dozen. (*b*) the mass of 3.50 mol of uranium atoms.

Solution

(*a*) $3.50 \text{ dozen} \left(\dfrac{3.00 \text{ pounds}}{1 \text{ dozen}} \right) = 10.5 \text{ pounds}$

(*b*) The atomic mass of uranium is found on the periodic table.

$3.50 \text{ mol U} \left(\dfrac{238 \text{ g U}}{1 \text{ mol U}} \right) = 833 \text{ g U}$ □

In summary, remember that we can use the molar *mass* to convert to or from *masses*, and Avogadro's *number* to convert to or from *numbers* of individual formula units. The following figure may help us remember how to convert moles to numbers of individual items or to mass, or vice versa.

EXAMPLE 7 (*a*) Calculate the number of molecules in 5.00 mol of NH_3. (*b*) Calculate the mass of 5.00 mol of NH_3.

Solution

(a) $5.00 \, \text{mol NH}_3 \left(\dfrac{6.02 \times 10^{23} \, \text{molecules NH}_3}{1 \, \text{mol NH}_3} \right)$

$\qquad\qquad\qquad\qquad = 3.01 \times 10^{24} \, \text{molecules NH}_3$

(b) $5.00 \, \text{mol NH}_3 \left(\dfrac{17.0 \, \text{g NH}_3}{1 \, \text{mol NH}_3} \right) = 85.0 \, \text{g NH}_3$ $\qquad$ □

To convert from masses to numbers of individual formula units or vice versa, use two steps in the figure above.

EXAMPLE 8 Calculate the number of molecules in $56.7 \, \text{g NH}_3$.

Solution

$$56.7 \, \text{g NH}_3 \left(\frac{1 \, \text{mol NH}_3}{17.0 \, \text{g NH}_3} \right) = 3.34 \, \text{mol NH}_3$$

$$3.34 \, \text{mol NH}_3 \left(\frac{6.02 \times 10^{23} \, \text{molecules NH}_3}{1 \, \text{mol NH}_3} \right)$$

$$= 2.01 \times 10^{24} \, \text{molecules NH}_3$$

Once we get more experience doing these types of problems, we may solve them in a single step:

$$56.7 \, \text{g NH}_3 \left(\frac{1 \, \text{mol NH}_3}{17.0 \, \text{g NH}_3} \right) \left(\frac{6.02 \times 10^{23} \, \text{molecules NH}_3}{1 \, \text{mol NH}_3} \right)$$

$$= 2.01 \times 10^{24} \, \text{molecules NH}_3 \qquad □$$

The subscripts in the chemical formula tell us how many moles of atoms of each element are present in a mole of the compound. For example, there are 8 moles of carbon atoms, 18 moles of hydrogen atoms, and 1 mole of oxygen atoms in each mole of octanol, $C_8H_{18}O$. In doing problems involving the numbers of moles of atoms in a given number of moles of compound, be sure to identify the substance after writing the unit involved.

EXAMPLE 9 How many moles of potassium are present in $1.40 \, \text{mol}$ of K_3PO_4, a compound used as a fertilizer?

Solution

$$1.40 \, \text{mol K}_3PO_4 \left(\frac{3 \, \text{mol K}}{1 \, \text{mol K}_3PO_4} \right) = 4.20 \, \text{mol K}$$

$$\text{from the}$$
$$\text{chemical formula} \qquad □$$

4.3 Percent Composition

The subscripts in the formula of a compound give the mole ratio of atoms of the elements in the compound. For example, H_2SO_4 has a mole ratio of 2 mol of hydrogen atoms to 1 mol of sulfur atoms to 4 mol of oxygen atoms. The percent composition refers to the mass ratio of the elements converted to percentage. To get the percent composition, take an arbitrary quantity of the compound (1.00 mol is easiest), convert each number of moles of the elements to grams with the molar masses of the atoms, then calculate the percentage by dividing the mass of each element by the total mass in the given quantity of compound (in this case, 1.00 mol).

EXAMPLE 10 Calculate the percent composition of NH_4NO_3, another fertilizer.

Solution The masses are calculated as shown above:

$$2\,\text{mol N}\left(\frac{14.01\,\text{g N}}{1\,\text{mol N}}\right) = 28.02\,\text{g N}$$

$$4\,\text{mol H}\left(\frac{1.008\,\text{g H}}{1\,\text{mol H}}\right) = 4.032\,\text{g H}$$

$$3\,\text{mol O}\left(\frac{16.00\,\text{g O}}{1\,\text{mol O}}\right) = 48.00\,\text{g O}$$

$$\text{Total} = 80.05\,\text{g}$$

(Note that we use 16.00 g/mol of oxygen atoms; this problem has nothing to do with oxygen molecules, O_2.)

The percentage of each element is the mass of the element divided by the total mass, times 100% to convert to percent:

$$\frac{4.032\,\text{g H}}{80.05\,\text{g}} \times 100.0\% = 5.037\%\,\text{H}$$

$$\frac{28.02\,\text{g N}}{80.05\,\text{g}} \times 100.0\% = 35.00\%\,\text{N}$$

$$\frac{48.00\,\text{g O}}{80.05\,\text{g}} \times 100.0\% = 59.95\%\,\text{O}$$

$$\text{Total} = 99.99\%$$

We should always check our answer to see that it is reasonable! A total between 99.5% and 100.5% is reasonable. □

4.4 Empirical Formulas

Empirical formula problems should be done with at least three significant digits in each value. If fewer significant digits are used, rounding errors may yield an incorrect formula.

We have learned how to convert a formula to percent composition; we will now do the opposite—convert a percent composition to the empirical formula. The **empirical formula** of a compound is its simplest formula, having the smallest possible set of integral subscripts. Thus CH_2 is an empirical formula, but C_2H_4 is not, because its subscripts can both be divided by 2. The empirical formula tells the mole ratio of the atoms of each element to those of every other element in the compound. If we start with a set of masses for the elements in the compound, we can change them to moles as shown in Section 4.2. We then have to make that set of moles into an integral set of moles, and use those integers as subscripts in our formula.

EXAMPLE 11 Calculate the empirical formula of glucose, a simple sugar, if a certain sample contains 393.4 g of carbon, 66.07 g of hydrogen, and 524.2 g of oxygen.

Solution We first change each of the masses to moles:

$$393.4\,g\,C\left(\frac{1\,mol\,C}{12.01\,g\,C}\right) = 32.76\,mol\,C$$

$$66.07\,g\,H\left(\frac{1\,mol\,H}{1.008\,g\,H}\right) = 65.55\,mol\,H$$

$$524.2\,g\,O\left(\frac{1\,mol\,O}{16.00\,g\,O}\right) = 32.76\,mol\,O$$

We now have a mole ratio of these elements, but it is not an integer ratio. The easiest way to get an integer ratio is to divide all of these moles by the magnitude of the smallest:

$$\frac{32.76\,mol\,C}{32.76} = 1.000\,mol\,C \qquad \frac{32.76\,mol\,O}{32.76} = 1.000\,mol\,O$$

$$\frac{65.55\,mol\,H}{32.76} = 2.001\,mol\,H$$

The ratio is close enough to a $1:2:1$ ratio to deduce the empirical formula to be CH_2O. □

Two complications often arise. Instead of masses of the elements, a problem is usually stated in terms of percentages of the elements. If we assume that we have a 100.0-g sample, the percentages are equal to the masses in grams. Then we proceed as above. The second complication is the division by the magnitude of the smallest number of moles may not give all integers, but some decimal fractions in addition to integers. We can change the fractional part of the decimal fraction to a common fraction, then multiply every number of moles by the denominator of that fraction. (We had the same problem in Section 3.3 with the law of multiple proportions.)

EXAMPLE 12   Calculate the empirical formula of a compound composed of 52.9% carbon and 47.1% oxygen.

Solution   We first change each of the percentages to masses and those to moles:

$$52.9\,g\ C\left(\frac{1\,mol\ C}{12.0\,g\ C}\right) = 4.41\,mol\ C$$

$$47.1\,g\ O\left(\frac{1\,mol\ O}{16.0\,g\ O}\right) = 2.94\,mol\ O$$

The attempt to get integral numbers of moles produces

$$\frac{4.41\,mol\ C}{2.94} = 1.50\,mol\ C \qquad \frac{2.94\,mol\ O}{2.94} = 1.00\,mol\ O$$

The 1.50 is equal to $1\frac{1}{2}$ or $\frac{3}{2}$, so we multiply *every* number of moles by 2 (the denominator of $\frac{3}{2}$).

$$\frac{1.50\,mol\ C \times 2}{1.00\,mol\ O \times 2} = \frac{3\,mol\ C}{2\,mol\ C}$$

and the empirical formula is C_3O_2 (for carbon suboxide). □

4.5 Molecular Formulas

Covalent compounds exist as molecules, and their (molecular) formulas have some integral multiple of the set of subscripts in the empirical formula. The **molecular formula** gives all the information that the empirical formula gives, and in addition it gives the ratio of the number of moles of every element to the number of moles of the compound as a whole. To get the molecular formula from the empirical formula and the molecular mass, determine the mass corresponding to the empirical formula and divide that into the molecular mass. Use the integral result to multiply each subscript in the empirical formula (including the understood values equal to 1).

EXAMPLE 13 Determine the molecular formula of a compound with empirical formula CH_2 and molecular mass 98.0 amu.

Solution
The empirical formula mass is 12.0 amu + 2(1.0 amu) = 14.0 amu.

There are (98.0 amu)/(14.0 amu) = 7 empirical formula units in each molecule. The molecular formula is thus C_7H_{14}. □

On examinations, the empirical formula is often not given, but a percentage composition is given instead along with a molecular mass. Then we have a two-step solution; first find the empirical formula as in Section 4.4 and then find the molecular formula as just shown.

Leading Questions

1. One oxygen atom has a mass 1.33 times that of a carbon atom. What is the ratio of masses of (a) 2 oxygen atoms to 2 carbon atoms? (b) 1 dozen oxygen atoms to 1 dozen carbon atoms? (c) 200 oxygen atoms to 200 carbon atoms? (d) 1 mol of oxygen atoms to 1 mol of carbon atoms?

2. (a) Calculate the number of dozens of oranges in 60 oranges. (b) Calculate the number dozens of pairs of socks in 60 pairs of socks. (c) Calculate the number of moles of Al atoms in 3.01×10^{24} Al atoms. (d) Calculate the number of moles of H_2 molecules in 3.01×10^{24} H_2 molecules.

3. What is the molar mass of (a) oxygen atoms? (b) oxygen gas?

4. Which section of Chapter 4 is limited to only one type of formula unit?

Answers to Leading Questions

1. All these ratios are 1.33 to 1.

2. (a) $60 \text{ oranges} \left(\dfrac{1 \text{ dozen oranges}}{12 \text{ oranges}} \right) = 5 \text{ dozen oranges}$

(b) $60 \text{ pairs of socks} \left(\dfrac{1 \text{ dozen pairs of socks}}{12 \text{ pairs of socks}} \right)$
$$= 5 \text{ dozen pairs of socks}$$

(c) $3.01 \times 10^{24} \text{ Al atoms} \left(\dfrac{1 \text{ mol Al}}{6.02 \times 10^{23} \text{ Al atoms}} \right) = 5.00 \text{ mol Al}$

(d) $3.01 \times 10^{24} \text{ H}_2 \text{ molecules} \left(\dfrac{1 \text{ mol H}_2}{6.02 \times 10^{23} \text{ H}_2 \text{ molecules}} \right)$
$$= 5.00 \text{ mol H}_2$$

3. (a) 16.0 g/mol (b) 32.0 g/mol (of O_2 molecules)

4. Section 4.5. It calculates molecular formulas that exist only for covalent compounds that form molecules.

Supplementary Problems

1. In a 5.00-g sample of carbon, how many of the atoms have a mass of 12.01 amu?

2. Calculate the atomic mass of an element if its average atom has a mass (a) 2.25 times that of carbon. (b) 2.42 times that of the element in part (a).

3. Calculate the atomic mass of an element if 60.4% of the atoms have a mass of 68.9257 amu and the rest have a mass of 70.9249 amu.

4. Calculate the percentage of bromine atoms that have a mass of 78.9183 amu and the percentage that have a mass of 80.9163 amu. The atomic mass of bromine is 79.909 amu, and these are the only two naturally occurring isotopes.

5. Calculate the formula mass of (a) $(NH_4)_2HPO_4$ (one type of fertilizer); (b) C_2H_5OH (ethyl alcohol); (c) P_4 (one form of elemental phosphorus).

6. Determine the molar mass of (a) $(NH_4)_2HPO_4$; (b) C_2H_5OH; (c) P_4.

7. (a) Calculate the number of dozens of oranges in 84 oranges. (b) Calculate the number of moles of Al atoms in 5.75×10^{24} Al atoms. (c) Calculate the number of moles of H_2 molecules in 5.75×10^{24} H_2 molecules. (d) Calculate the number of moles of H atoms in 5.75×10^{24} H_2 molecules.

8. Calculate the number of aluminum atoms in a can containing 25.0 g of aluminum.

9. Calculate the number of moles of ethylene glycol, $C_2H_6O_2$, used as antifreeze in cars, that are in 47.7 g of $C_2H_6O_2$.

10. Calculate the mass in grams of 5.00×10^{20} H_2O molecules.

11. Calculate the number of moles of hydrogen atoms in 17.4 g of $(NH_4)_2SO_4$.

12. Calculate the percent composition of borax, $Na_2B_2O_7$, used in commercial laundry processes.

13. Calculate the empirical formula of "hypo," used in photographic development, consisting of 29.1% Na, 40.5% S, and 30.4% O.

14. Calculate the percent composition of rubbing alcohol, C_3H_8O.

15. Calculate the molecular formula of a compound with molar mass 104 g/mol composed of 92.3% carbon and 7.7% hydrogen.

16. Consider the formula of hydrazinium nitrate, $N_2H_6(NO_3)_2$. (a) Calculate its molar mass. (b) Calculate the number of moles of the compound in 17.4 g of it. (c) Calculate the number of moles of nitrogen atoms in that quantity of compound. (d) Calculate the number of individual nitrogen atoms in that quantity.

17. Calculate the number of individual nitrogen atoms in 151 g of ammonium azide, NH_4N_3.

Solutions to Supplementary Problems

1. None. The 12.01 amu is the atomic mass—the weighted average of all the isotopes of carbon. (The same reasoning tells us that no American family has 2.3 children.)

2. (a) $2.25(12.01\,\text{amu}) = 27.0\,\text{amu}$
   (b) $2.42(27.0\,\text{amu}) = 65.3\,\text{amu}$

3. $\dfrac{(60.4\%)(68.9257\,\text{amu}) + (39.6\%)(70.9249\,\text{amu})}{100\%} = 69.7\,\text{amu}$

4. Let x = the percentage of the 78.9183 amu isotope, then $(100 - x)$ = the percentage of the other isotope.

$$\frac{x(78.9183\,\text{amu}) + (100 - x)(80.9163\,\text{amu})}{100} = 79.909\,\text{amu}$$

$$78.9183x + 8091.63 - 80.9163x = 7990.9$$
$$-1.998x = -100.7$$
$$x = 50.40\%$$
$$\text{and } (100 - x) = 49.60\%$$

5. (a) $2(14.0\,\text{amu}) + 9(1.0\,\text{amu}) + 31.0\,\text{amu} + 4(16.0\,\text{amu})$
   $= 132.0\,\text{amu}$ (b) $46.0\,\text{amu}$ (c) $4(31.0\,\text{amu}) = 124\,\text{amu}$

6. (*a*) 132.0 g/mol   (*b*) 46.0 g/mol   (*c*) 124 g/mol
(The numbers are the same as those in the prior problem, but the units of molar mass are grams per mole.)

7. (*a*) $84 \, \text{oranges} \left(\dfrac{1 \, \text{dozen oranges}}{12 \, \text{oranges}} \right) = 7 \, \text{dozen oranges}$

(*b*) $5.75 \times 10^{24} \, \text{Al atoms} \left(\dfrac{1 \, \text{mol Al}}{6.02 \times 10^{23} \, \text{Al atoms}} \right) = 9.55 \, \text{mol Al}$

(*c*) $5.75 \times 10^{24} \, \text{H}_2 \, \text{molecules} \left(\dfrac{1 \, \text{mol H}_2}{6.02 \times 10^{23} \, \text{H}_2 \, \text{molecules}} \right)$
$$= 9.55 \, \text{mol H}_2$$

(*d*) $5.75 \times 10^{24} \, \text{H}_2 \, \text{molecules} \left(\dfrac{2 \, \text{H atoms}}{1 \, \text{H}_2 \, \text{molecule}} \right) \times$
$$\left(\dfrac{1 \, \text{mol H atoms}}{6.02 \times 10^{23} \, \text{H atoms}} \right) = 19.1 \, \text{mol H atoms}$$

There are Avogadro's number of particles in a mole of particles, no matter what type of particles they are.

8. $25.0 \, \text{g Al} \left(\dfrac{1 \, \text{mol Al}}{27.0 \, \text{g Al}} \right) \left(\dfrac{6.02 \times 10^{23} \, \text{atoms Al}}{1 \, \text{mol Al}} \right)$
$$= 5.57 \times 10^{23} \, \text{atoms Al}$$

9. $47.7 \, \text{g C}_2\text{H}_6\text{O}_2 \left(\dfrac{1 \, \text{mol C}_2\text{H}_6\text{O}_2}{62.0 \, \text{g C}_2\text{H}_6\text{O}_2} \right) = 0.769 \, \text{mol C}_2\text{H}_6\text{O}_2$

10. $5.00 \times 10^{20} \, \text{H}_2\text{O molecules} \left(\underbrace{\dfrac{1 \, \text{mol H}_2\text{O}}{6.02 \times 10^{23} \, \text{H}_2\text{O molecules}}}_{\text{Avogadro's number}} \right) \times$
$$\underbrace{\left(\dfrac{18.0 \, \text{g H}_2\text{O}}{1 \, \text{mol H}_2\text{O}} \right)}_{\text{molar mass}} = 0.0150 \, \text{g H}_2\text{O}$$

11. $17.4 \, \text{g (NH}_4)_2\text{SO}_4 \underbrace{\left(\dfrac{1 \, \text{mol (NH}_4)_2\text{SO}_4}{132 \, \text{g (NH}_4)_2\text{SO}_4} \right)}_{\text{molar mass}} \underbrace{\left(\dfrac{8 \, \text{mol H}}{1 \, \text{mol (NH}_4)_2\text{SO}_4} \right)}_{\text{from chemical formula}}$
$$= 1.05 \, \text{mol H atoms}$$

12.

$$2 \, \text{Na} \quad 2 \, \text{mol} \times 22.99 \, \text{g/mol} = \quad 45.98 \, \text{g}$$
$$2 \, \text{B} \quad 2 \, \text{mol} \times 10.81 \, \text{g/mol} = \quad 21.62 \, \text{g}$$
$$7 \, \text{O} \quad 7 \, \text{mol} \times 16.00 \, \text{g/mol} = 112.0 \, \text{g}$$
$$\text{Total} = 179.6 \, \text{g}$$

$$\% \, \text{Na} = \dfrac{45.98 \, \text{g Na}}{179.6 \, \text{g total}} \times 100\% = 25.60\% \, \text{Na}$$

$$\% B = \frac{21.62 \text{ g B}}{179.6 \text{ g total}} \times 100\% = 12.04\% \text{ B}$$

$$\% O = \frac{112.0 \text{ g O}}{179.6 \text{ g total}} \times 100\% = 62.36\% \text{ O}$$

$$\text{Total} = 100.00\%$$

13. Assume 100.0 g of sample:

$$29.1 \text{ g Na} \left(\frac{1 \text{ mol Na}}{23.0 \text{ g Na}} \right) = 1.27 \text{ mol Na}$$

$$40.5 \text{ g S} \left(\frac{1 \text{ mol S}}{32.1 \text{ g S}} \right) = 1.26 \text{ mol S}$$

$$30.4 \text{ g O} \left(\frac{1 \text{ mol O}}{16.0 \text{ g O}} \right) = 1.90 \text{ mol O}$$

Dividing each of these numbers of moles by the smallest magnitude yields

$$\frac{1.27 \text{ mol Na}}{1.26} = 1.01 \text{ mol Na} \qquad \frac{1.26 \text{ mol S}}{1.26} = 1.00 \text{ mol S}$$

$$\frac{1.90 \text{ mol O}}{1.26} = 1.51 \text{ mol O}$$

The ratio of $1 : 1 : 1.5$ is equal to $2 : 2 : 3$, and the empirical formula is $Na_2S_2O_3$.

14.

$$3 \text{ C} \quad 3 \text{ mol} \times 12.01 \text{ g/mol} = 36.03 \text{ g C}$$

$$8 \text{ H} \quad 8 \text{ mol} \times 1.008 \text{ g/mol} = 8.064 \text{ g H}$$

$$1 \text{ O} \quad 1 \text{ mol} \times 16.00 \text{ g/mol} = 16.00 \text{ g O}$$

$$\text{Total} = 60.09 \text{ g}$$

$$\% C = \frac{36.03 \text{ g C}}{60.09 \text{ g total}} \times 100\% = 59.96\% \text{ C}$$

$$\% H = \frac{8.064 \text{ g H}}{60.09 \text{ g total}} \times 100\% = 13.42\% \text{ H}$$

$$\% O = \frac{16.00 \text{ g O}}{60.09 \text{ g total}} \times 100\% = 26.63\% \text{ O}$$

$$\text{Total} = 100.01\%$$

15. Assume 100.0 g of sample:

$$92.3\,g\,C\left(\frac{1\,mol\,C}{12.0\,g\,C}\right)=7.69\,mol\,C$$

$$7.7\,g\,H\left(\frac{1\,mol\,H}{1.0\,g\,H}\right)=7.7\,mol\,H$$

Since these numbers of moles are equal, the mole ratio is $1:1$; the empirical formula is CH. The empirical formula mass is therefore 13 amu, which divides into 104 amu exactly 8 times. The molecular formula is C_8H_8.

16. (a) $4\,mol\,N(14.0\,g/mol)+6\,mol\,H(1.0\,g/mol)+$
$$6\,mol\,O(16.0\,g/mol)=158\,g$$

(b) $17.4\,g\,N_2H_6(NO_3)_2\left(\dfrac{1\,mol\,N_2H_6(NO_3)_2}{158\,g\,N_2H_6(NO_3)_2}\right)$
$$=0.110\,mol\,N_2H_6(NO_3)_2$$

(c) $0.110\,mol\,N_2H_6(NO_3)_2\left(\dfrac{4\,mol\,N}{1\,mol\,N_2H_6(NO_3)_2}\right)=0.440\,mol\,N$

(d) $0.440\,mol\,N\left(\dfrac{6.02\times10^{23}\,N\,atoms}{1\,mol\,N}\right)=2.65\times10^{23}\,N\,atoms$

17. This problem is similar to the prior problem, but is not stated in steps.

$$4\,mol\,N(14.0\,g/mol)+4\,mol\,H(1.008\,g/mol)=60.0\,g$$

$$151\,g\,NH_4N_3\left(\frac{1\,mol\,NH_4N_3}{60.0\,g\,NH_4N_3}\right)\left(\frac{4\,mol\,N}{1\,mol\,NH_4N_3}\right)\times$$

$$\left(\frac{6.02\times10^{23}\,N\,atoms}{1\,mol\,N}\right)=6.06\times10^{24}\,N\,atoms$$

Chapter 5

Stoichiometry

5.1 Mole Relationships in Chemical Reactions

Stoichiometry is the subject that tells the quantity of one substance that reacts with some quantity of anything else in a chemical reaction. The coefficients of the balanced chemical equation give the *mole ratios* of every substance in the reaction to every other substance. Therefore it is imperative to write a balanced chemical equation for every problem involving a chemical reaction. The equation

$$6\,Li + N_2 \rightarrow 2\,Li_3N$$

states that lithium and nitrogen gas react in a 6 mol to 1 mol ratio, and that for every 6 mol of lithium used up, 2 mol of lithium nitride is produced. The ratio of coefficients of any two substances in a chemical equation can be used as a factor to solve a problem.

EXAMPLE 1 (*a*) How many moles of Mg_3N_2 will be produced by reaction of 1.50 mol of Mg with excess N_2? (*b*) How many moles of Mg are required to react with 3.50 mol of oxygen gas?

Solution

(*a*) $3\,Mg(s) + N_2(g) \rightarrow Mg_3N_2(s)$
We use the ratio of moles of Mg_3N_2 to moles of Mg because moles of magnesium are given and moles of Mg_3N_2 are asked for:

$$1.50\;\text{mol Mg}\left(\frac{1\;\text{mol Mg}_3\text{N}_2}{3\;\text{mol Mg}}\right) = 0.500\;\text{mol Mg}_3\text{N}_2$$

(*b*) We must remember that oxygen gas is diatomic: O_2.

$$2 \, Mg(s) + O_2(g) \rightarrow 2 \, MgO(s)$$

$$3.50 \text{ mol } O_2\left(\frac{2 \text{ mol Mg}}{1 \text{ mol } O_2}\right) = 7.00 \text{ mol Mg} \qquad \square$$

5.2 Mass Relationships

Conversions of moles of one substance to moles of any other in the balanced chemical equation is straightforward; just remember that it is *moles* not mass that is related to the coefficients in the equation. However, stoichiometry problems often give students more trouble than they should because the problems are often asked in terms of masses or other quantities that can be related to moles of reactant or product. These problems are multistep problems, but should not present too much difficulty because each individual step is straight-forward.

EXAMPLE 2   What mass of Li_3N will be produced by the reaction of 2.75 g of lithium metal with excess nitrogen gas?

Solution   The balanced chemical equation (6 Li + N_2 → 2 Li_3N) gives the *mole ratio*. We must first change the mass to moles, as we did in Section 4.2. *Note well*: The coefficient in the balanced chemical equation has nothing to do with the conversion of mass to moles or vice versa. Indeed, we did such conversions before we learned how to balance equations!

$$2.75 \text{ g Li}\left(\frac{1 \text{ mol Li}}{6.94 \text{ g Li}}\right) = 0.396 \text{ mol Li}$$

(*Note:* We use 1 mol of Li in the factor, not the number in the balanced equation.) Then we convert the number of moles of Li used to moles of Li_3N produced, using the ratio from the balanced equation:

$$0.396 \text{ mol Li}\left(\frac{2 \text{ mol } Li_3N}{6 \text{ mol Li}}\right) = 0.132 \text{ mol } Li_3N$$

Finally we convert that number of moles of Li_3N to mass, again as in Section 4.2:

$$0.132 \text{ mol } Li_3N\left(\frac{34.8 \text{ g } Li_3N}{1 \text{ mol } Li_3N}\right) = 4.59 \text{ g } Li_3N \qquad \square$$

We can diagram the overall process as we did in Chapter 4.

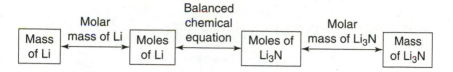

5.3 Other Conversions

Any quantity that can be converted to moles of reactant or product may be presented in the statement of a problem. Examples are number of formula units of reactant or product, or number of moles of an element in one of the reactants or products, as well as data on solutions or gases that will be presented later (in Chapters 6 and 7). In any case, merely convert the quantity given to moles, use the balanced chemical equation as presented in Section 5.1 to determine the number of moles of reactant or product that was asked about, and finish the problem as required.

EXAMPLE 3 Calculate the mass of oxygen gas produced by the thermal decomposition of 9.97×10^{21} formula units of $KClO_3$. KCl is the other product.

Solution

$$2\,KClO_3(s) \xrightarrow{\text{heat}} 2\,KCl(s) + 3\,O_2(g)$$

9.97×10^{21} formula units $KClO_3 \times$

$$\left(\frac{1\ \text{mol}\ KClO_3}{6.02 \times 10^{23}\ \text{formula units of}\ KClO_3} \right) = 0.0166\ \text{mol}\ KClO_3$$

Next, find the number of moles of oxygen, the substance that was asked about:

$$0.0166\ \text{mol}\ KClO_3 \left(\frac{3\ \text{mol}\ O_2}{2\ \text{mol}\ KClO_3} \right) = 0.0249\ \text{mol}\ O_2$$

Finally, find the mass of oxygen:

$$0.0249\ \text{mol}\ O_2 \left(\frac{32.0\ \text{g}\ O_2}{1\ \text{mol}\ O_2} \right) = 0.797\ \text{g}\ O_2$$

As we gain experience, we may want to combine all three steps into one, which may help precision by minimizing rounding errors:

$$9.97 \times 10^{21} \text{ units KClO}_3 \left(\frac{1 \text{ mol KClO}_3}{6.02 \times 10^{23} \text{ units KClO}_3} \right) \times$$

Avogadro's number

$$\left(\frac{3 \text{ mol O}_2}{2 \text{ mol KClO}_3} \right)\left(\frac{32.0 \text{ g O}_2}{1 \text{ mol O}_2} \right) = 0.795 \text{ g O}_2$$

equation   molar mass
stoichiometry

EXAMPLE 4 Calculate the number of moles of nitrogen atoms in the NH_4NO_3 produced by the reaction of 2.10 mol of NH_3 with HNO_3.

Solution

$$NH_3(aq) + HNO_3(aq) \rightarrow NH_4NO_3(aq)$$

$$2.10 \text{ mol NH}_3 \left(\frac{1 \text{ mol NH}_4NO_3}{1 \text{ mol NH}_3} \right)\left(\frac{2 \text{ mol N}}{1 \text{ mol NH}_4NO_3} \right)$$

$$= 4.20 \text{ mol N atoms} \quad \square$$

5.4 Limiting Quantities Problems

So far, the quantity of only one reactant or product has been given in the statement of the problem. We have assumed or have been told that a sufficient or more than sufficient quantity has been present of any other reactant(s). If the quantities of two (or more) quantities of reactants are specified, however, there is no assurance that they all will react completely. For example, if we are making baloney sandwiches with a slab of baloney and two slices of bread for each, how many sandwiches can we make (a) with 10 slabs of baloney and 16 slices of bread? (b) with 10 slabs of baloney and 24 slices of bread? In case (a), we run out of bread before we run out of baloney, and we can make only eight sandwiches (despite the fact that we have more slices of bread than slabs of baloney). We have two slabs of baloney in excess. In case (b), we can make 10 sandwiches before we run out of baloney. We have four slices of bread left over. These are examples of limiting quantities problems, and the same principles apply to chemical reactions. When one of the reactants is used up, the reaction stops and no more product can be produced. That reactant is called the **limiting quantity**, and the reactant that is left over is said to have been present *in excess*.

62

EXAMPLE 5 Consider the equation 2 Na(s) + Cl$_2$(g) → 2 NaCl(s). Calculate the quantity of sodium chloride that can be prepared by the reaction of (*a*) 0 mol of sodium and 1 mol chlorine. (*b*) 2 mol of sodium and 1 mol of chlorine. (*c*) 2 mol sodium and 2 mol chlorine.

Solution

(*a*) No NaCl can be prepared if there is no sodium.
(*b*) 2 mol, exactly as predicted by the balanced equation.
(*c*) 2 mol, which is the sum of the quantities of parts (*a*) and (*b*). That is, after the 2 mol Na reacts with 1 mol Cl$_2$, as in part (*b*), there is no sodium left to react with the second mole of Cl$_2$. We then have the situation described in part (*a*). □

To solve limiting quantities problems, the first step is to recognize that it is such a problem. In these problems, the quantities of two (or more) reactants are given. Make sure that all the quantities are in moles, or convert them to moles. Select one of the quantities and calculate how much of the other(s) will react with that quantity, as we did in Section 5.1. If we calculated that we *need* more moles of the second reactant than is present, then the second reactant is in limiting quantity. If we calculated that we *have* more moles of the second reactant than is needed, the first reactant is in limiting quantity. *We use the number of moles of limiting reactant to calculate the quantity of reaction that will occur.*

Note that the balanced chemical equation gives the mole ratios *that react*, not necessarily the ratios *present* at the start of the reaction.

EXAMPLE 6 Calculate the number of moles of Na$_2$SO$_4$ that will be produced by the reaction of 7.50 mol of NaOH with 3.50 mol of H$_2$SO$_4$.

Solution

$$H_2SO_4(aq) + 2\,NaOH(aq) \rightarrow Na_2SO_4(aq) + 2\,H_2O(l)$$

We can start with the quantity of either reactant.

$$3.50 \text{ mol } H_2SO_4 \left(\frac{2 \text{ mol NaOH}}{1 \text{ mol } H_2SO_4} \right) = 7.00 \text{ mol NaOH required}$$

Since 7.00 mol of NaOH is needed to react with all the acid, and 7.50 mol of NaOH is present in the beginning, the NaOH is in excess and the H$_2$SO$_4$ is in limiting quantity. We base further calculations on the limiting quantity:

$$3.50 \text{ mol } H_2SO_4 \left(\frac{1 \text{ mol } Na_2SO_4}{1 \text{ mol } H_2SO_4} \right) = 3.50 \text{ mol } Na_2SO_4$$

If we had started our calculation with the 7.50 mol of NaOH, we would have come to the same conclusion. Try it. □

Leading Questions

1. What can be calculated for a chemical reaction from the knowledge of the number of moles of the first reactant that reacts?
2. How can we recognize a limiting quantities problem?
3. What is the importance of the balanced chemical equation in solving stoichiometry problems?

Answers to Leading Questions

1. We can calculate the number of moles of every other substance involved in the reaction.
2. Quantities of two or more reactants are given.
3. The equation gives the mole ratios of all the substances that react or are produced in the reaction.

Supplementary Problems

1. Calculate the number of moles of titanium(IV) oxide for paint pigments that can be produced by the reaction of 4.18 mol of oxygen gas with excess titanium.
2. Calculate the number of moles of sodium required to react with 17.56 mol of liquid bromine.
3. Calculate the number of moles of each reagent required to yield 3.32 mol of NO according to the following equation, one step in the industrial production of nitric acid:

$$4 NH_3(g) + 5 O_2(g) \rightarrow 4 NO(g) + 6 H_2O(l)$$

4. Write the equation for the reaction in which 1.00 mol of H_3PO_4 reacts with exactly 2.00 mol of KOH.
5. Calculate the mass of aluminum chloride that can be produced by the reaction of 293 g of chlorine gas with excess aluminum.
6. Calculate the mass of sodium required to react with 2.788 kg of liquid bromine.

7. Calculate the mass of each reagent required to yield 99.6 g of NO according to the following equation, one step in the industrial production of nitric acid:

$$4\,NH_3(g) + 5\,O_2(g) \rightarrow 4\,NO(g) + 6\,H_2O(l)$$

8. Calculate the number of moles of aluminum chloride that can be produced by the reaction of 7.11×10^{24} molecules of chlorine gas with excess aluminum.

9. Calculate the mass of sodium required to react with 1.62×10^{20} molecules of liquid bromine.

10. Calculate the number of molecules of each reagent required to yield 1.23 g of NO according to the following equation:

$$4\,NH_3(g) + 5\,O_2(g) \rightarrow 4\,NO(g) + 6\,H_2O(l)$$

11. Calculate the number of moles of Na_2SO_4 that will be produced by the reaction of 1.40 mol of Na_2O and 1.76 mol of SO_3.

12. Calculate the mass of Na_2SO_4 that will be produced by the reaction of 4.40 mol of aqueous NaOH and 1.76 mol of aqueous H_2SO_4.

13. Calculate the mass of Na_2SO_4 that will be produced by the reaction of 89.7 g of aqueous NaOH and 64.8 g of aqueous H_2SO_4.

14. Calculate the mass of H_3PO_4 that can be produced by reaction of water with the quantity of P_4O_{10} that contains 5.00 mol of phosphorus atoms.

15. A sample of 4.50 g of $Ba(OH)_2$ is treated with a sample of HCl containing 4.44×10^{21} molecules. (a) What can we tell from the mass of $Ba(OH)_2$ and its molar mass? (b) What can we tell from the number of molecules of HCl and Avogadro's number? (c) What equation can we predict for a reaction of these compounds from their formulas? (d) What can we tell from the results of (a) to (c)? (e) What final conclusions can we draw?

16. A sample of 4.50 g of $Ba(OH)_2$ is treated with a sample of HCl containing 4.44×10^{21} molecules. (a) Calculate the number of moles of $Ba(OH)_2$. (b) Calculate the number of moles of HCl. (c) Write a balanced equation for the reaction that takes place. (d) Which reactant is in limiting quantity? (e) How much excess reactant will remain after any reaction?

17. A sample of 4.50 g of $Ba(OH)_2$ is treated with a sample of HCl containing 4.44×10^{21} molecules. How much excess reactant will remain after any reaction?

18. When 15.0 mg of an unknown compound of carbon, hydrogen, and oxygen was burned in excess oxygen gas, water and carbon dioxide were formed. The water was trapped in one cylinder (by reaction with a certain compound) and the carbon dioxide was trapped in another. The water cylinder gained 12.3 mg of mass, and the carbon dioxide cylinder gained 30.0 mg. (a) What mass of carbon dioxide was produced by the reaction? (b) What mass of water was produced by the reaction? (c) How many millimoles of each was produced? (d) How many millimoles of carbon was in the original sample? (e) How many millimoles of hydrogen was in the original sample? (f) How many milligrams of each element was in the original sample? (g) How many milligrams of oxygen was there in the original sample. (h) What is the empirical formula of the sample?

19. When 25.0 mg of an unknown compound of carbon, hydrogen, and oxygen was burned in excess oxygen gas, water and carbon dioxide were formed. The water was trapped in one cylinder (by reaction with a certain compound) and the carbon dioxide was trapped in another. The water cylinder gained 23.7 mg of mass, and the carbon dioxide cylinder gained 43.4 mg. What is the empirical formula of the sample?

20. (a) Calculate the number of grams of $CaCO_3$ that react with 25.0 g of $HClO_4$ according to the equation

$$CaCO_3(s) + 2\,HClO_4(aq) \rightarrow Ca(ClO_4)_2(aq) + H_2O(l) + CO_2(g)$$

(b) Explain why the *mass ratio* in this reaction is equal to the ratio of moles of reactants.

21. Explain why many of the problems in this chapter seem similar to others.

22. Calculate the number of grams of carbon that react with 2.50 metric tons (2.50×10^6 g) of Al_2O_3 in the industrial production of aluminum at high temperature according to the following equation: Al_2O_3(special solution) + 3 C(s) $\rightarrow$ 2 Al(l) + 3 CO(g).

23. Calculate the mass of sulfuric acid (the chemical produced in the largest tonnage in the world) produced by the reaction of 5.00 metric tons (5.00×10^6 g) of sulfur in the following sequence of reactions:

$$S(s) + O_2(g) \rightarrow SO_2(g)$$

$$SO_2(g) + \tfrac{1}{2}\,O_2(g) \rightarrow SO_3(g)$$

$$SO_3(g) + H_2O(l) \rightarrow H_2SO_4(l)$$

24. Calculate the mass of an iron ore containing 13.7% Fe_2O_3 that requires 2.00×10^6 g of carbon to reduce the Fe_2O_3 to iron metal at high temperature:

$$Fe_2O_3(s) + 3\, C(s) \rightarrow 2\, Fe(l) + 3\, CO(g)$$

Solutions to Supplementary Problems

1. $Ti(s) + O_2(g) \rightarrow TiO_2(s)$

$$4.18 \text{ mol } O_2\left(\frac{1 \text{ mol } TiO_2}{1 \text{ mol } O_2}\right) = 4.18 \text{ mol } TiO_2$$

2. $2\, Na(s) + Br_2(l) \rightarrow 2\, NaBr(s)$

$$17.56 \text{ mol } Br_2\left(\frac{2 \text{ mol } Na}{1 \text{ mol } Br_2}\right) = 35.12 \text{ mol } Na$$

3. $3.32 \text{ mol } NO\left(\dfrac{4 \text{ mol } NH_3}{4 \text{ mol } NO}\right) = 3.32 \text{ mol } NH_3$

$3.32 \text{ mol } NO\left(\dfrac{5 \text{ mol } O_2}{4 \text{ mol } NO}\right) = 4.15 \text{ mol } O_2$

4. Note that these two reagents are stated to have reacted, not merely to have been mixed. The equation represents the reacting ratio, therefore the coefficient of H_3PO_4 is 1 and that of KOH is 2:

$$H_3PO_4(aq) + 2\, KOH(aq) \rightarrow K_2HPO_4(aq) + 2\, H_2O(l)$$

5. $2\, Al(s) + 3\, Cl_2(g) \rightarrow 2\, AlCl_3(s)$

$$293 \text{ g } Cl_2\left(\frac{1 \text{ mol } Cl_2}{70.9 \text{ g } Cl_2}\right) = 4.13 \text{ mol } Cl_2$$

$$4.13 \text{ mol } Cl_2\left(\frac{2 \text{ mol } AlCl_3}{3 \text{ mol } Cl_2}\right)\left(\frac{133 \text{ g } AlCl_3}{1 \text{ mol } AlCl_3}\right) = 366 \text{ g } AlCl_3$$

Alternatively, a complete solution in one step may be obtained:

$$293 \text{ g } Cl_2\left(\frac{1 \text{ mol } Cl_2}{70.9 \text{ g } Cl_2}\right)\left(\frac{2 \text{ mol } AlCl_3}{3 \text{ mol } Cl_2}\right)\left(\frac{133 \text{ g } AlCl_3}{1 \text{ mol } AlCl_3}\right)$$

$$= 366 \text{ g } AlCl_3$$

6. $2 \, Na(s) + Br_2(l) \rightarrow 2 \, NaBr(s)$

$$2788 \, g \, Br_2 \left(\frac{1 \, mol \, Br_2}{158.8 \, g \, Br_2} \right) = 17.56 \, mol \, Br_2$$

This problem is now related to Supplementary Problem 2.

$$17.56 \, mol \, Br_2 \left(\frac{2 \, mol \, Na}{1 \, mol \, Br_2} \right) \left(\frac{22.99 \, g \, Na}{1 \, mol \, Na} \right) = 807.4 \, g \, Na$$

7. $99.6 \, g \, NO \left(\dfrac{1 \, mol \, NO}{30.0 \, g \, NO} \right) = 3.32 \, mol \, NO$

This problem is now related to Supplementary Problem 3.

$$3.32 \, mol \, NO \left(\frac{4 \, mol \, NH_3}{4 \, mol \, NO} \right) = 3.32 \, mol \, NH_3$$

$$3.32 \, mol \, NO \left(\frac{5 \, mol \, O_2}{4 \, mol \, NO} \right) = 4.15 \, mol \, O_2$$

To get the masses:

$$3.32 \, mol \, NH_3 \left(\frac{17.0 \, g \, NH_3}{1 \, mol \, NH_3} \right) = 56.4 \, g \, NH_3$$

$$4.15 \, mol \, O_2 \left(\frac{32.0 \, g \, O_2}{1 \, mol \, O_2} \right) = 133 \, g \, O_2$$

8. $2 \, Al(s) + 3 \, Cl_2(g) \rightarrow 2 \, AlCl_3(s)$

$$7.11 \times 10^{24} \, molecules \, Cl_2 \left(\frac{1 \, mol \, Cl_2}{6.02 \times 10^{23} \, molecules \, Cl_2} \right)$$

$$= 11.8 \, mol \, Cl_2$$

$$11.8 \, mol \, Cl_2 \left(\frac{2 \, mol \, AlCl_3}{3 \, mol \, Cl_2} \right) = 7.87 \, mol \, AlCl_3$$

9. $2 \, Na(s) + Br_2(l) \rightarrow 2 \, NaBr(s)$

$$1.62 \times 10^{20} \, molecules \, Br_2 \left(\frac{1 \, mol \, Br_2}{6.02 \times 10^{23} \, molecules \, Br_2} \right)$$

$$= 2.69 \times 10^{-4} \, mol \, Br_2$$

$$2.69 \times 10^{-4} \, mol \, Br_2 \left(\frac{2 \, mol \, Na}{1 \, mol \, Br_2} \right) = 5.38 \times 10^{-4} \, mol \, Na$$

$$5.38 \times 10^{-4} \text{ mol Na}\left(\frac{23.0 \text{ g Na}}{1 \text{ mol Na}}\right) = 0.0124 \text{ g Na}$$

10.
$$1.23 \text{ g NO}\left(\frac{1 \text{ mol NO}}{30.0 \text{ g NO}}\right)\left(\frac{4 \text{ mol NH}_3}{4 \text{ mol NO}}\right) \times$$

$$\left(\frac{6.02 \times 10^{23} \text{ molecules NH}_3}{1 \text{ mol NH}_3}\right) = 2.47 \times 10^{22} \text{ molecules NH}_3$$

$$1.23 \text{ g NO}\left(\frac{1 \text{ mol NO}}{30.0 \text{ g NO}}\right)\left(\frac{5 \text{ mol O}_2}{4 \text{ mol NO}}\right) \times$$

$$\left(\frac{6.02 \times 10^{23} \text{ molecules O}_2}{1 \text{ mol O}_2}\right) = 3.09 \times 10^{22} \text{ molecules O}_2$$

11. $Na_2O(s) + SO_3(g) \rightarrow Na_2SO_4(s)$
Because the equation has a 1 : 1 mole ratio of reactants, and there is more SO_3 than Na_2O, the Na_2O is limiting. It is therefore used for the rest of the problem:

$$1.40 \text{ mol Na}_2O\left(\frac{1 \text{ mol Na}_2SO_4}{1 \text{ mol Na}_2O}\right) = 1.40 \text{ mol Na}_2SO_4$$

12. $2 \text{ NaOH(aq)} + H_2SO_4(aq) \rightarrow Na_2SO_4(aq) + 2 H_2O(l)$

$$4.40 \text{ mol NaOH}\left(\frac{1 \text{ mol H}_2SO_4}{2 \text{ mol NaOH}}\right) = 2.20 \text{ mol H}_2SO_4 \text{ needed}$$

There are 1.76 mol of H_2SO_4 present, but 2.20 needed to react with all the base, so the H_2SO_4 is in limiting quantity.

$$1.76 \text{ mol H}_2SO_4\left(\frac{1 \text{ mol Na}_2SO_4}{1 \text{ mol H}_2SO_4}\right)\left(\frac{142 \text{ g Na}_2SO_4}{1 \text{ mol Na}_2SO_4}\right)$$

$$= 2.50 \times 10^2 \text{ g Na}_2SO_4$$

13. $89.7 \text{ g NaOH}\left(\frac{1 \text{ mol NaOH}}{40.0 \text{ g NaOH}}\right) = 2.24 \text{ mol NaOH}$

$$64.8 \text{ g H}_2SO_4\left(\frac{1 \text{ mol H}_2SO_4}{98.0 \text{ g H}_2SO_4}\right) = 0.661 \text{ mol H}_2SO_4$$

$$2.24 \text{ mol NaOH}\left(\frac{1 \text{ mol } H_2SO_4}{2 \text{ mol NaOH}}\right) = 1.12 \text{ mol } H_2SO_4 \text{ needed}$$

The H_2SO_4 is limiting, so:

$$0.661 \text{ mol } H_2SO_4\left(\frac{1 \text{ mol } Na_2SO_4}{1 \text{ mol } H_2SO_4}\right)\left(\frac{142 \text{ g } Na_2SO_4}{1 \text{ mol } Na_2SO_4}\right)$$

$$= 93.9 \text{ g } Na_2SO_4$$

14. $P_4O_{10}(s) + 6 H_2O(l) \rightarrow 4 H_3PO_4(aq)$

$$5.00 \text{ mol P}\left(\frac{1 \text{ mol } P_4O_{10}}{4 \text{ mol P}}\right)\left(\frac{4 \text{ mol } H_3PO_4}{1 \text{ mol } P_4O_{10}}\right)\left(\frac{98.0 \text{ g } H_3PO_4}{1 \text{ mol } H_3PO_4}\right)$$

$$= 4.90 \times 10^2 \text{ g } H_3PO_4$$

(This problem could have been stated as a chemical formula problem, as in Section 4.2. Because the phosphorus atoms must go into the phosphoric acid, and there is one mole of phosphorus atoms in each mole of the acid, it is obvious that the phosphorus can make 5.00 mol of the acid.)

15. (a) The number of moles of $Ba(OH)_2$. (b) The number of moles of HCl. (c) $Ba(OH)_2 + 2 HCl \rightarrow BaCl_2 + 2 H_2O$.
They will react because one is an acid and the other a base, and they will react in a $1:2$ ratio. (d) From the numbers of moles of each and the balanced chemical equation, we can tell the reactant that is in limiting quantity. (e) The numbers of moles of each substance produced and of the excess reactant.

16. (a) $4.50 \text{ g } Ba(OH)_2 \left(\frac{1 \text{ mol } Ba(OH)_2}{171 \text{ g } Ba(OH)_2}\right) = 0.0263 \text{ mol } Ba(OH)_2$

(b) $4.44 \times 10^{21} \text{molecules HCl} \left(\frac{1 \text{ mol HCl}}{6.02 \times 10^{23} \text{ molecules HCl}}\right)$

$$= 0.00738 \text{ mol HCl}$$

(c) $Ba(OH)_2(aq) + 2 HCl(aq) \rightarrow BaCl_2(aq) + 2 H_2O(l)$

(d) $0.00738 \text{ mol HCl} \left(\frac{1 \text{ mol } Ba(OH)_2}{2 \text{ mol HCl}}\right)$

$$= 0.00369 \text{ mol } Ba(OH)_2 \text{ needed}$$

The HCl is limiting.
(e) $0.0263 \text{ mol of } Ba(OH)_2 \text{ present} - 0.00369 \text{ mol } Ba(OH)_2 \text{ used up}$
$$= 0.0226 \text{ mol } Ba(OH)_2 \text{ excess}$$

17. This problem is the same as Problem 16, but it is not stated in parts.
18. (a) 30.0 mg   (b) 12.3 mg

   (c) $30.0 \text{ mg CO}_2\left(\dfrac{1 \text{ mmol CO}_2}{44.0 \text{ mg CO}_2}\right) = 0.682 \text{ mmol CO}_2$

      $12.3 \text{ mg H}_2\text{O}\left(\dfrac{1 \text{ mmol H}_2\text{O}}{18.0 \text{ mg H}_2\text{O}}\right) = 0.683 \text{ mmol H}_2\text{O}$

   (d) The same number of millimoles of carbon is in the reactant as in the CO_2 produced.

$$0.682 \text{ mmol CO}_2\left(\dfrac{1 \text{ mmol C}}{1 \text{ mmol CO}_2}\right) = 0.682 \text{ mmol C}$$

   (e) The same number of millimoles of hydrogen atoms are in the reactant as in the H_2O produced. That is twice the number of millimoles of water:

$$0.683 \text{ mmol H}_2\text{O}\left(\dfrac{2 \text{ mmol H}}{1 \text{ mmol H}_2\text{O}}\right) = 1.37 \text{ mmol H}$$

   (f) $0.682 \text{ mmol C}\left(\dfrac{12.0 \text{ mg C}}{1 \text{ mmol C}}\right) = 8.18 \text{ mg C}$

      $1.37 \text{ mmol H}\left(\dfrac{1.008 \text{ mg H}}{1 \text{ mmol H}}\right) = 1.38 \text{ mg H}$

   (g) $15.0 \text{ mg} - 8.18 \text{ mg} - 1.38 \text{ mg} = 5.4 \text{ mg oxygen}$
   (h) $5.4 \text{ mg O}\left(\dfrac{1 \text{ mmol O}}{16.0 \text{ mg O}}\right) = 0.34 \text{ mmol O}$
There are 0.682 mmol C, 1.37 mmol H, and 0.34 mmol O in the sample, which gives a ratio of 2 mmol C to 4 mmol H to 1 mmol O and an empirical formula C_2H_4O.

19. This problem is similar to the prior problem except that it is not stated in steps.

$$43.4 \text{ mg CO}_2\left(\dfrac{1 \text{ mmol CO}_2}{44.0 \text{ mg CO}_2}\right)\left(\dfrac{1 \text{ mmol C}}{1 \text{ mmol CO}_2}\right) = 0.986 \text{ mmol C}$$

$$23.7 \text{ mg H}_2\text{O}\left(\dfrac{1 \text{ mmol H}_2\text{O}}{18.0 \text{ mg H}_2\text{O}}\right)\left(\dfrac{2 \text{ mmol H}}{1 \text{ mmol H}_2\text{O}}\right) = 2.63 \text{ mmol H}$$

$$0.986 \text{ mmol C}\left(\dfrac{12.0 \text{ mg C}}{1 \text{ mmol C}}\right) = 11.8 \text{ mg C}$$

$$2.63 \text{ mmol H}\left(\frac{1.008 \text{ mg H}}{1 \text{ mmol H}}\right) = 2.65 \text{ mg H}$$

$$25.0 \text{ mg} - 11.8 \text{ mg} - 2.65 \text{ mg} = 10.6 \text{ mg oxygen}$$

$$10.6 \text{ mg O}\left(\frac{1 \text{ mmol O}}{16.0 \text{ mg O}}\right) = 0.663 \text{ mmol O}$$

There are 0.986 mmol C, 2.63 mmol H, and 0.663 mmol O in the sample, which gives a ratio of 1.5 mmol C to 4 mmol H to 1 mmol O and an empirical formula $C_3H_8O_2$.

20. (*a*) $25.0 \text{ g HClO}_4\left(\dfrac{1 \text{ mol HClO}_4}{100 \text{ g HClO}_4}\right)\left(\dfrac{1 \text{ mol CaCO}_3}{2 \text{ mol HClO}_4}\right) \times$

$$\left(\frac{100 \text{ g CaCO}_3}{1 \text{ mol CaCO}_3}\right) = 12.5 \text{ g CaCO}_3$$

(*b*) The mass ratio is the same as the mole ratio because the molar masses just happen to be equal.

21. Many problems in this set of problems seem the same because essentially they are the same with some review problem steps added. The set is intended to demonstrate to us that once we understand the material, there is not as much to learn as we might have thought.

22. $2.50 \times 10^6 \text{ g Al}_2O_3\left(\dfrac{1 \text{ mol Al}_2O_3}{102 \text{ g Al}_2O_3}\right)\left(\dfrac{3 \text{ mol C}}{1 \text{ mol Al}_2O_3}\right)\left(\dfrac{12.0 \text{ g C}}{1 \text{ mol C}}\right)$

$$= 8.82 \times 10^5 \text{ g C}$$

23. $5.00 \times 10^6 \text{ g S}\left(\dfrac{1 \text{ mol S}}{32.1 \text{ g S}}\right)\left(\dfrac{1 \text{ mol H}_2SO_4}{1 \text{ mol S}}\right)\left(\dfrac{98.1 \text{ g H}_2SO_4}{1 \text{ mol H}_2SO_4}\right)$

$$= 1.53 \times 10^7 \text{ g H}_2SO_4$$

24. $2.00 \times 10^6 \text{ g C}\left(\dfrac{1 \text{ mol C}}{12.0 \text{ g C}}\right)\left(\dfrac{1 \text{ mol Fe}_2O_3}{3 \text{ mol C}}\right)\left(\dfrac{160 \text{ g Fe}_2O_3}{1 \text{ mol Fe}_2O_3}\right)$

$$= 8.89 \times 10^6 \text{ g Fe}_2O_3$$

$$8.89 \times 10^6 \text{ g Fe}_2O_3\left(\frac{100 \text{ g ore}}{13.7 \text{ g Fe}_2O_3}\right) = 6.49 \times 10^7 \text{ g ore}$$

Chapter 6

Concentration Calculations

6.1 Molarity

The most common unit of concentration in chemistry is **molarity**, defined as the number of moles of solute dissolved per liter (or cubic decimeter) of solution. It can also be defined as the number of millimoles of solute per milliliter of solution. The symbol for molarity is an *italic capital M*; its unit is **molar**, symbolized M. (Some books use M for both.) Do not use lowercase letters for either! We use *mol* as an abbreviation for *mole*; we do not use either capital M or lowercase m.

We must be sure to understand the difference between concentration and quantity of solute.

EXAMPLE 1 A cup labeled A has two lumps of sugar in it and is filled with tea. A cup labeled B has one lump of sugar, and is half filled. (*a*) Which cup, if either, has more sugar in it? (*b*) In which cup, if either, is the tea sweeter?

Solution (*a*) Cup A has more sugar. (Two lumps is more than one.) (*b*) The tea is equally sweet in each, because the **concentration** of sugar is the same in each. Be sure to note in each chemistry problem the difference between *quantity* of solute and *concentration* of solute! □

EXAMPLE 2 If 2.00 L of solution contains 4.50 mol of solute, what is the molarity of the solution?

Solution The molarity (concentration) is defined as the number of moles of solute per liter of solution:

$$M = \frac{\text{moles of solute}}{\text{L of solution}} = \frac{4.50 \text{ mol}}{2.00 \text{ L}} = 2.25 \text{ M} \qquad \square$$

EXAMPLE 3 Show that a solution containing 4.50 mmol of solute in 2.00 mL of solution is also 2.25 M.

Solution

$$\frac{4.50 \text{ mmol}}{2.00 \text{ mL}} \left(\frac{1 \text{ mol}}{1000 \text{ mmol}} \right) \left(\frac{1000 \text{ mL}}{1 \text{ L}} \right) = \frac{2.25 \text{ mol}}{1.00 \text{ L}}$$

$$= 2.25 \text{ M} \qquad \square$$

Because molarity is a ratio, it can be used as a factor in solving problems. Wherever the symbol M appears, it can be replaced by mol/L or mmol/mL, and for 1/M, their reciprocals can be substituted.

EXAMPLE 4 Calculate the number of moles of solute contained in 3.00 L of 4.00 M solution.

Solution As with most factor label method solutions, put down the *quantity* first, then multiply it by the appropriate ratio:

$$3.00 \text{ L} \left(\frac{4.00 \text{ mol}}{1 \text{ L}} \right) = 12.0 \text{ mol}$$

We can see from Fig. 6-1 that this answer is correct. $\qquad \square$

EXAMPLE 5 Calculate the volume of a 2.80 M solution that contains 4.00 mol of solute.

Solution The reciprocal of the ratio corresponding to molarity is used:

$$4.00 \text{ mol} \left(\frac{1 \text{ L}}{2.80 \text{ mol}} \right) = 1.43 \text{ L} \qquad \square$$

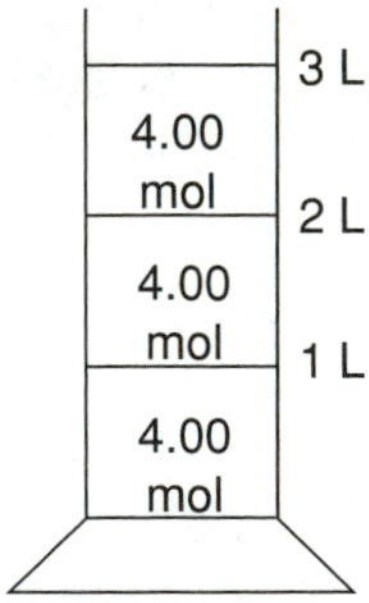

Fig. 6-1 Number of Moles of Solute in a Solution. The number of moles is the molarity times the volume. There are 12.0 mol in 3.00 L of this solution.

If a solution is diluted with solvent, its number of moles of solute *does not change*, but its molarity gets lower.

EXAMPLE 6   Calculate the molarity of 1.50 L of a 2.50 M solution after it has been diluted to 4.50 L.

Solution   The initial number of moles of solute is calculated just as in Example 4.

$$1.50\,L\left(\frac{2.50\ mol}{1\ L}\right) = 3.75\ mol$$

Addition of more solvent does not change the number of moles of solute, so that same number of moles of solute is used for the final solution. The 3.75 mol of solute is now dissolved in 4.50 L of solution:

$$\frac{3.75\ mol}{4.50\ L} = 0.833\ M$$

It should be noted that tripling the volume has caused the molarity to be reduced to one-third its original value.   □

6.2   Titration

The method used most often for determining the molarity of a solution (as well as numbers of moles of solid reagents) is **titration**. For example, a solution of HCl, whose concentration is known, and a solution of NaOH, whose concentration is to be determined, are titrated. The NaOH solution is added to a carefully measured volume of HCl solution, the addition being stopped when exactly the correct stoichiometric quantity has been added according to the balanced chemical equation, and the volume of the NaOH solution is carefully measured. An **indicator**, a chemical that changes color at the point where the proper quantity of one chemical has been added to the other, signals the end of the titration. An acid-base indicator is a compound that has a very intense color in acidic or basic solution, or a different intense color in each. The **end point** is a point in the titration at the point where the ratio of moles of the reactants added is the same as that ratio in the balanced chemical equation.

EXAMPLE 7   If 45.70 mL of NaOH has been added to 25.00 mL of a solution of 3.000 M HCl when the end point is reached, what is the concentration of the base?

Solution   The balanced equation for the reaction is

$$HCl(aq) + NaOH(aq) \rightarrow NaCl(aq) + H_2O(l)$$

The number of millimoles of acid is

$$25.00 \text{ mL HCl} \left(\frac{3.000 \text{ mmol}}{1 \text{ mL}} \right) = 75.00 \text{ mmol HCl}$$

The titration is stopped when the number of millimoles of NaOH is equal to the number of millimoles of HCl, so the concentration of the base is

$$\frac{75.00 \text{ mmol NaOH}}{45.70 \text{ mL}} = 1.641 \text{ M NaOH} \qquad \square$$

EXAMPLE 8   If 45.70 mL of NaOH has been added to 25.00 mL of a solution of 3.000 M H_2SO_4 when the acid is completely neutralized, what is the concentration of the base?

Solution   The balanced equation for the reaction is

$$H_2SO_4(aq) + 2 \text{ NaOH}(aq) \rightarrow Na_2SO_4(aq) + 2 \text{ H}_2O(l)$$

The number of millimoles of acid is

$$25.00 \text{ mL} \left(\frac{3.000 \text{ mmol}}{1 \text{ mL}} \right) = 75.00 \text{ mmol H}_2SO_4$$

According to the balanced chemical equation, the titration is stopped when the number of millimoles of NaOH is *twice* the number of millimoles of H_2SO_4, so the concentration of the base is

$$\frac{150.0 \text{ mmol NaOH}}{45.70 \text{ mL}} = 3.282 \text{ M NaOH}$$

Note that in this case the molarity times the volume of the acid is *not* equal to the molarity times the volume of the base: $M_1 V_1 \neq M_2 V_2$ $\qquad \square$

EXAMPLE 9   A 0.200 M solution of NaOH is treated with a 0.200 M solution of HCl. At the equivalence point (where the reaction is just completed), (*a*) what would be the concentration of NaOH if no reaction had occurred? (*b*) What is the concentration of the NaCl produced?

Solution   (*a*) Because the concentrations of acid and base are equal, the volume has been doubled by the addition of the HCl solution. Therefore, the concentration would have been halved, to 0.100 M. (*b*) The concentration of NaCl is 0.100 M.

Alternate solution: V liters of each solution are used, containing $0.200V$ mol of each reactant. Therefore $0.200V$ mol of NaCl is produced, in the $1:1:1:1$ ratio of reactants and products:

$$HCl(aq) + NaOH(aq) \rightarrow NaCl(aq) + H_2O(l)$$

The concentration is

$$\frac{0.200V \text{ mol}}{2.00V \text{ liters}} = 0.100 \text{ M}$$

(The volume V cancels out, no matter what its value. If we try using 10.0 mL, 24.0 mL, 2.00 L or any other volume for each solution, we get the same result each time.) $\square$

6.3 Molality

Another concentration unit used by chemists is **molality**, symbolized by an *italic*, lowercase *m*. It is defined as the number of moles of solute per *kilogram* of *solvent*. The unit of molality is **molal**, symbolized by a regular (not italic) m. (Some texts use regular m for both.) Note well the differences between molarity and molality; the denominator of molality involves a *mass* not a *volume*, and it is the mass of the *solvent*, not the *solution*. Great care must be taken to avoid confusing molarity and molality because their names as well as their units and symbols are so similar. We must be sure to use the standard notation so that we do not confuse ourselves!

Many molality problems do not differ in solving technique from molarity problems. As usual, be very careful with the units.

EXAMPLE 10 Calculate the molality of a solution containing 0.500 mol of solute in 250 g of solvent.

Solution

$$m = \frac{0.500 \text{ mol}}{0.250 \text{ kg}} = 2.00 \text{ m} \qquad \square$$

EXAMPLE 11 Calculate the mass of water required to prepare a 4.00 m aqueous solution of NH_3 using 25.0 g of NH_3.

Solution

$$25.0 \text{ g NH}_3 \left(\frac{1 \text{ mol NH}_3}{17.0 \text{ g NH}_3} \right) \left(\frac{1 \text{ kg H}_2O}{4.00 \text{ mol NH}_3} \right) = 0.368 \text{ kg H}_2O \qquad \square$$

6.4 Mole Fraction

Another way to measure concentration is with **mole fraction**, defined as the number of moles of a given component of a solution divided by the total number of moles in the solution. No component needs to be defined as the solvent with mole fraction. The mole fraction of component A is symbolized X_A; it has no units because the unit *moles* in the numerator and the unit *moles* in the denominator cancel each other.

EXAMPLE 12 Calculate the mole fraction of alcohol and of water in a solution containing 2.00 mol of alcohol and 8.00 mol of water.

Solution

$$X_{alcohol} = \frac{2.00 \text{ mol alcohol}}{10.00 \text{ mol total}} = 0.200$$

$$X_{water} = \frac{8.00 \text{ mol water}}{10.00 \text{ mol total}} = 0.800 \qquad \square$$

As is evident from Example 12, the total of all mole fractions in any given solution is 1.00 (just as the total of all percentages in a given sample is 100%).

Both molality and mole fraction are intensive properties, which is useful for an easy method to convert from one to the other. In such a problem, we can assume that we have any quantity of solution that will make our solving process easiest.

EXAMPLE 13 Calculate the mole fraction of ammonia in a 2.00 m solution of NH_3 in water.

Solution Assume 1.00 kg of water. Then there are 2.00 mol of ammonia and

$$1.00 \text{ kg H}_2\text{O} \left(\frac{1000 \text{ g H}_2\text{O}}{1 \text{ kg H}_2\text{O}} \right) \left(\frac{1 \text{ mol H}_2\text{O}}{18.0 \text{ g H}_2\text{O}} \right) = 55.6 \text{ mol H}_2\text{O}$$

$$X_{NH_3} = \frac{2.00 \text{ mol NH}_3}{57.6 \text{ mol total}} = 0.0347 \qquad \square$$

For ease of solution of such problems, we should always assume a quantity of solution such that the value of the concentration is equal in magnitude to the number of moles of one of the components, as in the last example (2.00 m and 2.00 mol because 1.00 kg was selected) and in the next.

EXAMPLE 14 The mole fraction of alcohol in water is 0.100. Calculate its molality.

Solution   Assume a total of 1.000 mol of solution. Then there are 0.100 mol of alcohol and 0.900 mol of water. The mass of water (in kilograms) is

$$0.900 \text{ mol H}_2\text{O} \left(\frac{18.0 \text{ g H}_2\text{O}}{1 \text{ mol H}_2\text{O}} \right) \left(\frac{1 \text{ kg H}_2\text{O}}{1000 \text{ g H}_2\text{O}} \right) = 0.0162 \text{ kg H}_2\text{O}$$

$$m_{\text{alcohol}} = \frac{0.100 \text{ mol}}{0.0162 \text{ kg}} = 6.17 \text{ m} \qquad \square$$

Leading Questions

1. List the differences between molarity and molality.
2. Explain why molality is not used with titrations.

Answers to Leading Questions

1. The one-letter difference in the spelling, the capital letters for molarity and molar in contrast to the lowercase designations for molality and molal, the volume for molarity as opposed to mass for molality, and the fact that *solution* is designated for molarity and *solvent* for molality are the major differences.
2. Titrations are done by volume, and molality does not deal easily with volumes.

Supplementary Problems

1. Calculate the molarity of a 250-mL solution containing 80.0 mmol of solute.
2. Calculate the concentration of a 500-mL solution containing 1.71 mol of solute.
3. Calculate the volume of a 2.00 M solution containing 4.22 mol of solute.
4. Calculate the number of moles of solute required to make 50.00 mL of 1.500 M solution.
5. Calculate the molarity of a solution after 1.70 L of 2.06 M solution is diluted to 2.50 L.
6. Calculate the concentration of HCl if 25.00 mL of the solution takes 41.72 mL of 4.000 M NaOH to neutralize it.
7. Calculate the concentration of H_3PO_4 if 25.00 mL of the solution takes 38.98 mL of 4.000 M NaOH to completely neutralize it.

8. (a) Calculate the number of moles of a solid unknown acid, HA, that is present if 17.40 mL of 3.00 M NaOH is required to neutralize it. (b) Calculate the molar mass of the acid if 4.17 g of the acid was used in part (a).

9. Calculate the molarity, molality, and mole fraction of a solution of 0.0150 mol of NaCl in 50.0 g of water if the solution has a density of 1.02 g/mL.

10. Calculate the mole fraction of each component in a solution of 50.0 g CH_3OH and 75.0 g of H_2O.

11. A 0.100 M solution of NaOH is treated with a 0.100 M solution of HNO_3. At the equivalence point (where the reaction is just completed), what is the concentration of the $NaNO_3$ produced?

12. Calculate the molar mass of an acid, H_2A, if 6.66 g of the acid required 22.22 mL of 3.000 M NaOH to completely neutralize it.

13. A solution was 2.40 m and contained 245 g of solvent. Calculate the molality of the solution after dilution with 125 g more of solvent.

14. Calculate the molality of an alcohol in aqueous solution if the mole fraction of the alcohol is 0.150.

15. Calculate the molar mass of an unknown base, B, with molecules that each react with two hydrogen ions, if 7.99 g of the base is neutralized by 41.44 mL of 3.000 M HCl.

$$B(s) + 2\ HCl(aq) \rightarrow BH_2Cl_2(aq)$$

16. Calculate the molality of an aqueous solution 2.24 M in sucrose, $C_{12}H_{22}O_{11}$. (Assume that the density of the solution is 2.05 g/mL.)

Solutions to Supplementary Problems

1. $\dfrac{80.0\ \text{mmol}}{250\ \text{mL}} = 0.320\ \text{M}$

2. $\dfrac{1.71\ \text{mol}}{0.500\ \text{L}} = 3.42\ \text{M}$ (Watch the units!)

3. $4.22\ \text{mol}\left(\dfrac{1\ \text{L}}{2.00\ \text{mol}}\right) = 2.11\ \text{L}$

4. $50.00\ \text{mL}\left(\dfrac{1.500\ \text{mmol}}{1\ \text{mL}}\right)\left(\dfrac{0.001\ \text{mol}}{1\ \text{mmol}}\right) = 0.07500\ \text{mol}$

5. The number of moles of solute in the initial solution is calculated first:

$$1.70\ \text{L}\left(\dfrac{2.06\ \text{mol}}{1\ \text{L}}\right) = 3.50\ \text{mol}$$

The same number of moles of solute is present in the final solution:

$$\frac{3.50 \text{ mol}}{2.50 \text{ L}} = 1.40 \text{ M}$$

6. The number of millimoles of base is

$$41.72 \text{ mL} \left(\frac{4.000 \text{ mmol NaOH}}{1 \text{ mL}} \right) = 166.9 \text{ mmol NaOH}$$

$$HCl(aq) + NaOH(aq) \rightarrow NaCl(aq) + H_2O(l)$$

According to the balanced chemical equation, the same number of millimoles of acid is needed, so the concentration of the acid is:

$$\frac{166.9 \text{ mmol HCl}}{25.00 \text{ mL}} = 6.676 \text{ M HCl}$$

In a one-step solution:

$$\frac{41.72 \text{ mL} \left(\dfrac{4.000 \text{ mmol NaOH}}{1 \text{ mL}} \right) \left(\dfrac{1 \text{ mmol HCl}}{1 \text{ mmol NaOH}} \right)}{25.00 \text{ mL HCl}}$$

$$= 6.675 \text{ M HCl}$$

7. The number of millimoles of base is

$$38.98 \text{ mL} \left(\frac{4.000 \text{ mmol NaOH}}{1 \text{ mL}} \right) = 155.9 \text{ mmol NaOH}$$

$$H_3PO_4(aq) + 3 \text{ NaOH}(aq) \rightarrow Na_3PO_4(aq) + 3 \text{ H}_2O(l)$$

According to the balanced chemical equation, one-third the number of millimoles of acid is needed, so the concentration of the acid is:

$$\frac{51.97 \text{ mmol H}_3PO_4}{25.00 \text{ mL}} = 2.079 \text{ M H}_3PO_4$$

8. (a) $17.40 \text{ mL} \left(\dfrac{3.00 \text{ mmol NaOH}}{1 \text{ mL}} \right) = 52.2 \text{ mmol NaOH}$

Because the acid has only one ionizable hydrogen atom, as denoted by the formula HA,

$$HA(s) + NaOH(aq) \rightarrow NaA(aq) + H_2O(l)$$

the quantity of HA is also 52.2 mmol.

(b) $\dfrac{4170 \text{ mg HA}}{52.2 \text{ mmol HA}} = 79.9 \text{ mg/mmol} = 79.9 \text{ g/mol}$

9. The molality may be calculated immediately:

$$m = \dfrac{0.0150 \text{ mol}}{0.0500 \text{ kg}} = 0.300 \text{ m}$$

The mole fraction requires that the mass of water be changed to moles first:

$$50.0 \text{ g} \left(\dfrac{1 \text{ mol}}{18.0 \text{ g}} \right) = 2.78 \text{ mol}$$

$$X_{\text{NaCl}} = \dfrac{0.0150 \text{ mol}}{(2.78 \text{ mol} + 0.0150 \text{ mol})} = 0.00536$$

(Note the significant digits in the denominator.)

The molarity requires the volume of the solution, which can be calculated from the density of the solution and its total mass. The mass of the NaCl is

$$0.0150 \text{ mol} \left(\dfrac{58.5 \text{ g NaCl}}{1 \text{ mol NaCl}} \right) = 0.878 \text{ g}$$

The total mass is 50.9 g, and the volume is

$$50.9 \text{ g} \left(\dfrac{1 \text{ mL}}{1.02 \text{ g}} \right) = 49.9 \text{ mL}$$

$$M = (0.0150 \text{ mol})/(0.0499 \text{ L}) = 0.301 \text{ M}$$

10. The numbers of moles must be calculated first:

$$50.0 \text{ g CH}_3\text{OH} \left(\dfrac{1 \text{ mol CH}_3\text{OH}}{32.0 \text{ g CH}_3\text{OH}} \right) = 1.56 \text{ mol CH}_3\text{OH}$$

$$75.0 \text{ g H}_2\text{O} \left(\dfrac{1 \text{ mol H}_2\text{O}}{18.0 \text{ g H}_2\text{O}} \right) = 4.17 \text{ mol H}_2\text{O}$$

$$4.17 \text{ mol H}_2\text{O} + 1.56 \text{ mol CH}_3\text{OH} = 5.73 \text{ mol total}$$

$$X_{\text{H}_2\text{O}} = \dfrac{4.17 \text{ mol H}_2\text{O}}{5.73 \text{ mol total}} = 0.728$$

$$X_{\text{CH}_3\text{OH}} = 1.000 - 0.728 = 0.272$$

11. $HNO_3(aq) + NaOH(aq) \rightarrow NaNO_3(aq) + H_2O(l)$

The volumes of acid and base must be equal at the equivalence point because the concentrations are equal and the numbers of moles are the same. Therefore the volume of the solution has doubled, and the concentrations of the sodium ion and the nitrate ion have each been halved to 0.0500 M. The hydrogen ion and hydroxide ion have been completely used up, so the sodium nitrate is 0.0500 M.

12. Because the acid has two ionizable hydrogen atoms, as denoted by the formula H_2A, the equation is

$$H_2A(s) + 2\,NaOH(aq) \rightarrow Na_2A(aq) + 2\,H_2O(l)$$

$$22.22\ mL\left(\frac{3.000\ mmol\ NaOH}{1\ mL}\right) = 66.66\ mmol\ NaOH$$

The quantity of H_2A is

$$66.66\ mmol\ NaOH\left(\frac{1\ mmol\ H_2A}{2\ mmol\ NaOH}\right) = 33.33\ mmol\ H_2A$$

$$\frac{6.66\ g\ H_2A}{0.03333\ mol\ H_2A} = 200\ g/mol\ H_2A = 2.00 \times 10^2\ g/mol\ H_2A$$

13. The number of moles of solute in the initial solution was

$$0.245\ kg\ solvent\left(\frac{2.40\ mol\ solute}{1\ kg\ solvent}\right) = 0.588\ mol\ solute$$

After the dilution, there is still that same 0.588 mol of solute, but now it is in 0.370 kg of solvent. The new molality is

$$\frac{0.588\ mol\ solute}{0.370\ kg\ solvent} = 1.59\ m$$

14. Assume that we have a total of 1.000 mol of solute plus solvent. Then there are 0.150 mol alcohol and

$$0.850\ mol\ H_2O\left(\frac{18.0\ g\ H_2O}{1\ mol\ H_2O}\right) = 15.3\ g\ H_2O = 0.0153\ kg\ H_2O$$

The molality is $\dfrac{0.150\ mol\ alcohol}{0.0153\ kg\ H_2O} = 9.80\ m$ alcohol

15. This is similar to Problem 12.

$$41.44 \text{ mL} \left(\frac{3.000 \text{ mmol HCl}}{1 \text{ mL}} \right) = 124.3 \text{ mmol HCl}$$

The quantity of B is

$$124.3 \text{ mmol HCl} \left(\frac{1 \text{ mmol B}}{2 \text{ mmol HCl}} \right) = 62.15 \text{ mmol B}$$

$$\frac{7.99 \text{ g B}}{0.06215 \text{ mol B}} = 129 \text{ g/mol B}$$

16. Assuming that we have 1.00 L of solution, we have 2.05 kg = 2050 g of solution and 2.24 mol of sucrose.

$$2.24 \text{ mol } C_{12}H_{22}O_{11} \left(\frac{344 \text{ g } C_{12}H_{22}O_{11}}{1 \text{ mol } C_{12}H_{22}O_{11}} \right) = 771 \text{ g } C_{12}H_{22}O_{11}$$

The mass of water then is 2050 g − 771 g = 1280 g = 1.28 kg.
The molality of the sucrose is (2.24 mol)/(1.28 kg) = 1.75 m.
Note the large difference between the molarity and the molality in this relatively concentrated solution.

Chapter 7

Gas Laws

7.1 Laws for a Given Sample of Gas

The gas laws require us for the first time to use algebraic equations in solving problems. (We could have used equations earlier, for example, as early as density calculations in Section 2.4, but the factor label method proved to be easier in most cases.)

It would be good to review the section Scientific Calculations (Section 1.1) before attempting this chapter. Pay careful attention to the units. In solving elementary gas law equations, the units of volume and of pressure must be the same every place they appear in each equation; the units of temperature not only must be the same, but must be *kelvins*!

Be sure to read each example carefully. It makes a great deal of difference if the problem states that the volume increased 5.0 L or increased *to* 5.0 L. In contrast, there is no essential difference in the following statements:

A 1.00-L sample of gas at 150 kPa and 25°C is compressed to 0.500 L at 25°C.
A 1.00-L sample of gas at 150 kPa and 25°C is compressed to 0.500 L at constant temperature.

Memorize the values of the constants that enable the conversions between kilopascals (kPa) and atmospheres (atm) as well as other units of pressure, and between Celsius and Kelvin temperatures:

$$1.000 \text{ atm} = 101.3 \text{ kPa} = 760.0 \text{ torr} = 760.0 \text{ mm Hg}$$

$$K = {}^\circ C + 273 \quad \text{or} \quad T = t + 273$$

Problems relating pressure and volume (Boyle's law problems), those relating temperature and volume (Charles' law problems), and those involving all three (combined gas law problems) are generally stated with all but one of the variables given. We are to determine that variable. For solving these types of problems, it is very useful to tabulate the quantities, especially if any of the units need to be converted. Know the conditions applicable for each of these types of problems:

Boyle's law   given sample of gas,
                     temperature constant $P_1 V_1 = P_2 V_2$
Charles' law   given sample of gas,
                     pressure constant,
                     temperature in kelvins $V_1/T_1 = V_2/T_2$
combined gas law   given sample of gas,
                     temperature in kelvins

$$P_1 V_1/T_1 = P_2 V_2/T_2$$

Every gas law that includes temperature must have the temperature in *kelvins*—**absolute temperature**!

In **Boyle's law**, pressure and volume are inversely proportional. That means that when the pressure goes down, the volume goes up, and vice versa:

Up

$$P_1 V_1 = P_2 V_2$$

Down

In **Charles' law**, when the temperature goes up, the volume goes up, and vice versa:

Up

$$V_1/T_1 = V_2/T_2$$

Up

Both these generalities tend to happen for the **combined gas law**.

EXAMPLE 1   (*a*) Calculate the final volume if a 1.50-L sample of gas at 105 kPa is changed to 1.22 atm at constant temperature. (*b*) Calculate the final volume if a 1.50-L sample of gas at 788 torr is changed to 1.22 atm at constant temperature.

Solution

(*a*) Using Boyle's law: $P_1 V_1 = P_2 V_2$

Dividing both sides by P_2 yields:
$$\frac{P_1 V_1}{P_2} = \frac{P_2 V_2}{P_2} = V_2$$

	P	V
1	105 kPa	1.50 L
2	1.22 atm $=$ 124 kPa	V_2

$$V_2 = P_1 V_1 / P_2 = (105 \text{ kPa})(1.50 \text{ L})/(124 \text{ kPa}) = 1.27 \text{ L}$$

This volume is reasonable, since the volume will decrease because of the increased pressure.

(b) Using Boyle's law:
$$P_1 V_1 = P_2 V_2$$

Dividing both sides by P_2 yields:
$$\frac{P_1 V_1}{P_2} = \frac{P_2 V_2}{P_2} = V_2$$

	P	V
1	788 torr	1.50 L
2	1.22 atm $=$ 927 torr	V_2

$$V_2 = P_1 V_1 / P_2 = (788 \text{ torr})(1.50 \text{ L})/(927 \text{ torr}) = 1.28 \text{ L}$$

This volume is essentially the same as in part (a) because the pressure and volume are both about the same, despite the difference in units. □

From now on, we will follow our usual practice of using liters rather than cubic decimeters, but we will use some pressures in kilopascals and some in torr, as well as some in atmospheres.

EXAMPLE 2 Calculate the initial volume if a sample of gas at 75°C is changed to 1.50 L at 25°C at constant pressure.

Solution Using Charles' law:

	T	V
1	75°C $=$ 348 K	V_1
2	25°C $=$ 298 K	1.50 L

$$V_1 = T_1 V_2 / T_2 = (348 \text{ K})(1.50 \text{ L})/(298 \text{ K}) = 1.75 \text{ L}$$

This volume is reasonable, since the volume will decrease because of the decreased temperature. Note that the volume is *not* decreased to one-third of its initial value because the volume is *not* proportional to the Celsius temperature. □

EXAMPLE 3 Calculate the final volume if a 1.50-L sample of gas at 905 torr and 10°C is changed to 1.000 atm at 100°C.

Solution Using the combined gas law:

	P	V	T
1	905 torr	1.50 L	10°C = 283 K
2	1.000 atm = 760.0 torr	V_2	100°C = 373 K

$$V_2 = \frac{P_1 V_1 T_2}{P_2 T_1} = \frac{(905 \text{ torr})(1.50 \text{ L})(373 \text{ K})}{(760.0 \text{ torr})(283 \text{ K})} = 2.35 \text{ L}$$

This volume is reasonable, since the volume will increase because of the decreased pressure and also because of the increased temperature. ☐

EXAMPLE 4 An 8.00-L sample of gas at 99.0 kPa and 25°C is compressed. What is its final pressure at 25°C if the gas (*a*) is compressed 2.00 L? (*b*) is compressed to 2.00 L?

Solution

(*a*) Since the volume is compressed 2.00 L and it started at 8.00 L, V_2 is 8.00 L − 2.00 L = 6.00 L. P_2 is given by Boyle's law:

$$P_2 = \frac{P_1 V_1}{V_2} = \frac{(99.0 \text{ kPa})(8.00 \text{ L})}{(6.00 \text{ L})} = 132 \text{ kPa}$$

(*b*) V_2 is 2.00 L. Again P_2 is given by Boyle's law:

$$P_2 = \frac{P_1 V_1}{V_2} = \frac{(99.0 \text{ kPa})(8.00 \text{ L})}{(2.00 \text{ L})} = 396 \text{ kPa} \qquad ☐$$

7.2 Moles of Gas

There are at least two distinct methods of calculating the number of moles in a sample of gas. The first involves the combined gas law, and the second the ideal gas law.

Molar Volume Calculations

A gas at 0°C and 1.000 atm = 101.3 kPa is said to be at **standard temperature and pressure**, abbreviated **STP**. Under these conditions, 1.00 mol of an ideal gas occupies 22.4 L. All real gases occupy approximately 22.4 L at STP. This volume is called the **molar volume** of a gas, but the word *molar* here means *per mole*, and has nothing to do with molarity (Section 6.1). Thus measurement at STP of the volume of a sample of gas enables calculation of the number of moles of gas in the sample, and vice versa.

EXAMPLE 5 (*a*) Calculate the volume occupied by 0.750 mol of O_2 at STP. (*b*) Calculate the number of moles of N_2 that occupies 7.00 L at STP.

Solution

(*a*) $0.750 \text{ mol} \left(\dfrac{22.4 \text{ L (at STP)}}{1.00 \text{ mol}} \right) = 16.8 \text{ L}$

(*b*) $7.00 \text{ L} \left(\dfrac{1 \text{ mol}}{22.4 \text{ L (at STP)}} \right) = 0.313 \text{ mol}$ □

If the sample of gas is not at STP, we can use the combined gas law to calculate what its volume would be at STP, then convert that volume to number of moles. Similarly, if the number of moles are given, we can use the molar volume to calculate the volume at STP and then convert that with the combined gas law to any temperature and pressure required. (See Fig. 7-1.)

EXAMPLE 6 Calculate the number of moles of O_2 that occupies 17.2 L at 25°C and 751 torr.

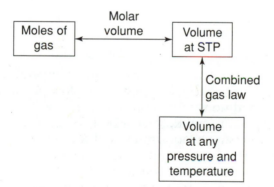

Fig. 7-1 Two Step Mole-Volume Problem. To convert moles of a gas to a volume at any temperature and pressure, first convert the moles to volume at STP with the molar volume (first arrow), then convert the volume to the required volume at the given conditions with the combined gas law. If given the *P-V-T* data, use the combined gas law first, then the molar volume. Where do we start? Where the complete data are given. Work toward the answer required.

Solution First, calculate the volume that the gas would occupy at STP:

$$V_2 = \frac{P_1 V_1 T_2}{P_2 T_1} = \frac{(751 \text{ torr})(17.2 \text{ L})(273 \text{ K})}{(760 \text{ torr})(298 \text{ K})} = 15.6 \text{ L}$$

Then calculate the number of moles:

$$15.6 \text{ L}\left(\frac{1.00 \text{ mol}}{22.4 \text{ L (at STP)}}\right) = 0.696 \text{ mol} \qquad \square$$

EXAMPLE 7 Calculate the volume occupied by 0.151 mol of Cl_2 at 100°C and 73.7 kPa.

Solution At STP:

$$0.151 \text{ mol}\left(\frac{22.4 \text{ L (at STP)}}{1.00 \text{ mol}}\right) = 3.38 \text{ L}$$

Under the specified conditions:

$$V_2 = \frac{P_1 V_1 T_2}{P_2 T_1} = \frac{(101.3 \text{ kPa})(3.38 \text{ L})(373 \text{ K})}{(73.7 \text{ kPa})(273 \text{ K})} = 6.35 \text{ L} \qquad \square$$

The Ideal Gas Law

The ideal gas law

$$PV = nRT$$

applies to any sample of any gas at any temperature and pressure. (Real gases obey this law best under low-pressure and high-temperature conditions.) The constant R in the equation is often given in units L·atm/mol·K, so it is best to express the volume in liters and the pressure in atmospheres. If R is given in L·kPa/mol·K, we will express the volume in liters and the pressure in kilopascals. As usual, the temperature *must be in kelvins!* Memorize the value of R in the ideal gas law equation in metric units, and convert to the value in kilopascals by multiplying by 101.3 kPa/atm.

$R = 0.0821$ L·atm/mol·K   (note well the zero after the decimal point)

or $R = 8.31$ L·kPa/mol·K

The typical ideal gas law problem gives three of the four variables (P, V, n, T) and asks for the fourth. (See Fig. 7-2.)

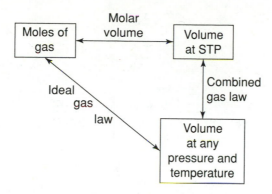

Fig. 7-2   Conversion of Moles of Gas to Volume at Any Temperature and Pressure. In addition to the method in Fig. 7-1, we may use the ideal gas equation to do either conversion—moles of gas to volume or vice versa.

EXAMPLE 8   Calculate the number of moles of gas in a sample occupying 245 mL at 409 torr at 38°C.

Solution

$$P = 409 \text{ torr} = 0.538 \text{ atm} \qquad V = 245 \text{ mL} = 0.245 \text{ L}$$

$$T = 38°C + 273° = 311 \text{ K}$$

Dividing both sides of $PV = nRT$ by RT to isolate the n yields:

$$\frac{PV}{RT} = \frac{nRT}{RT} = n$$

$$n = \frac{PV}{RT} = \frac{(0.538 \text{ atm})(0.245 \text{ L})}{(0.0821 \text{ L·atm/mol·K})(311 \text{ K})} = 0.00516 \text{ mol} \qquad \square$$

EXAMPLE 9   Calculate the number of moles of gas in a sample occupying 532 mL at 0.555 atm at −14°C.

Solution

$$P = 0.555 \text{ atm} \qquad V = 532 \text{ mL} = 0.532 \text{ L}$$

$$T = -14°C + 273° = 259 \text{ K}$$

$$n = \frac{PV}{RT} = \frac{(0.555 \text{ atm})(0.532 \text{ L})}{(0.0821 \text{ L·atm/mol·K})(259 \text{ K})} = 0.0139 \text{ mol} \qquad \square$$

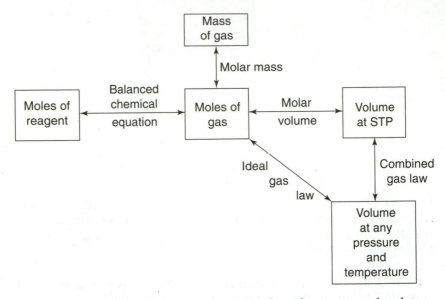

Fig. 7-3   Additional Conversions. Moles of a gas may be determined from other data, such as moles of another reagent in a chemical reaction or mass and molar mass. Conversely, these values may be determined from gas data by working in the opposite direction on the figure. Again, start with the data provided and work toward the answer required. (Remember the boy scouts.)

Using the Number of Moles of Gas

We can use the number of moles of gas, calculated from these gas laws, as we would use moles of any substance. For example, we can use it in a stoichiometry problem. (See Fig. 7-3.)

EXAMPLE 10   Calculate the number of moles of $KClO_3$ that must be decomposed to produce 45.0 L of oxygen at STP.

Solution   The number of moles of oxygen can be calculated from the molar volume of oxygen or from the ideal gas law as

$$45.0 \text{ L}\left(\frac{1 \text{ mol O}_2}{22.4 \text{ L (at STP)}}\right) = 2.01 \text{ mol O}_2$$

$$\text{or} \quad n = \frac{PV}{RT} = \frac{(1.00 \text{ atm})(45.0 \text{ L})}{(0.0821 \text{ L·atm/mol·K})(273 \text{ K})} = 2.01 \text{ mol O}_2$$

To find the number of moles of $KClO_3$ from the number of moles of oxygen requires the balanced chemical equation (Section 5.1):

$$2\ KClO_3(s) \rightarrow 3\ O_2(g) + 2\ KCl(s)$$

$$2.01\ mol\ O_2\left(\frac{2\ mol\ KClO_3}{3\ mol\ O_2}\right) = 1.34\ mol\ KClO_3 \qquad \square$$

Sometimes it is necessary to use the ideal gas law twice in the same problem.

EXAMPLE 11   On a space station, a 10.0-L steel drum of oxygen gas at 25°C and 101.3 kPa pressure springs a leak, and 8.00 g of gas escapes before the leak is plugged. What is the final pressure of the oxygen in the drum at 25°C?

Solution   Even if we cannot see how to complete this problem, we do know that from the initial P-V-T data, we can solve for the initial number of moles of oxygen:

$$n = \frac{PV}{RT} = \frac{(101.3\ kPa)(10.0\ L)}{(8.31\ L \cdot kPa/mol \cdot K)(298\ K)} = 0.409\ mol$$

We also can tell what fraction of a mole of oxygen escaped:

$$8.00\ g\ O_2\left(\frac{1\ mol\ O_2}{32.0\ g\ O_2}\right) = 0.250\ mol\ O_2$$

Knowing the original number of moles of O_2 and the number of moles that escaped enables us to calculate how much oxygen remains in the tank:

$$0.409\ mol - 0.250\ mol = 0.159\ mol$$

Because the drum is steel, it does not change volume; it is still 10.0 L, and

$$P = \frac{nRT}{V} = \frac{(0.159\ mol)(8.31\ L \cdot kPa/mol \cdot K)(298\ K)}{(10.0\ L)} = 39.4\ kPa \qquad \square$$

7.3 Dalton's Law of Partial Pressures

When gases are mixed, the volumes of the individual gases assume the total volume of the mixture, and therefore they are equal to each other and to the volume of the mixture. The temperatures of the individual gases are also the same as the temperature of the mixture. However, the pressures of the individual gases add up to the total pressure of the mixture, and the numbers of moles of the individual gases add up to the total number of moles of the mixture. This is a statement of **Dalton's law of partial pressures**. For example, for a mixture of two gases, using the subscripts 1 and 2 to denote the individual gases:

$$V_1 = V_2 = V_{total} \qquad P_1 + P_2 = P_{total}$$

$$T_1 = T_2 = T_{total} \qquad n_1 + n_2 = n_{total}$$

The ideal gas law can be used with any individual gas in the mixture or with the mixture as a whole. The pressure of the mixture gives the total number of moles in the mixture, but if a partial pressure (pressure of an individual gas, P_i) is used, the number of moles of that gas (n_i) is calculated:

$$P_{total} V = n_{total} RT \qquad \text{or} \qquad P_i V = n_i RT$$

$$(i \text{ is a number such as } 1, 2, 3 \dots)$$

EXAMPLE 12 In a mixture of argon and helium, the volume of the argon is 2.00 L, the temperature of the helium is 27°C, and the total pressure is 725 torr. (*a*) What is the volume of the mixture? (*b*) What is the temperature of the mixture? (*c*) What is the number of moles of gas in the mixture?

Solution (*a*) Since gases in a mixture each have the volume of the mixture, in this case the volume of the mixture is equal to the volume of the argon, 2.00 L. (*b*) The temperature of the mixture (and of the argon) is the same as that of the helium, 27°C. (*c*) The number of moles of mixture is given by the pressure, volume, and temperature of the mixture:

$$725 \text{ torr}\left(\frac{1 \text{ atm}}{760 \text{ torr}}\right) = 0.954 \text{ atm}$$

$$n = \frac{PV}{RT} = \frac{(0.954 \text{ atm})(2.00 \text{ L})}{(0.0821 \text{ L·atm/mol·K})(300 \text{ K})} = 0.0775 \text{ mol} \qquad \square$$

EXAMPLE 13 Show that the ratio of the pressures of two gases in a mixture is equal to the ratio of their numbers of moles.

Solution Dividing the ideal gas law equation for one gas by that for another (or for the whole mixture) enables us to cancel variables with equal values.
Since $V_1 = V_2 = V$ and $T_1 = T_2 = T$:

$$\frac{P_1}{P_2}\frac{V}{V} = \frac{n_1}{n_2}\frac{RT}{RT} = \frac{P_1}{P_2} = \frac{n_1}{n_2}$$

And similarly, starting with $P_{total} V_{total} = n_{total} R T_{total}$ instead of

$P_2 V_2 = n_2 R T_2$:

$$\frac{P_1}{P_{total}} = \frac{n_1}{n_{total}}$$

□

EXAMPLE 14 Calculate the oxygen pressure in a mixture of 0.500 mol of oxygen and 0.750 mol of nitrogen with a total pressure of 40.0 kPa.

Solution

$$\frac{P_{oxygen}}{P_{total}} = \frac{n_{oxygen}}{n_{total}}$$

$$\frac{P_{oxygen}}{40.0 \text{ kPa}} = \frac{0.500 \text{ mol}}{1.250 \text{ mol}}$$

$$P_{oxygen} = 16.0 \text{ kPa}$$

□

When a gas is collected over water, some of the water evaporates and its vapor forms a mixture with the other gas. Evaporation continues until the rate of evaporation of the liquid water equals the rate at which the water vapor condenses, and a state of **physical equilibrium** is achieved.

A mixture of a normal gas and water vapor behaves just like any other gas mixture *as long as no more water can evaporate and no water vapor can condense*. But when the gas mixture is in equilibrium with liquid water, any attempt to reduce the pressure of the water vapor will result in more liquid water evaporating. Any attempt at increasing the water *vapor pressure* (by reducing the volume, for example) will result in water vapor condensing. Thus the vapor pressure of water in equilibrium with liquid water is a constant at any given temperature. Tables of water vapor pressure at various temperatures are given in texts and typically the water vapor pressure at a specified temperature is given on exams.

EXAMPLE 15 (*a*) A mixture of oxygen and water vapor at a total pressure of 107 kPa is in equilibrium with liquid water at 25°C, at which temperature the water vapor pressure is 3.2 kPa. Calculate the pressure of the oxygen. (*b*) Oxygen is collected over water at 25°C under a barometric pressure of 107 kPa. ($P_{H_2O} = 3.2$ kPa) Calculate the pressure of the oxygen.

Solution

(*a*) The pressure of the oxygen is the total pressure minus the water vapor pressure:

$$P_{oxygen} = 107 \text{ kPa} - 3.2 \text{ kPa} = 104 \text{ kPa}$$

(*b*) This problem is merely another statement of the problem of part (*a*).

$$P_{oxygen} = 104 \text{ kPa} \qquad \square$$

7.4 The Law of Combining Volumes

The **law of combining volumes** states that if all the *gases* involved in a chemical reaction are measured (separately) at the same temperature and pressure, their volumes will be in the same ratio as their numbers of moles in the balanced chemical equation. It turns out that this law was very important historically, but is not really needed now. However, it can help do certain problems quickly.

Using the ideal gas law, we can prove that equal volumes of two separate samples of gases, both at the same temperature and pressure, will have equal numbers of moles:

Let V = volume of each gas
and T = absolute temperature of each gas
and P = pressure of each gas
Then $n = PV/RT$ for each gas.

Because every term on the right side of the last equation is the same for the two gases, the number of moles is the same also. Please note that this conclusion is true for *separate* samples of gas; there is no gas mixture in this discussion. Under these conditions, if the numbers of moles of two gases in a chemical reaction are equal, their volumes would be the same. If there were twice the number of moles of one gas than the other, the volume of that gas would be double that of the other. Because this is true, then the gases in a chemical reaction involving separate gases at equal temperature and equal pressure have their volumes proportional to the number of moles of gas—the coefficients in the balanced equation. For example,

$$N_2(g) + 3 H_2(g) \rightarrow 2 NH_3(g)$$

If all three gases are separate samples at the same temperature and pressure, the volume of the ammonia that is produced will be twice the volume of the nitrogen that reacts, and the volume of the hydrogen that reacts will be three times the volume of the nitrogen that reacts.

EXAMPLE 16 (*a*) If 6.00 L of hydrogen gas reacts with oxygen gas to form liquid water, what volume of oxygen will react, assuming that the oxygen is measured at the same temperature and pressure as the hydrogen. (*b*) Can the volume of the water be determined?

Solution

$$2\,H_2(g) + O_2(g) \rightarrow 2\,H_2O(l)$$

(*a*) Two types of solution are possible. The law of combining volumes states that the ratio of volumes of hydrogen to oxygen under these conditions is $2:1$, the same as the coefficients in the balanced equation, so the volume of oxygen is 3.00 L.

We can also determine the ratio of the number of moles of hydrogen to the number of moles of oxygen in terms of the ideal gas law:

$$\frac{n_{H_2}}{n_{O_2}} = \frac{V_{H_2}(P/RT)}{V_{O_2}(P/RT)} = \frac{6.00\ L}{V_{O_2}} = \frac{2\ mol\ H_2}{1\ mol\ O_2}$$

$$V_{O_2} = 3.00\ L$$

(See Supplementary Problem 6 if the use of variables for the pressure and temperature is difficult.)

(*b*) The volume of the water cannot be determined because, in this problem, it is not a gas. Again, it is important not only to remember the rules, but also when to use each one! □

7.5 Graham's Law

Effusion is the escape of a gas through small pores in its container. **Diffusion** is the passage of molecules of one gas through another gas. (For example, ammonia gas diffuses through air, and can be smelled on the far side of a room from where it is allowed to escape.)

Graham's Law states that, under equal conditions of temperature and pressure, the rate of effusion or diffusion of a gas is *inversely* proportional to the square root of its molar mass. The most useful mathematical form of this law involves the rates of two gases:

$$\frac{r_1}{r_2} = \sqrt{\frac{MM_2}{MM_1}}$$

The usual problem involving Graham's law asks for the ratio of rates of effusion or diffusion of two gases, or it gives the rate for one gas and asks the rate for another.

EXAMPLE 17   How many times faster does hydrogen gas effuse from a porous cup compared to oxygen gas under the same conditions of temperature and pressure?

Solution

$$\frac{r_{\text{hydrogen}}}{r_{\text{oxygen}}} = \sqrt{\frac{MM_{\text{oxygen}}}{MM_{\text{hydrogen}}}} = \sqrt{\frac{32.0 \text{ g/mol}}{2.02 \text{ g/mol}}} = \sqrt{15.8} = 3.98$$

$$r_{\text{hydrogen}} = 3.98(r_{\text{oxygen}})$$

Hydrogen effuses about four times as fast as oxygen under the same conditions of temperature and pressure. □

EXAMPLE 18 In a certain experiment, argon effuses from a porous cup at 4.00 mmol/minute. How fast would chlorine effuse under the same conditions?

Solution

$$\frac{r_{\text{chlorine}}}{r_{\text{argon}}} = \sqrt{\frac{MM_{\text{argon}}}{MM_{\text{chlorine}}}} = \sqrt{\frac{39.9 \text{ g/mol}}{70.9 \text{ g/mol}}} = 0.750$$

$$r_{\text{chlorine}} = (0.750)(4.00 \text{ mmol/minute}) = 3.00 \text{ mmol/minute}$$

Hints:

1. Once again, it is important to remember that hydrogen, nitrogen, oxygen, fluorine, and chlorine, when uncombined with other elements, are gases that exist as diatomic molecules.
2. For ease of solution, let the unknown rate appear in the numerator.
3. The proportion is inverse; if the rate of a given gas appears in the numerator, its molar mass is in the denominator, and vice versa. □

The *time* it takes for a gas to diffuse a certain distance is inversely proportional to its *rate* of diffusion. (The faster something moves, the less time it takes to reach its destination.) If a Graham's law problem asks for a time, the problem may be solved in terms of rates, and that information used to get the final answer.

EXAMPLE 19 If escaping ammonia gas can be smelled across a room in 5.00 minutes, how long would it take to smell chlorine gas under identical conditions?

Solution The rate ratio is calculated as usual:

$$\frac{r_{\text{ammonia}}}{r_{\text{chlorine}}} = \sqrt{\frac{MM_{\text{chlorine}}}{MM_{\text{ammonia}}}} = \sqrt{\frac{70.9 \text{ g/mol}}{17.0 \text{ g/mol}}} = 2.04$$

Because the ammonia diffuses 2.04 times as fast, the chlorine will take 2.04 times as long to get there:

$$\text{Time} = (2.04)\,(5.00 \text{ minutes}) = 10.2 \text{ minutes}$$

Note that the heavier gas (chlorine) takes longer to arrive (because it diffuses more slowly). □

7.6 Kinetic Molecular Theory Calculations

One of the postulates of the **kinetic molecular theory (KMT)** states that the average kinetic energy of the molecules of a gas is directly proportional to the *absolute* temperature.

$$\overline{KE} = 3RT/2N$$

where R is expressed in joules per mole per kelvin ($1\,J = 1\,L\cdot kPa$). T is absolute temperature and N is Avogadro's number. A line (called a *bar*) over a variable designates the quantity as an average. Thus $\overline{KE}$ means the average kinetic energy.

   If two samples of gas are at the same temperature, the average kinetic energies of their molecules are equal. That does not mean that the average velocities of their molecules are equal, however. If the gases are not the same, their molecules have different molecular masses. Because the kinetic energy is equal to half the mass times the square of the velocity, their velocities must be different.

$$\overline{KE} = \tfrac{1}{2}m\overline{v^2}$$

Since $\overline{KE}$ for the two gases is the same, but m is different, $\overline{v^2}$ must also be different. Thus the lighter gas molecules must travel faster on average. (This is the basis for Graham's law.)

EXAMPLE 20   Samples of hydrogen and nitrogen are at the same temperature. (*a*) Compare the average kinetic energies of their molecules. (*b*) Compare qualitatively the average velocities of their molecules.

   Solution
(*a*) Since the temperatures are the same, the average kinetic energies are the same.
(*b*) Since the mass of each hydrogen molecule is less than that of each nitrogen molecule, the average velocity of hydrogen molecules must be greater than that of nitrogen molecules. □

Leading Questions

1. State two ways to convert the number of moles of a gas to its volume, given all other factors.
2. To get the volume of a sample of gas given its temperature and pressure, does it matter which gas is under consideration (a) if the number of moles of gas is given? (b) if the mass of gas is given?
3. What calculation differences are there between two gases in a mixture and two gases in a chemical reaction measured separately?
4. What is the difference between a 2.00-L sample of gas being expanded (a) 5.00 L or (b) to 5.00 L?
5. Explain why Boyle's law cannot be used to solve Example 11.
6. Write equations like those in the text before Example 12 relating the pressures of three gases in a mixture, their temperatures, their numbers of moles, and their volumes.

Answers to Leading Questions

1. (a) Use the molar volume with the combined gas law or (b) use the ideal gas law.
2. (a) No. (b) Yes. The molar mass must be used to convert the mass to the number of moles.
3. Two gases in a mixture *must* have equal *volumes* and equal temperatures. Two separate samples of gas *may* have equal *pressures* and equal temperatures (as in problems involving the law of combining volumes).
4. (a) The final volume is 7.00 L. (b) The final volume is 5.00 L.
5. Boyle's law cannot be used because there is not a given sample of gas.
6. $V_1 = V_2 = V_3 = V_{total}$ $\qquad$ $P_1 + P_2 + P_3 = P_{total}$
   $T_1 = T_2 = T_3 = T_{total}$ $\qquad$ $n_1 + n_2 + n_3 = n_{total}$

Supplementary Problems

1. (a) Calculate the final pressure of a gas if a 22.4-mL sample of the gas at 78.0 kPa is expanded to 0.255 L at constant temperature.
   (b) Calculate the final pressure of a gas if a 49.1-mL sample of the gas at 755 torr is expanded to 0.123 L at constant temperature.
2. Calculate the initial temperature of a gas if a 0.380-L sample of the gas is changed at constant pressure to 555 mL at $-25°C$.

3. Calculate the final pressure of a gas if a 953-mL sample of the gas at 1.25 atm and 50°C is changed to 1.55 L at 75°C.

4. A 0.790-L sample of gas at 255 kPa and 25°C is compressed. What is its final pressure at 75°C if the volume (a) was lowered by 0.200 L? (b) was lowered 0.200 L? (c) was lowered to 0.200 L?

5. Calculate the pressure of 0.444 mol of gas in a sample occupying 666 mL at −8°C.

6. To show that the law of combining volumes works, do each of the following parts by calculating the number of moles of each reactant. (a) If 6.00 L of hydrogen gas reacts with oxygen gas to form liquid water, what volume of oxygen will react, assuming that the oxygen and hydrogen are both measured at 25°C and 785 torr. (b) If 6.00 L of hydrogen gas reacts with oxygen gas to form liquid water, what volume of oxygen will react, assuming that the oxygen and hydrogen are both measured at 53°C and 805 torr. (c) Repeat the process with other arbitrary values of temperature and pressure to be convinced that the law is true for *any* such values.

7. What pressure is exhibited by 0.250 mol of a gas in 10.0 L at 23°C?

8. Explain why in Dalton's law problems $\dfrac{n_1}{n_2} = \dfrac{P_1}{P_2}$

   but in combining volume problems $\dfrac{n_1}{n_2} = \dfrac{V_1}{V_2}$

9. If 4.88 g of a gas occupies 2.75 L at 103 kPa and 22°C, (a) calculate the number of moles of gas present. (b) Calculate the molar mass.

10. Calculate the volume at STP of 26.7 g of oxygen gas.

11. Calculate the volume occupied by 7.00 g of nitrogen gas at 25°C and 1.03 atm.

12. Calculate the pressure of oxygen in a mixture at 105.9 kPa containing 0.400 mol of oxygen and 0.200 mol of nitrogen.

13. (a) Calculate the number of moles in 4.00 L of a gas mixture at 25°C if the total pressure is 0.995 atm. (b) What difference does it make, if any, that the sample is a mixture and not a pure substance?

14. Calculate the rate of effusion of helium from a porous cup under the same conditions that CH_4 effuses at a rate of 20.0 mmol/minute.

15. Calculate the relative rates of effusion of $^{235}UF_6$ and $^{238}UF_6$ from a mixture of the two. The molar masses of ^{235}U and ^{238}U are 235.04 g/mol and 238.05 g/mol, respectively.

16. Calculate the time it would take for SO_2 to diffuse across a room under the same conditions that it takes an equal number of moles of NH_3 5.00 minutes to diffuse.

17. (a) Calculate the average kinetic energy of hydrogen molecules at 295 K. (b) Calculate their "average" velocities (u), using

$$\overline{KE} = \tfrac{1}{2}\, mu^2 \qquad \text{and} \qquad 1\,J = 1\ kg{\cdot}m^2/s^2$$

18. Calculate the volume of oxygen that reacts with CO to produce 4.00 L of CO_2, all measured at the same temperature and pressure.

19. As far as possible, determine the relative volumes of the substances involved in the following reaction in the open atmosphere at 500°C:

$$2\ C(s) + O_2(g) \rightarrow 2\ CO(g)$$

20. Determine the volume of oxygen collected over water at 25°C and 762 torr barometric pressure by decomposition of 1.00 g of $KClO_3$ ($P_{H_2O} = 24$ torr).

21. Calculate the molar mass of 4.88 g of a gas that occupies 2.75 L at 1.02 atm and 22°C.

22. Determine the molar mass of a gas whose density at 25°C and 1.00 atm pressure is 1.72 g/L.

23. Using the ideal gas law equation, the volume of a mole of gas at STP, and the value of R, determine the value of standard pressure (in kilopascals).

24. A 5.00-g sample of gas is contained in a 2.51-L vessel at 25°C and 1.10 atm pressure. The gas contains 81.8% carbon and the rest hydrogen. (a) What can be calculated from the pressure-volume-temperature data? (b) What can be calculated from the mass and the answer to part (a)? (c) What can be calculated from the percent composition data? (d) What can be calculated from the answers to parts (b) and (c)?

25. A 5.00-g sample of gas is contained in a 2.51-L vessel at 25°C and 1.10 atm pressure. The gas contains 81.8% carbon and the rest hydrogen. (a) Calculate the number of moles of gas in the sample. (b) Calculate the molar mass of the sample. (c) Calculate the empirical formula of the sample. (d) Calculate the molecular formula of the sample.

26. Calculate the molecular formula of a 4.70-g sample of gas contained in a 2.51-L vessel at 25°C and 1.09 atm pressure. The gas contains 85.7% carbon and the rest hydrogen.

Solutions to Supplementary Problems

1. (a)

	P	V
1	78.0 kPa	22.4 mL
2	P_2	0.255 L = 255 mL

$$P_2 = P_1V_1/V_2 = (78.0 \text{ kPa})(22.4 \text{ mL})/(255 \text{ mL}) = 6.85 \text{ kPa}$$

This pressure is reasonable, since the volume increased because of the decreased pressure.

(b)

	P	V
1	755 torr	49.1 mL = 0.0491 L
2	P_2	0.123 L

$$P_2 = P_1V_1/V_2 = (755 \text{ torr})(0.0491 \text{ L})/(0.123 \text{ L}) = 301 \text{ torr}$$

This pressure is reasonable, since the volume increased because of the decreased pressure.

2.

	T	V
1	T_1	0.380 L
2	$-25°C = 248$ K	555 mL = 0.555 L

$$T_1 = T_2V_1/V_2 = (248 \text{ K})(0.380 \text{ L})/(0.555 \text{ L}) = 1.70 \times 10^2 \text{ K}$$

This temperature is reasonable, since the volume will increase because of the increasing temperature.

3.

	P	V	T
1	1.25 atm	953 mL	50°C = 323 K
2	P_2	1550 mL	75°C = 348 K

$$P_2 = \frac{P_1V_1T_2}{V_2T_1} = \frac{(1.25 \text{ atm})(953 \text{ mL})(348 \text{ K})}{(1550 \text{ mL})(323 \text{ K})} = 0.828 \text{ atm}$$

This pressure is reasonable, since the volume will increase because of the decreased pressure and also because of the increased temperature.

4. Note the wording of the three parts: "(a) was lowered by 0.200 L? (b) was lowered 0.200 L? (c) was lowered to 0.200 L?" "Lowered by 0.200 L" and "lowered 0.200 L" mean the same thing. "Lowered to 0.200 L" gives a new final volume.

(a) V_2 is 0.790 L − 0.200 L = 0.590 L. P_2 is given by the combined gas law:

$$P_2 = \frac{P_1 V_1 T_2}{V_2 T_1} = \frac{(255 \text{ kPa})(0.790 \text{ L})(348 \text{ K})}{(0.590 \text{ L})(298 \text{ K})} = 399 \text{ kPa}$$

(b) V_2 is again 0.790 L − 0.200 L = 0.590 L. P_2 is again 399 kPa.

(c) V_2 is 0.200 L. P_2 is again given by the combined gas law:

$$P_2 = \frac{P_1 V_1 T_2}{V_2 T_1} = \frac{(255 \text{ kPa})(0.790 \text{ L})(348 \text{ K})}{(0.200 \text{ L})(298 \text{ K})} = 1180 \text{ kPa}$$

5. $n = 0.444$ mol $\qquad V = 666$ mL $= 0.666$ L
$T = -8°C + 273° = 265$ K

$$P = \frac{nRT}{V} = \frac{(0.444 \text{ mol})(8.31 \text{ L·kPa/mol·K})(265 \text{ K})}{(0.666 \text{ L})} = 1470 \text{ kPa}$$

6. (a) The number of moles of hydrogen is given by

$$n = \frac{PV}{RT} = \frac{[(785/760) \text{ atm}](6.00 \text{ L})}{(0.0821 \text{ L·atm/mol·K})(298 \text{ K})} = 0.253 \text{ mol}$$

According to the balanced chemical equation, the number of moles of oxygen is half that, 0.127 mol. The volume of oxygen is

$$V = \frac{nRT}{P} = \frac{(0.127 \text{ mol})(0.0821 \text{ L·atm/mol·K})(298 \text{ K})}{[(785/760) \text{ atm}]} = 3.01 \text{ L}$$

(b) The number of moles of hydrogen is given by

$$n = \frac{PV}{RT} = \frac{[(805/760) \text{ atm}](6.00 \text{ L})}{(0.0821 \text{ L·atm/mol·K})(326 \text{ K})} = 0.237 \text{ mol}$$

According to the balanced chemical equation, the number of moles of oxygen is half that, 0.119 mol. The volume of oxygen is

$$V = \frac{nRT}{P} = \frac{(0.119 \text{ mol})(0.0821 \text{ L·atm/mol·K})(326 \text{ K})}{(805/760) \text{ atm}} = 3.01 \text{ L}$$

(c) No matter what values are chosen, the same answer is found each time (within rounding error).

7. $P = nRT/V = $ (0.250 mol)(0.0821 L·atm/mol·K)(296 K)/(10.0 L)
$= 0.608$ atm

Alternatively, at STP, the gas would occupy

$$0.250 \text{ mol}\left(\frac{22.4 \text{ L (at STP)}}{1 \text{ mol}}\right) = 5.60 \text{ L}$$

The pressure is

$$P_2 = \frac{P_1V_1T_2}{V_2T_1} = \frac{(1.00 \text{ atm})(5.60 \text{ L})(296 \text{ K})}{(10.0 \text{ L})(273 \text{ K})} = 0.607 \text{ atm}$$

8. Dalton's law involves a mixture of gases, in which the *volumes* and *temperatures must be the same*; the law of combining volumes involves separate gases, with *pressures and temperatures specified as equal.*

9. (a) $n = \dfrac{PV}{RT} = \dfrac{(103 \text{ kPa})(2.75 \text{ L})}{(8.31 \text{ L·kPa/mol·K})(295 \text{ K})} = 0.116 \text{ mol}$

(b) $MM = \dfrac{4.88 \text{ g}}{0.116 \text{ mol}} = 42.1 \text{ g/mol}$

10. The molar volume is 22.4 L at STP. If we know the number of moles, we can immediately calculate the volume at STP. The number of moles is calculated from the mass with the molar mass:

$$26.7 \text{ g O}_2\left(\frac{1 \text{ mol O}_2}{32.0 \text{ g O}_2}\right) = 0.834 \text{ mol O}_2 \qquad \text{(Remember that oxygen gas is O}_2\text{!)}$$

$$0.834 \text{ mol O}_2\left(\frac{22.4 \text{ L (at STP)}}{1 \text{ mol O}_2}\right) = 18.7 \text{ L}$$

11. The number of moles of nitrogen gas is given by

$$7.00 \text{ g N}_2\left(\frac{1 \text{ mol N}_2}{28.0 \text{ g N}_2}\right) = 0.250 \text{ mol N}_2 \qquad \text{(Remember that nitrogen gas is N}_2\text{!)}$$

The volume is given by the ideal gas law:

$$V = \frac{nRT}{P} = \frac{(0.250 \text{ mol})(0.0821 \text{ L·atm/mol·K})(298 \text{ K})}{1.03 \text{ atm}} = 5.94 \text{ L}$$

or by the molar volume and the combined gas law:

$$0.250 \text{ mol} \left(\frac{22.4 \text{ L (at STP)}}{1 \text{ mol}} \right) = 5.60 \text{ L}$$

$$V_2 = \frac{P_1 V_1 T_2}{P_2 T_1} = \frac{(1.00 \text{ atm})(5.60 \text{ L})(298 \text{ K})}{(1.03 \text{ atm})(273 \text{ K})} = 5.93 \text{ L}$$

12. $\dfrac{P_{O_2}}{P_{\text{total}}} = \dfrac{n_{O_2}}{n_{\text{total}}}$

$$P_{O_2} = \frac{(105.9 \text{ kPa})(0.400 \text{ mol } O_2)}{0.600 \text{ mol total}} = 70.6 \text{ kPa}$$

13. (a) $V_{\text{STP}} = \dfrac{P_2 V_2 T_{\text{STP}}}{P_{\text{STP}} T_2} = \dfrac{(0.995 \text{ atm})(4.00 \text{ L})(273 \text{ K})}{(1.00 \text{ atm})(298 \text{ K})} = 3.65 \text{ L}$

$$3.65 \text{ L} \left(\frac{1 \text{ mol}}{22.4 \text{ L(at STP)}} \right) = 0.163 \text{ mol}$$

(b) It does not make any difference.

14. $\dfrac{r_{\text{He}}}{r_{CH_4}} = \sqrt{\dfrac{MM_{CH_4}}{MM_{\text{He}}}} = \sqrt{\dfrac{16.0 \text{ g/mol}}{4.00 \text{ g/mol}}} = \sqrt{4.00} = 2.00$

$$r_{\text{He}} = (2.00)(20.0 \text{ mmol/minute}) = 40.0 \text{ mmol/minute}$$

15. $MM_{235} = 235.04 \text{ g/mol} + 6(18.998 \text{ g/mol}) = 349.03 \text{ g/mol for } {}^{235}UF_6$
    $MM_{238} = 238.05 \text{ g/mol} + 6(18.998 \text{ g/mol}) = 352.04 \text{ g/mol for } {}^{238}UF_6$

$$\frac{r_{235}}{r_{238}} = \sqrt{\frac{352.04 \text{ g/mol}}{349.03 \text{ g/mol}}} = \sqrt{1.0086} = 1.0043$$

This very small difference is sufficient to separate the isotopes with repeated effusions.

16. $\dfrac{r_{NH_3}}{r_{SO_2}} = \sqrt{\dfrac{MM_{SO_2}}{MM_{NH_3}}} = \sqrt{\dfrac{64.1 \text{ g/mol}}{17.0 \text{ g/mol}}} = \sqrt{3.77} = 1.94$

Since the NH_3 travels 1.94 times as fast, the SO_2 will take 1.94 times as long:

$$1.94(5.00 \text{ minutes}) = 9.70 \text{ minutes}$$

17. (a) $\overline{KE} = \dfrac{3RT}{2N} = \dfrac{3(8.31 \text{ J/mol·K})(295 \text{ K})}{2(6.02 \times 10^{23}/\text{mol})} = 6.11 \times 10^{-21} \text{ J}$

(b) The mass of a molecule in kilograms is

$$2.016 \text{ amu}\left(\frac{1 \text{ g}}{6.02 \times 10^{23} \text{ amu}}\right)\left(\frac{1 \text{ kg}}{1000 \text{ g}}\right) = 3.35 \times 10^{-27} \text{ kg}$$

$$u = \sqrt{\frac{2\overline{KE}}{m}} = \sqrt{\frac{2(6.11 \times 10^{-21} \text{ J})}{3.35 \times 10^{-27} \text{ kg}}} = 1910 \text{ m/s}$$

(about 4300 miles per hour)

18. $2 \text{ CO(g)} + \text{O}_2\text{(g)} \rightarrow 2 \text{ CO}_2\text{(g)}$

The law of combining volumes requires 2.00 L of O_2 to react to produce the 4.00 L of CO_2:

$$4.00 \text{ L CO}_2\left(\frac{1 \text{ L O}_2}{2 \text{ L CO}_2}\right) = 2.00 \text{ L O}_2$$

19. The ratio of volumes of O_2 to CO is 1 : 2, according to the law of combining volumes. The ratio of volume of carbon to volume of oxygen or carbon monoxide cannot be determined because carbon is a solid.

20. The oxygen pressure is

$$P_{O_2} = P_{\text{barometric}} - P_{H_2O} = 762 \text{ torr} - 24 \text{ torr} = 738 \text{ torr}$$

$$= 0.971 \text{ atm}$$

$$1.00 \text{ g KClO}_3\left(\frac{1 \text{ mol KClO}_3}{122 \text{ g KClO}_3}\right)\left(\frac{3 \text{ mol O}_2}{2 \text{ mol KClO}_3}\right) = 0.0123 \text{ mol O}_2$$

The volume of oxygen gas at STP is determined from its number of moles:

$$0.0123 \text{ mol O}_2\left(\frac{22.4 \text{ L (at STP)}}{1 \text{ mol O}_2}\right) = 0.276 \text{ L}$$

The volume at the specified temperature and pressure is given by the combined gas law:

$$V_2 = \frac{P_{STP}V_{STP}T_2}{P_2 T_{STP}} = \frac{(760 \text{ torr})(0.276 \text{ L})((298 \text{ K})}{(738 \text{ torr})(273 \text{ K})} = 0.310 \text{ L}$$

The ideal gas law may be used in place of the last two steps:

$$V = \frac{nRT}{P} = \frac{(0.0123 \text{ mol})(0.0821 \text{ L·atm/mol·K})(298 \text{ K})}{0.971 \text{ atm}} = 0.310 \text{ L}$$

21. $$n = \frac{PV}{RT} = \frac{(1.02 \text{ atm})(2.75 \text{ L})}{(0.0821 \text{ L·atm/mol·K})(295 \text{ K})} = 0.116 \text{ mol}$$

$$MM = \frac{4.88 \text{ g}}{0.116 \text{ mol}} = 42.1 \text{ g/mol}$$

This is the same problem as Supplementary Problem 9, but is stated in atmospheres and is not stated in steps.

22. Assume a 1.00-L volume. The mass of gas in this volume is 1.72 g. The number of moles is given by the ideal gas law:

$$n = \frac{PV}{RT} = \frac{(1.00 \text{ atm})(1.00 \text{ L})}{(0.0821 \text{ L·atm/mol·K})(298 \text{ K})} = 0.0409 \text{ mol}$$

The molar mass is thus

$$MM = \frac{1.72 \text{ g}}{0.0409 \text{ mol}} = 42.1 \text{ g/mol}$$

23. The value is given by

$$P = nRT/V = (1.00 \text{ mol})(8.31 \text{ L·kPa/mol·K})(273 \text{ K})/(22.4 \text{ L})$$

$$= 101 \text{ kPa}$$

24. (*a*) The number of moles of gas.
(*b*) The molar mass of the gas.
(*c*) The empirical formula.
(*d*) The molecular formula. (See the next two problems.)

25. (*a*) $$n = \frac{PV}{RT} = \frac{(1.10 \text{ atm})(2.51 \text{ L})}{(0.0821 \text{ L·atm/mol·K})(298 \text{ K})} = 0.113 \text{ mol}$$
(*b*) MM = m/n = (5.00 g)/(0.113 mol) = 44.2 g/mol
(*c*) $81.8 \text{ g C}\left(\dfrac{1 \text{ mol C}}{12.0 \text{ g C}}\right) = 6.82 \text{ mol C}$

$$18.2 \text{ g H}\left(\frac{1 \text{ mol H}}{1.008 \text{ g H}}\right) = 18.1 \text{ mol H}$$

The mole ratio of H to C is

$$\frac{18.1 \text{ mol H}}{6.82 \text{ mol C}} = \frac{2.65 \text{ mol H}}{1 \text{ mol C}} = \frac{2.65 \text{ mol H} \times 3}{1 \text{ mol C} \times 3} = \frac{8 \text{ mol H}}{3 \text{ mol C}}$$

The empirical formula is C_3H_8.

(d) The empirical formula mass is 44.0 g/mol, equal within two significant digits to the molar mass, so the molecular formula is C_3H_8.

26. This problem is similar to Problem 25, but it is not stated in parts. The number of moles is given by

$$n = \frac{PV}{RT} = \frac{(1.09 \text{ atm})(2.51 \text{ L})}{(0.0821 \text{ L·atm/mol·K})(298 \text{ K})} = 0.112 \text{ mol}$$

The molar mass is

$$MM = m/n = (4.70 \text{ g})/(0.112 \text{ mol}) = 42.0 \text{ g/mol}$$

The empirical formula and molecular formula are calculated as in Chapter 4.

$$85.7 \text{ g C}\left(\frac{1 \text{ mol C}}{12.0 \text{ g C}}\right) = 7.14 \text{ mol C}$$

$$14.3 \text{ g H}\left(\frac{1 \text{ mol H}}{1.008 \text{ g H}}\right) = 14.2 \text{ mol H}$$

The mole ratio of C to H is $1:2$, so the empirical formula is CH_2. The empirical formula mass is 14.0 g/mol, and the molar mass is 42.0 g/mol, so there are $(42.0/14.0) = 3$ empirical formula units per molecule. The molecular formula is C_3H_6.

Chapter 8

Thermochemistry

8.1 Calorimetry

Measurement of heat is an indirect process; we measure heat by its effect on material samples. The heat required to change the temperature of a sample by a certain number of degrees is given by

$$q = mc\Delta t$$

where q is the heat *added* to the sample. If heat is removed from the sample, q has a negative value. The m is the mass of the sample, c is its specific heat capacity, called specific heat for short, and Δt is the *change in temperature*. (The Greek letter Δ is used generally in chemistry to mean "change in," so Δt means change in temperature, ΔV means change in volume, and Δm means change in mass, for example.) The change is always defined as the *final value minus the initial value*:

$$\Delta t = t_{final} - t_{initial} \quad \text{or} \quad \Delta t = t_2 - t_1$$

The *system* is defined as the portion of the universe under investigation. The rest of the universe is known as the *surroundings*. When heat is added to a system and the temperature rises, Δt is positive, and therefore q is positive because m and c are always positive. If heat is removed, the temperature falls, Δt is negative, and q is also negative. *Heat added to a system is positive; heat removed from a system is negative.* We must be especially careful in this chapter to make sure that we use the correct signs and the correct units.

The **specific heat** of a substance is defined as the heat required to raise the temperature of 1 gram of the substance 1°C. (See Table 8-1.) It takes 4.184 J to raise the temperature of 1.000 g of water from 14.5°C to 15.5°C, so the specific heat of water (at that temperature) is 4.184 J/g·°C. The specific heat of liquid water at other temperatures

Table 8-1 Specific Heat Capacities

Metals	c (J/g·°C)	
Aluminum	0.90	
Chromium	0.45	
Copper	0.385	
Gold	0.129	
Iron	0.442	
Monel metal	0.427	(66% Ni, 31.5% Cu)
Platinum	0.130	
Silver	0.24	
Zinc	0.388	

Water		
Solid (ice)	2.089	
Liquid	4.184	
Vapor	2.042	

is very nearly the same, so we will use that value no matter what the temperature, except in the most precise work (where the precise specific heat will be given). Remember the value 4.184 J/g·°C. (Perhaps a more familiar unit of heat is the calorie; 1 calorie is defined as 4.184 J, so the heat capacity of water is 1.000 cal/g·°C.)

The equation for heat can be used to calculate heat capacities, changes in temperature or final or initial temperatures, masses, or heat, if all of the others are given. Be sure to distinguish between the change in temperature and the individual temperatures, as well as between heat and specific heat!

Differences in temperature or *changes* in temperature are the same on the Celsius scale and the Kelvin scale.

EXAMPLE 1 Calculate the difference in temperature between the freezing point of water and the normal boiling point of water on the Celsius scale and on the Kelvin scale.

Solution

$$\Delta t = 100°C - 0°C = 100°C$$

$$\Delta T = 373\ K - 273\ K = 100\ K \qquad \square$$

EXAMPLE 2 Calculate the quantity of heat required to raise the temperature of 2.00 g of water 4.00°C.

Solution

$$q = mc\Delta t = (2.00\ g)(4.184\ J/g·°C)(4.00°C) = 33.5\ J$$

Note that it is the *change in temperature* that is included in this equation. □

EXAMPLE 3 Calculate the quantity of heat required to raise the temperature of 2.00 g of water from 21.00°C to 25.00°C.

Solution The change in temperature is 4.00°C, so this example is the same as the prior one. □

EXAMPLE 4 Calculate the quantity of heat required to change the temperature of 2.00 g of water from 25.00°C to 21.00°C.

Solution This time, the change in temperature is 21.00°C − 25.00°C = −4.00°C, so the quantity of heat is

$$q = mc\Delta t = (2.00 \text{ g})(4.184 \text{ J/g·°C})(-4.00°C) = -33.5 \text{ J}$$

The minus sign means that heat must be *removed* from the water. □

EXAMPLE 5 (*a*) Calculate the temperature change when 55.7 J of heat is added to 12.0 g of water at 22.0°C. (*b*) What is the final temperature?

Solution

(*a*) $q = mc\Delta t = (12.0 \text{ g})(4.184 \text{ J/g·°C})(\Delta t) = 55.7 \text{ J}$
    $\Delta t = 1.11°C$
(*b*) The final temperature is 1.11°C higher than the initial temperature, or

$$t_f = 22.0°C + 1.11°C = 23.1°C$$

Note the difference between the *change in temperature* and the *final temperature*! □

To what temperature would the water in Example 5 be warmed if 55.7 J of electrical energy or 55.7 J of energy from a chemical reaction had been added? It doesn't matter to the water what form of energy has been used; just the quantity of energy is important. (See Supplementary Problems 13, 21, and 22.)

EXAMPLE 6 What mass of water is heated 2.30°C when 87.4 J of heat is added to it?

Solution

$$q = mc\Delta t = (m)(4.184 \text{ J/g·°C})(2.30°C) = 87.4 \text{ J}$$
$$m = 9.08 \text{ g} \qquad \square$$

EXAMPLE 7 Calculate the heat capacity of a metal if 157 J raises the temperature of a 53.1-g sample of the metal from 15.7°C to 21.8°C.

Solution

$$q = mc\Delta t = (53.1 \text{ g})(c)(21.8°C - 15.7°C) = 157 \text{ J}$$
$$c = 0.48 \text{ J/g·°C}$$

(The temperature change has only two significant digits.) $\qquad \square$

If two samples at different temperatures are placed in thermal contact, the hotter one will be cooled and the colder one will be warmed. They will both wind up *at the same temperature*. The heat lost by one will be gained by the other, and no heat will be exchanged with the surroundings.

EXAMPLE 8 Calculate its specific heat if a 35.9-g sample of a metal at 58.0°C is immersed in 52.1 g of water at 16.3°C, warming the water to 20.7°C.

Solution The final temperature of the metal is also 20.7°C.

$$q = 0 = m_{water}c_{water}\Delta t_{water} + m_{metal}c_{metal}\Delta t_{metal}$$
$$0 = (52.1 \text{ g})(4.184 \text{ J/g·°C})(20.7°C - 16.3°C)$$
$$+ (35.9 \text{ g})(c)(20.7°C - 58.0°C)$$

Doing the subtractions and canceling some of the units yields

$$0 = (52.1)(4.184 \text{ J})(4.4) + (35.9 \text{ g})(c)(-37.3°C)$$
$$c = 0.72 \text{ J/g·°C} \qquad \text{Watch the signs.} \qquad \square$$

EXAMPLE 9 Calculate the final temperature after 30.0 g of a metal ($c = 0.950 \text{ J/g·°C}$) at 71.3°C is immersed in 155 g of water at 21.3°C.

Solution Note that both samples have the same final temperature, t, and that the final temperature must be between the two initial temperatures. (Since the two terms add up to zero, one must be positive and the other negative.)

$$q = 0 = m_{water}c_{water}\Delta t_{water} + m_{metal}c_{metal}\Delta t_{metal}$$

$$0 = (155\text{ g})(4.184\text{ J/g·°C})(t - 21.3\text{°C})$$

$$+ (30.0\text{ g})(0.950\text{ J/g·°C})(t - 71.3\text{°C})$$

Canceling the units *grams* in each term and dividing the entire equation by *joules* yields an equation that looks easier to work with:

$$0 = (155)(4.184/\text{°C})(t - 21.3\text{°C}) + (30.0)(0.950/\text{°C})(t - 71.3\text{°C})$$

Using the distributive law of algebra $\{ab(c - d) = abc - abd\}$ yields

$$0 = (649/\text{°C})t - 13{,}800 + (28.5/\text{°C})t - 2030$$

Then

$$(678/\text{°C})t = 15{,}800$$

$$t = 23.3\text{°C}$$

(Ask the instructor if all the units can be ignored in solving this equation, and merely add the °C at the end, since a temperature is required.)

Check:

$$0 = (155\text{ g})(4.184\text{ J/g·°C})(23.3\text{°C} - 21.3\text{°C})$$

$$+ (30.0\text{ g})(0.950\text{ J/g·°C})(23.3\text{°C} - 71.3\text{°C})$$

$$0 = 1300\text{ J} - 1370\text{ J}$$

(The two significant digits in $23.3 - 21.3$ limits the accuracy of this check, but the answer is acceptable.) ☐

8.2 Energies of Phase Change

When we heat a sample of matter, we generally expect that the sample will get warmer. That happens most of the time, but not when a pure substance is heated at a temperature at which it will change phase. For example, when heat is added to pure ice at 0°C, the ice melts and the system remains at 0°C until all the ice is melted. (It takes some energy to rearrange the particles that constitute the substance—it takes some potential energy rather than the kinetic energy of heat.)

When a sample changes phase, the heat involved is given a name associated with that particular phase change. For example,

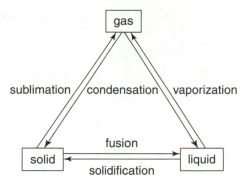

Fig. 8-1   Names of Phase Changes.

when **sublimation** occurs (a solid is changed directly to the gas phase), the heat involved is called the **heat of sublimation**. The most common changes of phase are shown in Fig. 8-1. Note that melting is formally called **fusion**, and evaporation is formally called **vaporization**. The word for changing from gas to either liquid or solid is **condensation**.

EXAMPLE 10   What is the name for the heat associated with the melting of a solid substance?

    Solution   Heat of fusion.   □

    Some heats of phase change are presented in Table 8-2. Two phase changes that are exactly opposite processes have heats with exactly the same magnitude but opposite signs. For example, the heat of fusion of water at 0°C is 6.00 kJ/mol; the heat of solidification of liquid water to ice at 0°C is −6.00 kJ/mol. Tabulated heats of phase change often have units different from those in a given problem; as usual, be careful with the units! Also note that since

Table 8-2   **Heats of Phase Change**

Substance	Process	Heat (kJ/mol)	Temperature (°C)
Water	Melting	6.00	0
Water	Boiling	40.6	100
Carbon dioxide	Subliming	162	−90
Ammonia	Boiling	23.3	−33
Phosphorus trichloride	Boiling	29.5	78
Sodium chloride	Melting	28.5	801

the phase change takes place at constant temperature, there is no °C as part of the unit and there is no Δt term in the equation to calculate the associated heat.

EXAMPLE 11 Calculate the heat required to melt 14.7 g of ice at 0°C.

Solution The problem is given in grams and the value from Table 8-2 is in moles, so a conversion factor is used:

$$14.7 \text{ g}\left(\frac{1 \text{ mol}}{18.0 \text{ g}}\right)\left(\frac{6.00 \text{ kJ}}{1 \text{ mol}}\right) = 4.90 \text{ kJ} \qquad \square$$

EXAMPLE 12 If it takes 439 J of heat to warm 14.7 g of ice to 0°C, how much heat would it take to warm the ice to the freezing point and then melt it? (See prior example.)

Solution The total heat required is the heat for the warming process plus the heat of fusion. As usual, watch out for the units and the significant digits!

$$4.90 \text{ kJ} + 439 \text{ J} = 4.90 \text{ kJ} + 0.439 \text{ kJ} = 5.34 \text{ kJ} \qquad \square$$

The last example indicates that to calculate the total heat required to heat a sample and to change its phase requires a separate calculation for each. For example, to calculate the heat required to change liquid water at 80°C to water vapor at 110°C, we have to calculate the heat required to warm the liquid to 100°C, the heat required to vaporize the water at 100°C, and the heat required to warm the vapor. Then we add the three terms to get the total heat for the process.

EXAMPLE 13 Calculate the heat required to change 45.0 g of liquid water at 80.0°C to water vapor at 110.0°C. Use the data of Tables 8-1 and 8-2.

Solution To calculate the heat used to warm the liquid water to 100°C takes a specific heat calculation:

$$q = mc\Delta t = (45.0 \text{ g})(4.184 \text{ J/g·°C})(20.0°C) = 3770 \text{ J}$$

To calculate the heat used to vaporize the water takes a heat of vaporization calculation:

$$45.0 \text{ g}\left(\frac{1 \text{ mol}}{18.0 \text{ g}}\right)\left(\frac{40.6 \text{ kJ}}{1 \text{ mol}}\right) = 102 \text{ kJ}$$

To calculate the heat used to warm the water vapor takes a specific heat calculation:

$$q = mc\Delta t = (45.0 \text{ g})(2.042 \text{ J/g·°C})(10.0°C) = 919 \text{ J}$$

The total heat required is $3.77 \text{ kJ} + 102 \text{ kJ} + 0.919 \text{ kJ} = 107 \text{ kJ}$.

Note that we cannot even combine the two specific heat calculations because liquid water and water vapor have different specific heat capacities. □

8.3 Enthalpy of Reaction

We are greatly interested in determining the energy associated with chemical reactions. Chemical manufacturers need to know how much energy it will take to produce their products, or how much energy they need to dissipate as their reactions proceed. Even better, they would like to use the energy produced by some reactions to make other reactions go so that they will not have to pay for extra fuel nor dump unwanted heat into the ecosphere. Everyone pays for energy sources—fuel for the furnace at home or the car, batteries for our portable electrical apparatus, and electricity for home and office use, for example. The price we pay for manufactured goods includes a good percentage for the energy that is used in the production and transportation of the goods.

Enthalpy change, ΔH, is a formal term for the heat associated with a process done at constant pressure with no energy exchange with the surroundings except expansion work. We loosely use the terms *heat* and *enthalpy change* interchangeably. For example, in the first sections of this chapter, we could have used ΔH instead of q in our equations. The enthalpy change of a process is named for the process; for example, the enthalpy of fusion is the enthalpy change associated with a fusion (melting) process. We need to define explicitly two enthalpy terms: enthalpy of combustion and enthalpy of formation. Enthalpy of combustion is the enthalpy of the burning process. If a substance can undergo two or more combustion reactions, the enthalpy of the reaction that goes furthest is by definition called the enthalpy of combustion. For example, carbon burns in limited oxygen supply to yield carbon monoxide, and in excess oxygen it produces carbon dioxide. Therefore, by definition, the enthalpy of combustion of carbon is the enthalpy change associated with the formation of carbon dioxide (in which more oxygen is combined).

The enthalpy of the reaction

$$CO(g) + \tfrac{1}{2} O_2(g) \rightarrow CO_2(g)$$

is the enthalpy of combustion of CO.

The **standard enthalpy of formation**, ΔH_f°, of a substance is the enthalpy change associated with the reaction of the elements of the substance in their standard states to produce the substance in its standard state. Thus the enthalpy of formation of carbon monoxide is the enthalpy change associated with the reaction

$$C(s) + \tfrac{1}{2} O_2(g) \rightarrow CO(g)$$

and that of carbon dioxide is the enthalpy change associated with the reaction

$$C(s) + O_2(g) \rightarrow CO_2(g)$$

The term **standard state** signifies the condition in which a substance is most stable at the temperature of the problem. (It has nothing to do with the standard temperature of the gas law problems, presented in Chapter 7.) Thus oxygen at 25°C is in its standard state as a gas in diatomic molecules. Ozone, O_3, is not the standard state of oxygen, nor is a sample of O atoms or liquid O_2.

There can be more than one name associated with the enthalpy change of a single reaction.

EXAMPLE 14 What names are associated with the enthalpy change of the following reaction?

$$H_2(g) + \tfrac{1}{2} O_2(g) \rightarrow H_2O(l)$$

Solution The enthalpy change for this reaction can be called the enthalpy of formation of water, the enthalpy of combustion of hydrogen, or the enthalpy of the reaction of hydrogen and oxygen. □

Enthalpy of formation data such as are presented in Table 8-3 allow us to calculate the enthalpy change of any reaction having its substances listed. There is no need to tabulate enthalpies of formation of *elements* in their standard states, however, because they are zero by definition. (The enthalpy required to change an element in its standard state to the element in its standard state is zero.)

Table 8-3 Enthalpies of Formation (kJ/mol)

BaO(s)	−559
$BaCO_3$(s)	−1217
$BaSO_4$(s)	−1465
CO(g)	−110
CO_2(g)	−393
H_2O(l)	−286
H_2O(g)	−242
HCl(g)	−92
NaCl(s)	−411
$NaHCO_3$(s)	−710
Na_2CO_3(s)	−1430
SO_2(g)	−297
SO_3(g)	−395
CH_4(g)	−74.5
C_2H_6(g)	−83.7

To calculate the enthalpy change of a chemical reaction, subtract the sum of the enthalpies of formation of the reactants from the sum of the enthalpies of formation of the products:

$$\Delta H = \Delta H_f(\text{products}) - \Delta H_f(\text{reactants})$$

EXAMPLE 15 Calculate the enthalpy change for the reaction of one mole of CH_4 with oxygen to yield carbon dioxide and water.

Solution

$$CH_4(g) + 2\,O_2(g) \rightarrow CO_2(g) + 2\,H_2O(l)$$

$$\Delta H = \Delta H_f(\text{products}) - \Delta H_f(\text{reactants})$$

$$= \Delta H_f(CO_2) + 2\Delta H_f(H_2O) - \Delta H_f(CH_4) - 2\Delta H_f(O_2)$$

$$= (-393\text{ kJ}) + 2(-286\text{ kJ}) - (-74.5\text{ kJ}) - 2(0\text{ kJ}) = -891\text{ kJ}$$

The enthalpy of formation of oxygen gas is zero by definition, since it is an element in its standard state. The other enthalpies of formation are obtained from Table 8-3. As usual, we must be careful with the signs and the units. Note specifically that the enthalpy of formation of water is −286 kJ/mol and that there are two moles present in the equation. Also note that when a sum is subtracted, it is equivalent to *subtracting each member* in the sum:

$$(a + b) - (c + d) = a + b - c - d \qquad \Box$$

If a different quantity from the number of moles in the equation is specified in the problem, calculate the value using the number of moles in the equation, then compute the value for the quantity specified in the problem.

EXAMPLE 16 Calculate the enthalpy change for the reaction of 23.7 g of CH_4 with oxygen to yield carbon dioxide and water.

Solution The number of kilojoules is calculated for 1 mol, just as was done in Example 15. Then ΔH is calculated for the 23.7 g specified in the problem:

$$\Delta H = 23.7 \text{ g } CH_4 \left(\frac{1 \text{ mol } CH_4}{16.0 \text{ g } CH_4} \right) \left(\frac{-891 \text{ kJ}}{1 \text{ mol } CH_4} \right) = -1320 \text{ kJ}$$

from the
prior problem $\qquad \Box$

EXAMPLE 17 Calculate the enthalpy change for the reaction of CH_4 with oxygen to yield carbon dioxide and 75.9 g of water.

Solution Again the result of Example 15 is used:

$$75.9 \text{ g } H_2O \left(\frac{1 \text{ mol } H_2O}{18.0 \text{ g } H_2O} \right) \left(\frac{-891 \text{ kJ}}{2 \text{ mol } H_2O} \right) = -1880 \text{ kJ}$$

Note that the −891 kJ enthalpy change of Example 15 is associated with *2 mol* of water in the balanced chemical equation! $\qquad \Box$

Hess's Law

If enthalpy of formation data are not available but other types of enthalpy data are, and if we can combine the chemical equations for the available reactions to give the desired reaction, we can combine the enthalpy changes in the same way. This is a statement of **Hess's law.** For example, consider the general reactions

$$\begin{aligned} A + 2\,B &\rightarrow C + 2\,D & \Delta H &= -20 \text{ kJ} \\ C + 2\,D &\rightarrow E & \Delta H &= 15 \text{ kJ} \end{aligned}$$

We can add these equations and add their associated enthalpy changes to get the enthalpy change for the reaction

$$A + 2B + \cancel{C} + \cancel{2D} \rightarrow E + \cancel{C} + \cancel{2D}$$
$$A + 2B \rightarrow E \qquad \Delta H = -5 \text{ kJ}$$

If we are given equations that add up to the one desired, it is simple to add them and their associated enthalpy changes. If the equations are not given in the form necessary, we may have to multiply them and their associated enthalpy changes by the same value, and/or reverse one or more of the equations and change the signs of the associated enthalpy changes.

EXAMPLE 18 Calculate the enthalpy change for the reaction

$$3\, C_2H_2(g) \rightarrow C_6H_6(l)$$

given the enthalpies of combustion of these compounds:

$$C_2H_2(g) \qquad -1305 \text{ kJ/mol}$$
$$C_6H_6(l) \qquad -3273 \text{ kJ/mol}$$

Solution Note that the data given are not enthalpies of formation; we cannot merely subtract the enthalpy of the reactants from the enthalpy of the products. However, we can write equations for the combustion reactions of the reagents given, both multiplied by factors to get the same integral numbers of moles of products:

$$\Delta H$$

(1) $6\,C_2H_2(g) + 15\,O_2(g) \rightarrow 12\,CO_2(g) + 6\,H_2O(l)$ $\quad 6(-1305 \text{ kJ})$

(2) $2\,C_6H_6(l) + 15\,O_2(g) \rightarrow 12\,CO_2(g) + 6\,H_2O(l)$ $\quad 2(-3273 \text{ kJ})$

We reverse the second of these equations, changing the sign of the ΔH value, then adding to the first equation, yielding

$$\Delta H$$

(1) $\quad 6\,C_2H_2(g) + 15\,O_2(g) \rightarrow 12\,CO_2(g) + 6\,H_2O(l)$ $\quad 6(-1305\,\text{kJ})$

(−2) $\quad 12\,CO_2(g) + 6\,H_2O(l) \rightarrow 2\,C_6H_6(l) + 15\,O_2(g)$ $\quad 2(+3273\,\text{kJ})$

(sum) $\qquad\qquad 6\,C_2H_2(g) \rightarrow 2\,C_6H_6(l)$ $\qquad\qquad -1284\,\text{kJ}$

Dividing this equation and its enthalpy change by 2 yields the answer required:

$$3\,C_2H_2(g) \rightarrow C_6H_6(l) \qquad \Delta H = -642\,\text{kJ} \qquad \square$$

Leading Questions

1. What are the two main mathematical equations presented in this chapter?
2. From the data of Table 8-2, determine the heat of condensation of water vapor to liquid water at 100°C.
3. When a warm metal bar is placed in cold water, is the value of q positive, negative, or zero (a) for the metal? (b) for the water? (c) for the whole system (metal plus water)?

Answers to Leading Questions

1. $q = mc\Delta t$ and $\Delta H = \Delta H_f(\text{products}) - \Delta H_f(\text{reactants})$
2. The heat of vaporization is given in the table as $+40.6$ kJ/mol, so the heat of condensation is -40.6 kJ/mol. (It is negative because heat is removed from the vapor to condense it to liquid.)
3. (a) The metal loses heat; q is negative. (b) The water gains heat; q is positive. (c) q is zero.

Supplementary Problems

1. Calculate the value in Kelvin of (a) 35°C. (b) 15°C. (c) Calculate the difference between these temperatures on each scale.
2. Calculate the quantity of heat required to raise the temperature of 42.7 g of iron 5.00°C.
3. Calculate the quantity of heat required to raise the temperature of 52.9 g of water vapor from 121°C to 135°C.
4. Calculate the final temperature after 935 J of heat is added to 112 g of water at 19.0°C.
5. Calculate the final temperature after 127 g of a metal ($c = 0.880$ J/g·°C) at 21.4°C is immersed in 338 g of water at 55.5°C.
6. Calculate the heat required to vaporize 138 g of water at 100°C.
7. If it took 533 J of heat to warm 138 g of water to 100°C, how much heat would it take to warm the water and vaporize it? (See prior problem.)
8. Calculate the specific heat of a metal if 18.5 g of the metal at 62.1°C is immersed in 77.4 g of water at 19.3°C, warming the water to 21.9°C.
9. Calculate the heat required to change 35.0 g of liquid water at 22.0°C to ice at −10.0°C. Use the data of Tables 8-1 and 8-2.

10. Write an equation to represent each of the following: (a) formation of PCl_3. (b) fusion of ice. (c) combustion of CH_4. (d) sublimation of $CO_2(s)$ (dry ice).

11. Calculate the enthalpy change for the reaction of one mole of C_2H_6 with oxygen to yield carbon dioxide and water.

12. Calculate the quantity of heat required to raise 100.0 g of water from 273.15 K to 293.15 K.

13. A chemical reaction raised the temperature of 200.0 g of a solution ($c = 4.17$ J/g·°C) by 1.43°C. (a) Calculate the quantity of heat added to the solution. (b) Calculate the quantity of heat released by the chemical reaction.

14. What mass of water rises 10.3°C in temperature when 1.24 kJ of heat is added to it?

15. Calculate the enthalpy change for the reaction of barium oxide with carbon dioxide to yield barium carbonate.

16. Calculate the enthalpy change for the reaction of 175 g of barium oxide with carbon dioxide to yield barium carbonate.

17. Calculate the enthalpy of combustion of carbon monoxide from the enthalpies of formation of carbon monoxide and carbon dioxide.

18. Calculate the enthalpy of the following reaction given the enthalpies of combustion in equations 1 to 3 below:

$$C_2H_2(g) + 2 H_2(g) \rightarrow C_2H_6(g)$$

(1) $C_2H_2(g) + 2.5 O_2(g) \rightarrow 2 CO_2(g) + H_2O(l)$ $\Delta H = -1305$ kJ
(2) $H_2(g) + \frac{1}{2} O_2(g) \rightarrow H_2O(l)$ $\Delta H = -286$ kJ
(3) $C_2H_6(g) + 3.5 O_2(g) \rightarrow 2 CO_2(g) + 3 H_2O(l)$ $\Delta H = -1560$ kJ

19. Calculate the enthalpy change for the reaction of C_2H_6 with 46.9 g of oxygen to yield carbon dioxide and water.

20. Calculate the final temperature of the water if 100.0 g of water at 20.0°C and 100.0 g of water at 68.0°C are mixed.

21. The enthalpy of neutralization of a strong acid with a strong base is -55.2 kJ/mol of water formed. If 100.0 mL of 1.00 M NaOH and 100.0 mL of 1.00 M HCl, both at 25.0°C, are mixed, assume that the heat capacity of the resulting solution is 4.18 J/g·°C and that the density of that solution is 1.02 g/mL. (a) Write a balanced chemical equation for the reaction. (b) Determine the number of moles of water that will be formed. (c) Determine the quantity of heat that the reaction will release. (d) How much heat is absorbed by the resulting solution? (e) Calculate the mass of the solution.
(f) Calculate the change in temperature of the solution.
(g) Calculate the final temperature of the solution.

22. The enthalpy of neutralization of a strong acid with a strong base is -55.2 kJ/mol of water formed. If 100.0 mL of 1.00 M NaOH at 27.0°C and 100.0 mL of 1.00 M HCl at 23.0°C, are mixed, calculate the temperature of the final solution. Assume that the heat capacity of each initial solution and of the final solution is 4.18 J/g·°C and that the density of the final solution is 1.02 g/mL.

23. Calculate the enthalpy change of the metal in Example 9.

Solutions to Supplementary Problems

1. (a) 308 K   (b) 288 K   (c) 20°C = 20 K *difference* in temperature.

2. $q = mc\Delta t = (42.7 \text{ g})(0.442 \text{ J/g·°C})(5.00°C) = 94.4 \text{ J}$

3. Note that the specific heat of water vapor is not the same as that of liquid water (Table 8-1):
$q = mc\Delta t = (52.9 \text{ g})(2.042 \text{ J/g·°C})(14°C) = 1500 \text{ J} = 1.5 \text{ kJ}$

4. $q = mc\Delta t = (112 \text{ g})(4.184 \text{ J/g·°C})(\Delta t) = 935 \text{ J}$
$\Delta t = 2.00°C$
The final temperature is 2.00°C higher than the initial temperature, or

$$19.0°C + 2.00°C = 21.0°C$$

5. $q = 0 = m_{water}c_{water}\Delta t_{water} + m_{metal}c_{metal}\Delta t_{metal}$

$0 = (338 \text{ g})(4.184 \text{ J/g·°C})(t - 55.5°C) +$

$$(127 \text{ g})(0.880 \text{ J/g·°C})(t - 21.4°C)$$

$t = 53.2°C$

6. $138 \text{ g}\left(\dfrac{1 \text{ mol}}{18.0 \text{ g}}\right)\left(\dfrac{40.6 \text{ kJ}}{1 \text{ mol}}\right) = 311 \text{ kJ}$

7. $311 \text{ kJ} + 533 \text{ J} = 311 \text{ kJ} + 0.533 \text{ kJ} = 312 \text{ kJ}$

8. $q = 0 = m_{water}c_{water}\Delta t_{water} + m_{metal}c_{metal}\Delta t_{metal}$

$0 = (77.4 \text{ g})(4.184 \text{ J/g·°C})(21.9°C - 19.3°C) +$

$$(18.5 \text{ g})(c_{metal})(21.9°C - 62.1°C)$$

$0 = (77.4)(4.184 \text{ J})(2.6) + (18.5 \text{ g})(c_{metal})(-40.2°C)$

$c_{metal} = 1.1 \text{ J/g·°C}$

9. To calculate the value of q for cooling the liquid water to the freezing point takes a specific heat calculation:

$$q = mc\Delta t = (35.0 \text{ g})(4.184 \text{ J/g·°C})(-22.0°C) = -3220 \text{ J}$$

To calculate value of q to freeze the water takes a heat of solidification calculation:

$$35.0 \text{ g}\left(\frac{1 \text{ mol}}{18.0 \text{ g}}\right)\left(\frac{-6.00 \text{ kJ}}{1 \text{ mol}}\right) = -11.7 \text{ kJ}$$

To calculate the value of q for cooling the ice takes a specific heat calculation:

$$q = mc\Delta t = (35.0 \text{ g})(2.089 \text{ J/g·°C})(-10.0°C) = -731 \text{ J}$$

The total heat required is $q = -3.22 \text{ kJ} + (-11.7 \text{ kJ}) + (-0.731 \text{ kJ})$
$$= -15.7 \text{ kJ}$$

10. (a) $P(s) + \frac{3}{2} Cl_2(g) \rightarrow PCl_3(l)$
(b) $H_2O(s) \rightarrow H_2O(l)$
(c) $CH_4(g) + 2 O_2(g) \rightarrow CO_2(g) + 2 H_2O(l)$
(d) $CO_2(s) \rightarrow CO_2(g)$

11. $C_2H_6(g) + \frac{7}{2} O_2(g) \rightarrow 2 CO_2(g) + 3 H_2O(l)$

$$\Delta H = \Delta H_f(\text{products}) - \Delta H_f(\text{reactants})$$

$$= 2\Delta H_f(CO_2) + 3\Delta H_f(H_2O) - \Delta H_f(C_2H_6) - \tfrac{7}{2}\Delta H_f(O_2)$$

$$= 2(-393 \text{ kJ}) + 3(-286 \text{ kJ}) - (-83.7 \text{ kJ}) - \tfrac{7}{2}(0 \text{ kJ}) = -1560 \text{ kJ}$$

Alternatively,

$$2 C_2H_6(g) + 7 O_2(g) \rightarrow 4 CO_2(g) + 6 H_2O(l)$$

$$\Delta H = \Delta H_f(\text{products}) - \Delta H_f(\text{reactants})$$

$$= 4\Delta H_f(CO_2) + 6\Delta H_f(H_2O) - 2\Delta H_f(C_2H_6) - 7\Delta H_f(O_2)$$

$$= 4(-393 \text{ kJ}) + 6(-286 \text{ kJ}) - 2(-83.7 \text{ kJ}) - 7(0 \text{ kJ}) = -3120 \text{ kJ}$$

This ΔH is for two moles of C_2H_6, so we divide this value by 2 to get the value per mole, -1560 kJ. Either method gives the same result.

12. $q = mc\Delta t = (100.0 \text{ g})(4.184 \text{ J/g·°C})(293.15 \text{ K} - 273.15 \text{ K}) = 8368 \text{ J}$
(The temperature change in kelvins is equal to the temperature change in degrees Celsius.)

13. (a) $q = mc\Delta t = (200.0 \text{ g})(4.17 \text{ J/g·°C})(1.43°C) = 1190 \text{ J}$
(b) $q = -1190 \text{ J}$ (The heat gained by the water, and therefore positive, was released by the chemical reaction, a loss of heat, with q having a negative value.)

14. Again, watch the units!

$$q = mc\Delta t = (m)(4.184 \text{ J/g·°C})(10.3°C) = 1240 \text{ J}$$

$$m = 28.8 \text{ g}$$

15. $BaO(s) + CO_2(g) \rightarrow BaCO_3(s)$
The data are from Table 8-3:

$$\Delta H = \Delta H_f(\text{products}) - \Delta H_f(\text{reactants})$$

$$= \Delta H_f(BaCO_3) - \Delta H_f(BaO) - \Delta H_f(CO_2)$$

$$= (-1217 \text{ kJ}) - (-559 \text{ kJ}) - (-393 \text{ kJ}) = -265 \text{ kJ}$$

16. The enthalpy change for 1 mol of BaO was calculated in the prior problem.

For 175 g of BaO, $175 \text{ g}\left(\dfrac{1 \text{ mol BaO}}{153 \text{ g BaO}}\right)\left(\dfrac{-265 \text{ kJ}}{1 \text{ mol BaO}}\right) = -303 \text{ kJ}$

17. $CO(g) + \frac{1}{2} O_2(g) \rightarrow CO_2(g)$

$$\Delta H = \Delta H_f(\text{products}) - \Delta H_f(\text{reactants})$$

$$= (-393 \text{ kJ}) - (-110 \text{ kJ}) - (0 \text{ kJ}) = -283 \text{ kJ}$$

18. We need $C_2H_2(g)$ on the left and we have it there in equation (1), so we leave equation (1) unchanged. We need 2 mol of hydrogen on the left, so we double equation (2) and its ΔH value. We need $C_2H_6(g)$ on the right, so we reverse equation (3) and change the sign of its ΔH value. We then add the three resulting ΔH values to get

$$(-1305 \text{ kJ}) + 2(-286 \text{ kJ}) + (+1560 \text{ kJ}) = -317 \text{ kJ}$$

(We could manipulate the equations and cancel the species that appear on both sides to reassure ourselves that the required equation is actually obtained.)

19. $C_2H_6(g) + 3.5\, O_2(g) \rightarrow 2\, CO_2(g) + 3\, H_2O(l)$
For 1 mol of C_2H_6:

$$\Delta H = \Delta H_f(\text{products}) - \Delta H_f(\text{reactants})$$

$$= 2(-393 \text{ kJ}) + 3(-286 \text{ kJ}) - (-83.7 \text{ kJ}) - 3.5(0 \text{ kJ})$$

$$= -1560 \text{ kJ}$$

For 46.9 g of O_2:

$$46.9 \text{ g } O_2\left(\frac{1 \text{ mol } O_2}{32.0 \text{ g } O_2}\right)\left(\frac{-1560 \text{ kJ}}{3.5 \text{ mol } O_2}\right) = -653 \text{ kJ}$$

20. $0 = m_{hot}C_{hot}\Delta t_{hot} + m_{cold}C_{cold}\Delta t_{cold}$
Since the masses are the same and the specific heats are the same, the magnitudes of the changes in temperatures must be the same: $\Delta t_{hot} = -\Delta t_{cold}$. The temperature is the average of those of the two samples, 44.0°C.

21. (a) $HCl(aq) + NaOH(aq) \rightarrow NaCl(aq) + H_2O(l)$
(b) There are present 0.100 mol of NaOH and 0.100 mol of HCl, so 0.100 mol of water will be formed.
(c) $(0.100 \text{ mol})(-55.2 \text{ kJ/mol}) = -5.52 \text{ kJ}$
(d) The heat absorbed by the solution is that released by the reaction, that is, $q = +5.52$ kJ.
(e) $(200.0 \text{ mL})(1.02 \text{ g/mL}) = 204 \text{ g}$
(f) The change in temperature is given by

$$q = mc\Delta t = (204 \text{ g})(4.18 \text{ J/g·°C})\Delta t = 5520 \text{ J}$$

$$\Delta t = 6.47°C$$

(g) The final temperature is $25.0°C + 6.47°C = 31.5°C$

22. The two solutions have equal masses and equal specific heats, so their temperature on mixing in the absence of any reaction would be 25.0°C. After that, this is the same problem as Problem 21.

23. $\Delta H = m_{metal}C_{metal}\Delta t_{metal} = (30.0 \text{ g})(0.950 \text{ J/g·°C})(23.3°C - 71.3°C)$
$= -1370 \text{ J}$

Chapter 9

Electrochemistry

There are two inherently different methods by which an electric current interacts with matter: (1) An electric current can cause a chemical reaction. (2) A chemical reaction can produce an electric current. The first of these is done in an **electrolysis cell**, and the second in a **voltaic cell**, also called a **galvanic cell**. Two entirely different sorts of calculations are generally used for the two kinds of cells. (Although the same type of calculations done for electrolysis cells can be done for voltaic cells, they are practically never asked for.)

To calculate the quantities of electricity and electrical energy interacting with matter, we must learn the electrical units involved:

1. The **coulomb**, C, is the unit of electric charge. The charge on 1.00 mol of electrons, called a Faraday (F), is 96,487 C, usually rounded to 96,500 C (a value to remember), and the charge on one electron is 1.60×10^{-19} C.
2. The **ampere**, A, is the unit of electric current. One ampere is the current involved in the passage past any point of 1 coulomb per second: $1 \text{ A} = 1 \text{ C/s}$.
3. A joule of energy is required to move a coulomb of charge through a potential of 1 volt. The **volt**, V, is the unit of *potential*, which is the "driving force" that causes charge to flow: $1 \text{ J} = (1 \text{ V})(1 \text{ C}) = (1 \text{ V})(1 \text{ A})(1 \text{ s})$.

9.1 Electrolysis Cells

In the middle of the nineteenth century, Michael Faraday discovered that in the electrolytic reduction of metals from their compounds, the mass of metal produced was directly proportional to the electric charge that passed, directly proportional to the atomic mass of the metal, and inversely proportional to the oxidation state of the metal in the compound. Thus, for a reaction

$$M^{n+} + n\, e^- \rightarrow M$$

(1) the more electricity that passed, the greater was the mass of metal produced. (2) the greater the atomic mass of M, the greater was the mass of metal produced. (3) the higher the value of n, the lower was the mass of metal produced.

These generalities are known as Faraday's laws. Fortunately, we do not have to worry about learning Faraday's laws in order to solve problems involving electrolysis cell reactions. All that we need to be able to do is to write net ionic equations for the reactions and remember the values for the constants listed above. As usual, we use dimensional analysis, starting with the quantity given.

EXAMPLE 1 Calculate the mass of copper metal produced from $CuSO_4$ solution by passage of a 3.00-A current for 7250 seconds.

Solution

$$Cu^{2+}(aq) + 2\, e^- \rightarrow Cu(s)$$

$$7250\ \text{s}\left(\underset{\substack{3.00\ \text{A}}}{\frac{3.00\ \text{C}}{1\ \text{s}}}\right)\left(\underset{\substack{\text{from the}\\ \text{definition}}}{\frac{1\ \text{mol e}^-}{96{,}500\ \text{C}}}\right)\left(\underset{\substack{\text{from the}\\ \text{equation}}}{\frac{1\ \text{mol Cu}}{2\ \text{mol e}^-}}\right)\left(\underset{\substack{\text{atomic}\\ \text{mass}}}{\frac{63.5\ \text{g Cu}}{1\ \text{mol Cu}}}\right) = 7.16\ \text{g Cu}$$

$\square$

EXAMPLE 2 Calculate the time required to deposit 7.00 g of silver from a solution of $AgNO_3$ with a current of 4.00 A.

Solution

$$Ag^+(aq) + e^- \rightarrow Ag(s)$$

$$7.00\ \text{g Ag}\left(\frac{1\ \text{mol Ag}}{108\ \text{g Ag}}\right)\left(\frac{1\ \text{mol e}^-}{1\ \text{mol Ag}}\right)\left(\frac{96{,}500\ \text{C}}{1\ \text{mol e}^-}\right)\left(\frac{1\ \text{s}}{4.00\ \text{C}}\right)$$

$$= 1560\ \text{s}\quad (26.1\ \text{minutes})\quad \square$$

If two quantities are given and the current is to be calculated, we convert the quantities given to coulombs and seconds and divide them to get the answer.

EXAMPLE 3 Calculate the current required to deposit 40.0 g of gold from $AuCl_3$ solution in 7.00 hours.

Solution

$$Au^{3+}(aq) + 3\ e^- \rightarrow Au(s)$$

$$40.0\ g\ Au\left(\frac{1\ mol\ Au}{197\ g\ Au}\right)\left(\frac{3\ mol\ e^-}{1\ mol\ Au}\right)\left(\frac{96{,}500\ C}{1\ mol\ e^-}\right) = 58{,}800\ C$$

$$7.00\ hours\left(\frac{3600\ s}{1\ hour}\right) = 25{,}200\ s$$

The current is $(58{,}800\ C)/(25{,}200\ s) = 2.33\ A$ □

Even if a metal is not produced, the ratio of moles of electrons involved in the reaction to moles of a chemical substance can be used to calculate the extent of the chemical reaction given in the balanced chemical equation.

EXAMPLE 4   Calculate the time required with a current of 10.5 A to reduce 50.0 g of PbO_2 to $PbSO_4$ in the lead storage cell (found in most automobile batteries).

$$PbO_2 + 4\ H^+ + SO_4^{2-} + 2\ e^- \rightarrow PbSO_4 + 2\ H_2O$$

Solution

$$50.0\ g\ PbO_2\left(\frac{1\ mol\ PbO_2}{239\ g\ PbO_2}\right)\left(\frac{2\ mol\ e^-}{1\ mol\ PbO_2}\right)\left(\frac{96{,}500\ C}{1\ mol\ e^-}\right) \times$$

$$\left(\frac{1\ s}{10.5\ C}\right) = 3850\ s$$

Note that despite the oxidation state of lead in the reactant being +4, the ratio of moles of electrons to moles of lead(IV) oxide is $2:1$ because the final product is not free lead. The number of moles of electrons involved is clearly given in the balanced equation no matter what the final product. □

The only new concepts that we used in solving these problems were the number of coulombs per mole of electrons and the fact that $1\ A = 1\ C/s$.

9.2 Voltaic Cells

If we place a metal electrode in a solution of its ions, and suitably connect it to another such combination of a different metal, we can produce an electric current. These combinations are called either

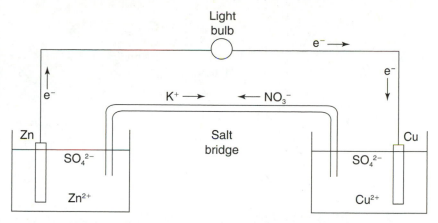

Fig. 9-1 Daniell Cell.

half-cells or, somewhat ambiguously, **electrodes**. The Daniell cell is a simple example of two electrodes connected to yield electricity (Fig. 9-1). Because different metals have different tendencies to lose electrons, one metal transfers electrons to the other, with the salt bridge serving to complete the electric circuit and prevent build-up of charge in any solution.

The quantitative measure of the tendency of a metal to lose electrons is the *potential* of that electrode. Potential is symbolized by ϵ or E. However, there cannot be a loss of electrons by any species unless there is a simultaneous gain of electrons by another. Thus it is impossible to measure the potential of a single electrode. Therefore, by convention, we set the potential of a standard hydrogen/hydrogen ion electrode at 0.000 V by definition, and determine the potential of other electrodes with it. This *standard hydrogen electrode* consists of hydrogen gas at 1.000 atm in contact with a 1.000 M solution of hydrogen ions, but neither of these can be connected to a wire, so an inert piece of metal (usually platinum) is used as the electrode. (See Fig. 9-2.) In general, the potential of a cell is the difference in the reduction potentials of the two electrodes. When the standard hydrogen half-cell is used with another half-cell, the cell potential is equal to the potential of the other half-cell, because the standard hydrogen half-cell potential is zero.

For example, the potential of a cell consisting of a copper electrode immersed in 1.000 M Cu^{2+} solution suitably connected to a standard hydrogen electrode just described has a potential of 0.34 V, with the copper ions being reduced. We assign the standard reduction potential of the Cu^{2+}/Cu half-cell to be 0.34 V. The potential

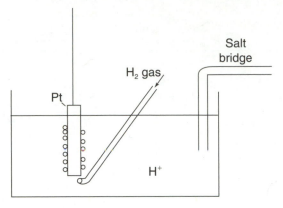

Fig. 9-2 Hydrogen/Hydrogen Ion Half-cell.

of a cell consisting of a zinc electrode immersed in 1.000 M Zn^{2+} solution suitably connected to a standard hydrogen electrode has a potential of 0.76 V, with the zinc metal being oxidized to Zn^{2+}. We assign the standard *oxidation* potential of the Zn^{2+}/Zn half-cell to be +0.76 V. *When we reverse the direction of the chemical reaction, we change the sign of the potential.* The standard *reduction* potential of the zinc half-cell is therefore −0.76 V.

The concentrations of its components affect the potential of a half-cell. We define a **standard half-cell**, denoted ϵ° or E°, to have all its components at **unit activity**:

1. Any solute in 1.000 M concentration is at unit activity.
2. Any gas at 1.000 atm (101.3 kPa) pressure is at unit activity.
3. Any pure solid is at unit activity.
4. Any pure liquid is at unit activity.
   (Water in dilute aqueous solution is included as at unit activity.)

We can make a table of **standard reduction potentials**, and use its values to calculate the potential of any cell consisting of two of its half-cells. See Table 9-1. The table of standard reduction potentials is a quantitative measure of the "activity series" learned earlier to enable us to predict whether a substitution reaction would proceed spontaneously. However, not only reductions of cations to metals, but any reduction half-reaction can be included in the table of standard reduction potentials.

To get an equation and corresponding potential for a complete reaction, we must add the equations for a reduction half-reaction and an oxidation half-reaction and add their corresponding potentials.

Table 9-1   Standard Reduction Potentials at 25°C

	ϵ^o (V)
$F_2(g) + 2\,e^- \rightarrow 2\,F^-(aq)$	2.87
$MnO_4^-(aq) + 8\,H^+(aq) + 5\,e^- \rightarrow Mn^{2+}(aq) + 4\,H_2O(l)$	1.51
$Ag^+(aq) + e^- \rightarrow Ag(s)$	0.80
$Fe^{3+}(aq) + e^- \rightarrow Fe^{2+}(aq)$	0.771
$Cu^{2+}(aq) + 2\,e^- \rightarrow Cu(s)$	0.34
$2\,H^+(aq) + 2\,e^- \rightarrow H_2(g)$	0.0000
$2\,H_2O(l) + 2\,e^- \rightarrow H_2(g) + 2\,OH^-(aq)$ (pure water)	−0.414
$Fe^{2+}(aq) + 2\,e^- \rightarrow Fe(s)$	−0.44
$Zn^{2+}(aq) + 2\,e^- \rightarrow Zn(s)$	−0.76
$2\,H_2O(l) + 2\,e^- \rightarrow H_2(g) + 2\,OH^-(aq)$ (1 M OH^-)	−0.828
$Na^+(aq) + e^- \rightarrow Na(s)$	−2.71

To calculate standard cell potentials from the half-cell potentials in Table 9-1, there are four principles that we must know: (1) When we reverse the direction of the chemical reaction, *we change the sign of the potential*. (2) If we multiply the coefficients in the equation by some number, *we do NOT change the potential*. Potential is an intensive property, and does not depend on the quantity of reagents. (3) When we add chemical equations for half-cells, we add the corresponding potentials. (4) A positive potential for a complete cell reaction means that the reaction proceeds spontaneously in the direction of the equation, and a negative potential means that the reaction goes spontaneously in the opposite direction.

To get an equation for an overall reaction with a positive potential from two half-reactions, reverse the half-reaction from the table with the smaller (or more negative) potential before adding the half-reactions. That is, reverse the equation lower in the table. In a table of reduction potentials listed in order of decreasing potentials, the reactants in a higher equation react spontaneously with the products in any equation below. For example, F_2 reacts spontaneously with Na. Also, Fe^{3+} reacts spontaneously with Cu when the species are at unit activity.

EXAMPLE 5   (*a*) Calculate the standard potential of the cell produced when the permanganate/manganese(II) half-cell is combined with the silver ion/silver half-cell. (*b*) State in which direction the spontaneous reaction occurs.

Solution

(*a*) The two half-cells from the table are

$$MnO_4^-(aq) + 8 H^+(aq) + 5 e^- \rightarrow Mn^{2+}(aq) + 4 H_2O(l) \qquad 1.51 \text{ V}$$

$$Ag^+(aq) + e^- \rightarrow Ag(s) \qquad 0.80 \text{ V}$$

We reverse the equation with the lower potential, and change the sign of the potential:

$$Ag(s) \rightarrow Ag^+(aq) + e^- \qquad -0.80 \text{ V}$$

We must multiply this equation by 5 to get the same number of electrons as are present in the reduction half-reaction. We *do not change* the potential:

$$5 Ag(s) \rightarrow 5 Ag^+(aq) + 5 e^- \qquad -0.80 \text{ V}$$

All that is left to do is to add these equations, and add the corresponding potentials:

$$5 Ag(s) + MnO_4^-(aq) + 8 H^+(aq) \rightarrow$$

$$Mn^{2+}(aq) + 4 H_2O(l) + 5 Ag^+(aq) \qquad 0.71 \text{ V}$$

(*b*) Since the potential is positive, the reaction goes spontaneously as written. □

The Nernst Equation

The actual potential of a cell (ϵ) depends not only on the standard potential (ϵ°) but also on the concentrations of the reactants and products in solution or their pressures in the gas phase (the things that can vary). Since the concentration of its components affects the potential of a cell, we can use a voltaic cell to measure a concentration if we know its standard potential and we measure its actual potential for the reaction. The pH meter is based on this principle. For either a cell or a half-cell, the potential is given by the **Nernst equation**. The Nernst equation for the general reaction

$$a A + b B \rightarrow c C + d D + n e^-$$

at 25°C is

$$\epsilon = \epsilon^\circ - \frac{0.0592}{n} \log \frac{[C]^c[D]^d}{[A]^a[B]^b}$$

where ϵ is the potential (often designated E in textbooks), ϵ° is the standard potential, and n is the number of moles of electrons in *either* the oxidation half-reaction *or* the reduction half-reaction. The value 0.0592 is $(RT/F)\ln 10$. The value of n for a complete reaction is the number of moles of electrons in either half-reaction, since the same electrons are involved in both. The electrons do not appear explicitly in the equation for the complete reaction, but they are present. The number of moles of electrons can be calculated by determining the total change in oxidation number for either the oxidizing agent or the reducing agent. The square brackets in the Nernst equation signify "concentration of," so [A] means the concentration of A, and has a numeric value. Each concentration is raised to the power equal to its coefficient in the balanced chemical equation.

EXAMPLE 6   What is the value of n in each of the following equations?

(a) $Fe^{3+} + e^- \rightarrow Fe^{2+}$
(b) $5 Fe^{2+} \rightarrow 5 Fe^{3+} + 5 e^-$
(c) $MnO_4^- + 8 H^+ + 5 e^- \rightarrow Mn^{2+} + 4 H_2O$
(d) $MnO_4^- + 8 H^+ + 5 Fe^{2+} \rightarrow Mn^{2+} + 4 H_2O + 5 Fe^{3+}$

Solution   (a) $n = 1$ (b) $n = 5$ (c) $n = 5$ (d) $n = 5$

It doesn't matter to n if the equation represents an oxidation, a reduction, or a complete reaction.   □

EXAMPLE 7   Calculate the value of ϵ for the oxidation of iron(II) to iron(III) in a solution of 0.100 M Fe^{2+} and 0.500 M Fe^{3+} according to each of the following equations:

(a) $Fe^{2+} \rightarrow Fe^{3+} + e^-$
(b) $5 Fe^{2+} \rightarrow 5 Fe^{3+} + 5 e^-$

Solution

(a) $\epsilon = \epsilon^\circ - \dfrac{0.0592}{1} \log \dfrac{[Fe^{3+}]}{[Fe^{2+}]}$

$= -0.771 - 0.0592 \log \dfrac{(0.500)}{(0.100)} = -0.771 - 0.0414$

$= -0.812$ V

(b)

$$\epsilon = \epsilon^0 - \frac{0.0592}{5} \log \frac{[Fe^{3+}]^5}{[Fe^{2+}]^5}$$

$$= -0.771 - \frac{0.0592}{5} \log \frac{(0.500)^5}{(0.100)^5}$$

$$= -0.771 - \frac{0.0592}{5} \log 5^5$$

$$= -0.771 - 0.0414 = -0.812 \text{ V}$$

As is apparent, there is no difference in the final potential. (This result stems from the algebraic identity $\log x^a = a \log x$.) ϵ *is an intensive property.* □

9.3 Relationship of Potential and Electrolysis

The tendency of an oxidation or reduction half-reaction to proceed can tell us what products to expect in an electrolysis reaction. For example, the reduction potential of sodium is far less (more negative) than that of water, so when we electrolyze a solution of sodium chloride, for example, water is reduced and not sodium ion. Electrolysis of a concentrated solution of sodium chloride produces chlorine along with the hydrogen, whereas electrolysis of a dilute solution of sodium chloride produces oxygen and hydrogen. To get sodium metal, we need to electrolyze molten (melted) sodium chloride in the absence of water altogether. Do not forget that aqueous solutions contain water as well as any solutes.

EXAMPLE 8 Calculate the mass of sodium produced from electrolysis of 10.0 g of sodium chloride dissolved in water by passage of 1.00 A for 40.0 minutes.

Solution None. Hydrogen will be produced instead. □

Leading Questions

1. What is the difference between ϵ and ϵ^0?
2. Calculate the ratio of the charge on a mole of electrons to the charge on one electron.
3. In the equation

$$MnO_4^- + 8 H^+ + 5 e^- \rightarrow Mn^{2+} + 4 H_2O$$

is the hydrogen ion concentration in the standard solution 1 M, 8 M, or 5 M?

Answers to Leading Questions

1. ϵ is the actual potential, $\epsilon°$ is the potential if all the reagents are 1 M (for solutes) or 1 atm (for gases).

2. $\dfrac{96{,}500 \text{ C/mol}}{1.60 \times 10^{-19} \text{ C/electron}} = 6.03 \times 10^{23}$ electrons/mol

   (Avogadro's number, within rounding error)

3. 1 M. Standard solutions are always 1 M in solute no matter what the coefficients are in the balanced chemical equation.

Supplementary Problems

1. Calculate the mass of copper metal produced from $CuCl_4^{2-}$ solution by passage of a 2.75-A current for 3.55 hours.

$$CuCl_4^{2-}(aq) + 2\,e^- \rightarrow Cu(s) + 4\,Cl^-(aq)$$

2. Calculate the current required to deposit 145 g of gold from $AuCl_4^-$ solution in (a) 225.0 minutes. (b) 3 hours and 45.0 minutes.

3. Calculate the standard potential of the cell composed of iron(III) and iron(II) half-cell suitably connected with an iron(II) and iron metal half-cell. Does the spontaneous reaction produce or use up iron(II)?

4. Calculate the value at 25°C of 2.303(RT/F), where 2.303 is the conversion factor between natural and common logarithms.

5. If the following half-cells combine to give a cell with a large positive potential, is the copper(I) ion stable in aqueous solution?

$$Cu^+(aq) \rightarrow Cu^{2+}(aq) + e^-$$

$$Cu^+(aq) + e^- \rightarrow Cu(s)$$

6. Calculate the standard cell potential of a cell composed of the zinc and silver half-cells.

7. Is hydrogen more easily produced from 1 M hydrogen ion solution, from 1 M hydroxide ion solution, or from pure water?

8. Calculate the concentration of silver ion necessary to get a cell potential of 0.00 V when connected to a standard copper electrode.

9. Calculate the concentration of hydrogen ions in a solution in contact with hydrogen gas at 1.000 atm if the half-cell reduction potential is 0.040 V.

10. Two electrolysis cells are connected in series to the same source of electricity. (The same electricity that passes through one then

passes through the other.) If 10.0 g of copper is deposited from $CuSO_4$ in the first, what mass of silver is deposited from silver nitrate from the second?

11. Calculate the time required to reduce 17.0 g of Sn^{2+} to tin metal with a current of 4.45 A.

12. A 1% change in concentration of which of the species in the following half-reaction will make the greatest change in potential?

$$Cr_2O_7{}^{2-} + 14\,H^+ + 6\,e^- \rightarrow 2\,Cr^{3+} + 7\,H_2O$$

Solutions to Supplementary Problems

1. $3.55 \text{ hours} \left(\dfrac{3600 \text{ s}}{1 \text{ hour}} \right) \left(\dfrac{2.75 \text{ C}}{1 \text{ s}} \right) \left(\dfrac{1 \text{ mol e}^-}{96,500 \text{ C}} \right) \left(\dfrac{1 \text{ mol Cu}}{2 \text{ mol e}^-} \right) \times$

$$\left(\dfrac{63.5 \text{ g Cu}}{1 \text{ mol Cu}} \right) = 11.6 \text{ g Cu}$$

2. (a) $AuCl_4{}^-(aq) + 3\,e^- \rightarrow Au(s) + 4\,Cl^-(aq)$

$$145 \text{ g Au} \left(\dfrac{1 \text{ mol Au}}{197 \text{ g Au}} \right) \left(\dfrac{3 \text{ mol e}^-}{1 \text{ mol Au}} \right) \left(\dfrac{96,500 \text{ C}}{1 \text{ mol e}^-} \right) = 213,000 \text{ C}$$

$$225.0 \text{ minutes} \left(\dfrac{60 \text{ s}}{1 \text{ min}} \right) = 13,500 \text{ s}$$

$$\dfrac{213,000 \text{ C}}{13,500 \text{ s}} = 15.8 \text{ A}$$

(b) Since 3 hours is 180 minutes, 3 hours and 45.0 minutes is 225.0 minutes, so this problem is exactly the same as that in part (a).

3. $Fe^{3+}(aq) + e^- \rightarrow Fe^{2+}(aq)$ 0.771 V
   $Fe^{2+}(aq) + 2\,e^- \rightarrow Fe(s)$ -0.44 V

Reversing the second of these equations yields

$$Fe(s) \rightarrow Fe^{2+}(aq) + 2\,e^- \qquad +0.44 \text{ V}$$

Multiplying the first equation by 2 to get two moles of electrons in each equation, without changing its potential, then adding this equation to the second yields:

$$2\,Fe^{3+}(aq) + Fe(s) \rightarrow 3\,Fe^{2+}(aq) \qquad 1.21 \text{ V}$$

Since the potential is positive, the reaction goes spontaneously as written; iron(II) is produced.

4. $2.303(RT/F) = (2.303)(8.31 \text{ J})(298 \text{ K})/(96,500 \text{ C}) = 0.0591 \text{ V}$
(The constant in the Nernst equation is essentially equal to this ratio.)

5. Cu^+ is not stable in aqueous solution. It reacts spontaneously with itself to produce copper metal and copper(II) ion.

6. $Ag^+(aq) + e^- \rightarrow Ag(s)$ 0.80 V
$Zn^{2+}(aq) + 2\,e^- \rightarrow Zn(s)$ -0.76 V
Doubling the silver half-reaction and reversing the zinc one, then adding, yields:

$$2\,Ag^+(aq) + 2\,e^- \rightarrow 2\,Ag(s) \quad\quad\quad 0.80 \text{ V}$$
$$Zn(s) \rightarrow Zn^{2+}(aq) + 2\,e^- \quad\quad +0.76 \text{ V}$$
$$2\,Ag^+(aq) + Zn(s) \rightarrow Zn^{2+}(aq) + 2\,Ag(s) \quad 1.56 \text{ V}$$

7. Hydrogen is most easily produced from 1 M H^+ because the reduction potential of this half-reaction is highest of the three.

8. $Cu(s) + 2\,Ag^+(aq) \rightarrow Cu^{2+}(aq) + 2\,Ag(s)$

$$\epsilon^\circ = 0.80 \text{ V} - 0.34 \text{ V} = 0.46 \text{ V}$$

$$\epsilon = \epsilon^\circ - \frac{0.0592}{2} \log \frac{[Cu^{2+}]}{[Ag^+]^2}$$

$$0.00 = 0.46 - \frac{0.0592}{2} \log(1.000/[Ag^+]^2)$$

$$\log\,(1/[Ag^+]^2) = 15.5$$

$$[Ag^+]^2 = 3 \times 10^{-16} \quad\quad \text{(Watch the signs!)}$$

$$[Ag^+] = 2 \times 10^{-8} \text{ M}$$

9. The Nernst equation enables us to calculate the concentration:

$$H^+(aq) + e^- \rightarrow \tfrac{1}{2}\,H_2(g)$$

$$\epsilon = \epsilon^\circ - 0.0592 \log \frac{P_{H_2}^{0.5}}{[H^+]}$$

$$0.040 = 0.000 - 0.0592 \log\{1.000/[H^+]\}$$

$$\log\,\{1.000/[H^+]\} = \frac{-0.040}{0.0592} = -0.68$$

$$\log\,[H^+] = +0.68 \quad\quad \text{(Watch the signs!)}$$

$$[H^+] = 4.8 \text{ M}$$

10. $Cu^{2+}(aq) + 2\,e^- \rightarrow Cu(s)$

$Ag^+(aq) + e^- \rightarrow Ag(s)$

Since the same number of moles of electrons pass through each one,

$$10.0\text{ g Cu}\left(\frac{1\text{ mol Cu}}{63.5\text{ g Cu}}\right)\left(\frac{2\text{ mol }e^-}{1\text{ mol Cu}}\right)\left(\frac{1\text{ mol Ag}}{1\text{ mol }e^-}\right)\left(\frac{108\text{ g Ag}}{1\text{ mol Ag}}\right)$$

$$= 34.0\text{ g Ag}$$

11. $$17.0\text{ g Sn}^{2+}\left(\frac{1\text{ mol Sn}^{2+}}{119\text{ g Sn}^{2+}}\right)\left(\frac{2\text{ mol }e^-}{1\text{ mol Sn}^{2+}}\right)\left(\frac{96,500\text{ C}}{1\text{ mol }e^-}\right)\left(\frac{1\text{ s}}{4.45\text{ C}}\right)$$

$$= 6200\text{ s}$$

12. A change in the H^+ concentration will affect the potential most because of the 14 power for H^+ in the Nernst equation.

Chapter 10

Equilibrium

Before studying this chapter, review Section 5.4 on limiting quantities problems and, before Section 10.2, Acid-Base Equilibrium, review net ionic equations from the textbook.

10.1 Equilibrium Constant Calculations

Chemical **equilibrium** is a state in which two exactly opposite chemical reactions occur in the same system at the same rate. Because the reactions do the opposite of each other, nothing appears to be happening.

Equilibrium constant calculations are rather straightforward, but we must keep several things in mind. (1) The values in the equilibrium constant expression are the *concentrations at equilibrium*. (2) The equilibrium constant expression has no addition or subtraction within it. (3) All the substances involved in the equilibrium constant expression are in the same solution (or the same gas mixture), and so have the same volume. (4) Pure solids and liquids, and the solvents for dilute solutions, do not appear in the equilibrium constant expression. (5) The equilibrium constant expression is written for a specific equilibrium equation; if we reverse the equation, the value of the new K is the reciprocal of the original one.

The **equilibrium constant expression** for a general equilibrium reaction

$$a \, A + b \, B \rightleftharpoons c \, C + d \, D$$

is

$$K = \frac{[C]^c [D]^d}{[A]^a [B]^b}$$

The square brackets mean "concentration of," so [A] means the concentration of A, and so on. All the terms in the equilibrium constant expression are *numbers*. Equilibrium constant problems are ordinarily done without expressly writing the units; only occasionally is it necessary to specify the units.

EXAMPLE 1 Determine the equilibrium constant expression for each of the following reactions:

(*a*) $2 CO(g) + O_2(g) \rightleftharpoons 2 CO_2(g)$

(*b*) $2 C(s) + O_2(g) \rightleftharpoons 2 CO(g)$

(*c*) $CH_3OH + HCOOH \rightleftharpoons HCOOCH_3 + H_2O$ (all in alcohol solution)

Solution

(*a*) $K = \dfrac{[CO_2]^2}{[CO]^2[O_2]}$

(*b*) $K = \dfrac{[CO]^2}{[O_2]}$ (Since carbon is solid, it is not included.)

(*c*) $K = \dfrac{[HCOOCH_3][H_2O]}{[CH_3OH][HCOOH]}$ (Water is included because the reaction is not in aqueous solution.)   □

In general, if we add up two or more chemical equations, the resulting equation will have an equilibrium constant equal to the product of the equilibrium constants of the original equations.

EXAMPLE 2 (*a*) Write equilibrium constant expressions for equations 1 to 3 below. (*b*) Determine the relationship of the K value for equation 3 to those of equations 1 and 2.

1. $X + Y \rightleftharpoons Z$
2. $Z \rightleftharpoons W + Q$
3. $X + Y \rightleftharpoons W + Q$

Solution

(*a*) (1) $K_1 = \dfrac{[Z]}{[X][Y]}$

    (2) $K_2 = \dfrac{[W][Q]}{[Z]}$

    (3) $K_3 = \dfrac{[W][Q]}{[X][Y]}$

(*b*) Adding equations 1 and 2 yields equation 3, for which $K_3 = K_1 K_2$. In multiplying the values of K_1 times K_2, the $[Z]$ term cancels out and the product is equal to K_3. This is a general result, no matter what equations are added. ☐

Calculation of Values of K

EXAMPLE 3 Calculate the value of the equilibrium constant for the reaction

$$A + 2\,B \rightleftharpoons C$$

if the concentrations at equilibrium are $[A] = 2.0$ M, $[B] = 1.5$ M, and $[C] = 0.010$ M.

Solution The equilibrium concentrations are given, so all we need do is write the equilibrium constant expression and substitute these values into it:

$$K = \frac{[C]}{[A][B]^2} = \frac{(0.010)}{(2.0)(1.5)^2} = 0.0022 \qquad \Box$$

EXAMPLE 4

(*a*) Using the data of Example 3, calculate the value of the equilibrium constant for the reaction

$$C \rightleftharpoons A + 2\,B$$

(*b*) What is the relationship between the value of K in Example 3 and the value of this K?

Solution

(*a*) Again, the equilibrium concentrations are given, so all we need do is write the equilibrium constant expression and substitute the values into it:

$$K = \frac{[A][B]^2}{[C]} = \frac{(2.0)(1.5)^2}{(0.010)} = 4.5 \times 10^2$$

(*b*) The two equilibrium constants are reciprocals of each other. ☐

In these examples, *equilibrium* concentrations were given. Much more often, *initial* concentrations for the reactants are given along with the equilibrium concentration of one substance, so we must calculate the equilibrium concentrations for all the other substances from the data given.

EXAMPLE 5 Calculate the value of the equilibrium constant for

$$A + 2\,B \rightleftharpoons C + 2\,D$$

if 1.20 mol of A and 1.70 mol of B are dissolved in 1.00 L of solution, whereupon 0.100 mol of C is produced at equilibrium.

Solution   Because all the substances are dissolved in the same solution, they all have the same volume, and therefore their numbers of moles are proportional to their molarities. Therefore, we can calculate the molarity ratios from the balanced chemical equation. First we write the balanced chemical equation and put under it rows for "Initial concentrations," "Change due to reaction," and "Equilibrium concentrations." We then put the data given in the problem into our table. We assume that there is no C or D present initially, since none was mentioned.

	A	+ 2 B	$\rightleftharpoons$ C	+ 2 D
Initial concentration (M)	1.20	1.70	0.000	0.000
Change due to reaction (M)				
Equilibrium concentration (M)			0.100	

It is obvious that the 0.100 mol/L of C must have been produced by the reaction, since there was none present before the reaction. As soon as we place that 0.100 in the "Change due to reaction" row, we know enough to calculate every other value in that row, because *the change due to a reaction is governed by the coefficients in the balanced chemical equation*. The ratio of coefficients in this problem is 1:2:1:2, so the ratio of changes of concentrations in this problem is 0.100:0.200:0.100:0.200.

	A	+ 2 B	$\rightleftharpoons$ C	+ 2 D
Initial concentration (M)	1.20	1.70	0.000	0.000
Change due to reaction (M)	0.100	0.200	0.100	0.200
Equilibrium concentration (M)			0.100	

The equilibrium concentration of each **reactant** is its initial concentration **minus** the change, since the reactants are used up by the reaction. The equilibrium concentration of each **product** is its initial concentration **plus** the change, since the products are produced by the reaction. We now have all the equilibrium concentrations:

	A	**+ 2 B**	**⇌ C**	**+ 2 D**
Initial concentration (M)	1.20	1.70	0.000	0.000
Change due to reaction (M)	0.100	0.200	0.100	0.200
Equilibrium concentration (M)	1.10	1.50	0.100	0.200

We put the equilibrium concentrations into the equilibrium constant expression and solve:

$$K = \frac{[C][D]^2}{[A][B]^2} = \frac{(0.100)(0.200)^2}{(1.10)(1.50)^2} = 0.00162$$

Note that the concentrations of B and D are squared, as required by the equilibrium constant expression. Note also that we got those concentrations from the stoichiometry of the problem, and we did not double the B or D concentration. The D concentration happens to be twice the C concentration, but it is *the* D concentration that we square. Please also note that the "Change due to reaction" row in the final table is the only row that is in the ratio of the balanced chemical equation. □

EXAMPLE 6   Calculate the value of the equilibrium constant for

$$2 Z + Q \rightleftharpoons 2 E$$

if 1.20 mol of Z and 1.70 mol of Q are placed in a 2.00-L solution and allowed to come to equilibrium, at which point the concentration of E is 0.400 M.

Solution   Note specifically that the volume is 2.00 L so the initial *concentrations* of Z and Q are 0.600 M and 0.850 M, respectively. The equilibrium *concentration* of E was given in the problem, so we don't have to calculate that using the volume of the solution. The rest of the problem is just like the one in Example 5.

	2 Z	**+ Q**	**⇌ 2 E**
Initial concentration (M)	0.600	0.850	0.000
Change due to reaction (M)	0.400	0.200	0.400
Equilibrium concentration (M)	0.200	0.650	0.400

$$K = \frac{[E]^2}{[Z]^2[Q]} = \frac{(0.400)^2}{(0.200)^2(0.650)} = 6.15$$ □

Calculating Equilibrium Concentrations Using the Value of K

We can calculate all the equilibrium concentrations from initial concentration values if we are given the value of K. We let one of the equilibrium concentrations be represented by an unknown variable, say x, and solve the equilibrium constant expression algebraically.

EXAMPLE 7 For the reaction $A + B \rightleftharpoons 2Z$, $K = 4.0 \times 10^{-4}$, calculate the equilibrium concentration of Z if 0.500 mol of A and 0.500 mol of B are dissolved in 1.00 L of solution and allowed to come to equilibrium.

Solution

	A	+ B	$\rightleftharpoons$ 2 Z
Initial concentration	0.500	0.500	0.000
Change due to reaction	x	x	$2x$
Equilibrium concentrations	$0.500-x$	$0.500-x$	$2x$

$$K = \frac{[Z]^2}{[A][B]} = \frac{(2x)^2}{(0.500 - x)^2} = 4.0 \times 10^{-4}$$

We could solve this equation using the quadratic formula, but it is easier to notice that the left side is a perfect square, so we can take the square root of both sides, giving:

$$\frac{(2x)}{(0.500 - x)} = 0.020$$

$$2x = (0.500 - x)(0.020) = 0.010 - 0.020x$$

$$2.020x = 0.010$$

$$x = 0.0050$$

$$2x = [Z] = 0.010$$

Check:

$$K = \frac{[Z]^2}{[A][B]} = \frac{[2(0.0050)]^2}{(0.500 - 0.0050)^2} = 4.1 \times 10^{-4}$$

The value is 4.1×10^{-4} (to two significant digits), so the process works. Please note carefully that we squared $(2x)$, which is the concentration of Z. (It happens to be twice something else, but that does not matter.) Also note that we did not finish the problem when we found the value of x, because we had let [Z] equal $2x$. (We did that so that the change in concentration of A and B would not be fractional. See the table above.) Also note that a check is a very good idea to see that our calculation is correct. □

Taking the square root of an equation generally loses one of the roots, but in chemistry problems the root that is lost is generally an impossible answer anyway, like a negative concentration. However, we are not always so lucky to have an equation that we can take the square root of. Rather than go through the process of solving quadratic equations (or cubic or higher-order equations), we generally use an approximation method to solve for unknown concentrations. We will neglect very small quantities *when added to* or *subtracted from* larger quantities, but not when the small quantity is multiplied or divided. In general, we should attempt to neglect small values when added to or subtracted from larger ones, then check to see that our approximation is valid. An error less than 5% (or even somewhat more) is generally acceptable.

EXAMPLE 8 Consider the general reaction: $A + 2B \rightleftharpoons C$, with $K = 1.00 \times 10^{-8}$. Calculate the equilibrium concentration of A, B, and C after 1.50 mol of A and 2.50 mol of B are dissolved in 1.00 L of solution and allowed to come to equilibrium.

Solution

	A	+	**2 B**	$\rightleftharpoons$	**C**
Initial concentration (M)	1.50		2.50		0.00
Change due to reaction (M)	x		$2x$		x
Equilibrium concentrations	$1.50 - x$		$2.50 - 2x$		x

$$K = \frac{[C]}{[A][B]^2} = \frac{x}{(1.50 - x)(2.50 - 2x)^2} = 1.00 \times 10^{-8}$$

With a value of K so low, it is expected that the numerator of the equilibrium constant expression will be very small. That is, x, and even $2x$, should be negligible compared to 1.50 or 2.50, so we will neglect them and get

$$K = \frac{[C]}{[A][B]^2} = \frac{x}{(1.50)(2.50)^2} = 1.00 \times 10^{-8}$$

$$x = 9.38 \times 10^{-8} \text{ M} = [C]$$

$$[A] = 1.50 - 9.38 \times 10^{-8} = 1.50 \text{ M}$$

$$[B] = 2.50 - 2(9.38 \times 10^{-8}) = 2.50 \text{ M}$$

The value of x (and even $2x$) is certainly negligible when subtracted from the larger quantities.
Check:

$$K = \frac{[C]}{[A][B]^2} = \frac{9.38 \times 10^{-8}}{[1.50 - 9.38 \times 10^{-8}][2.50 - 2(9.38 \times 10^{-8})]^2}$$

$$= 1.00 \times 10^{-8}$$

The agreement is almost exact. □

10.2 Acid–Base Equilibrium

It is a good idea to review the textbook discussion of net ionic equations if necessary before attempting this section.

Weak acids and weak bases undergo equilibrium reactions with water. In dilute aqueous solution, the reaction can be represented in either of the following ways, with acetic acid used as an example:

$$HC_2H_3O_2(aq) + H_2O(l) \rightleftharpoons C_2H_3O_2{}^-(aq) + H_3O^+(aq)$$

or in shortened form:

$$HC_2H_3O_2(aq) \rightleftharpoons C_2H_3O_2{}^-(aq) + H^+(aq)$$

The H_3O^+ ion is called the **hydronium ion**. (It is a hydrogen ion attached to a water molecule, and is more real than a free hydrogen ion in aqueous solution, because the hydrogen ion has no electrons.) We will regard H^+ and H_3O^+ to be two different ways to represent the same ion. Use whichever form the textbook uses.

Weak acids react only to a slight extent with water; that is, their equilibria lie far toward the un-ionized form. Most acids are weak; the only common strong acids are HCl, HBr, HI, $HClO_3$, $HClO_4$, HNO_3, and H_2SO_4. If an acid has an equilibrium constant with a value less than 1, it is a weak acid. Constants are not given for strong acids because they can be regarded as 100% ionized.

Tabulated values of equilibrium constants for weak acids and bases, by definition, correspond to the equation with the un-ionized molecules on the left side of the equation. That is not to say that the reverse reactions cannot proceed; indeed they proceed to a far greater extent than the forward reaction, but the tabulated values are for the un-ionized molecules reacting to form ions.

We write equilibrium constant expressions for the reactions of weak acids with water, just as we did for regular equilibria, but remember that liquids such as water in dilute solutions are not included in the equilibrium constant expression. The expressions for the two forms of the equations for the ionization of acetic acid are

$$K_a = \frac{[C_2H_3O_2^-][H_3O^+]}{[HC_2H_3O_2]} \quad \text{or} \quad K_a = \frac{[C_2H_3O_2^-][H^+]}{[HC_2H_3O_2]}$$

Note that neither expression has the concentration of water in it. The concentration of pure water is 55.6 M, and in a dilute solution that might drop to 55.4 M. Thus the concentration of water might be thought to be a constant that has been incorporated into the equilibrium constant. The constant for the ionization of a weak acid is called the **acid dissociation constant**, and is symbolized K_a.

A weak base like ammonia in water also is in equilibrium to a slight extent:

$$NH_3(aq) + H_2O(l) \rightleftharpoons NH_4^+(aq) + OH^-(aq)$$

Its equilibrium constant, the **base dissociation constant**, is symbolized K_b, with the subscript denoting *base*. This constant also has no concentration of water included:

$$K_b = \frac{[NH_4^+][OH^-]}{[NH_3]}$$

We can do equilibrium constant calculations with acid-base equilibria just as we did with regular equilibria. (It turns out that these equilibria are inherently easier because there are few coefficients different from 1 in the balanced equations.)

EXAMPLE 9 Calculate the value of the equilibrium constant for the dissociation of acetic acid if the hydrogen ion concentration in 0.100 M acetic acid solution is 1.35×10^{-3} M.

Solution

$$HC_2H_3O_2(aq) \rightleftharpoons C_2H_3O_2^-(aq) + H^+(aq)$$

	$HC_2H_3O_2$	$C_2H_3O_2^-$	H^+
Initial concentrations (M)	0.100	0.000	0.000
Change due to reaction (M)	1.35×10^{-3}	1.35×10^{-3}	1.35×10^{-3}
Equilibrium concentrations (M)	0.099	1.35×10^{-3}	1.35×10^{-3}

$$K_a = \frac{[C_2H_3O_2^-][H^+]}{[HC_2H_3O_2]} = \frac{(1.35 \times 10^{-3})^2}{0.099} = 1.84 \times 10^{-5}$$

The accepted value of K_a for acetic acid is 1.8×10^{-5}. ☐

The equilibria of weak bases can be handled in the same way.

EXAMPLE 10 Calculate the value of the equilibrium constant for the ionization of ammonia if 0.100 M NH_3 has a hydroxide ion concentration of 1.35×10^{-3} M.

Solution

$$H_2O(l) + NH_3(aq) \rightleftharpoons NH_4^+(aq) + OH^-(aq)$$

		$H_2O(l) + NH_3(aq)$	$\rightleftharpoons NH_4^+(aq)$	$+ OH^-(aq)$
Initial concentrations (M)		0.100	0.000	0.000
Change due to reaction (M)		1.35×10^{-3}	1.35×10^{-3}	1.35×10^{-3}
Equilibrium concentrations (M)		0.099	1.35×10^{-3}	1.35×10^{-3}

$$K_b = \frac{[NH_4^+][OH^-]}{[NH_3]} = \frac{(1.35 \times 10^{-3})^2}{0.099} = 1.84 \times 10^{-5}$$

Just by coincidence, acetic acid and ammonia have the same values for their dissociation constants, 1.8×10^{-5}. □

EXAMPLE 11 Calculate the hydroxide ion concentration of a 0.350 M solution of ammonia: $K_b = 1.8 \times 10^{-5}$.

Solution

$$H_2O(l) + NH_3(aq) \rightleftharpoons NH_4^+(aq) + OH^-(aq)$$

		$H_2O(l) + NH_3(aq)$	$\rightleftharpoons NH_4^+(aq)$	$+ OH^-(aq)$
Initial concentrations (M)		0.350	0.000	0.000
Change due to reaction (M)		x	x	x
Equilibrium concentrations (M)		$0.350 - x$	x	x

$$K_b = \frac{[NH_4^+][OH^-]}{[NH_3]} = \frac{x^2}{0.350 - x} = 1.8 \times 10^{-5}$$

Neglecting x when subtracted from a larger number, just as we did with regular equilibria, yields

$$\frac{x^2}{0.350} = 1.8 \times 10^{-5}$$

So

$$x^2 = 6.3 \times 10^{-6} \quad \text{and} \quad x = 2.5 \times 10^{-3} = [OH^-]$$

The approximation caused an error of less than 1%. □

What would **LeChatelier's principle** predict about adding 0.200 M NH_4Cl to the solution of Example 11? This salt is composed of ammonium ions and chloride ions. The ammonium ions ought to shift the equilibrium of the ammonia ionization to the left, decreasing the hydroxide ion concentration.

EXAMPLE 12 Calculate the hydroxide ion concentration of a 0.350 M solution of ammonia that also has 0.200 M ammonium chloride in it. For NH_3, $K_b = 1.8 \times 10^{-5}$.

Solution The equilibrium that we are considering is still the ionization of the ammonia. The only difference here is that there is a nonzero initial concentration of ammonium ion.

$$H_2O(l) + NH_3(aq) \rightleftharpoons NH_4^+(aq) + OH^-(aq)$$

Initial			
concentrations (M)	0.350	0.200	0.000
Change due			
to reaction (M)	x	x	x
Equilibrium			
concentrations (M)	$0.350 - x$	$0.200 + x$	x

Neglecting x when added to or subtracted from a larger quantity yields

$$K_b = \frac{[NH_4^+][OH^-]}{[NH_3]} = \frac{x(0.200)}{0.350} = 1.8 \times 10^{-5}$$

$$x = [OH^-] = 3.2 \times 10^{-5} \text{ M}$$

The approximations are valid. Just as predicted by LeChatelier's principle, the hydroxide ion concentration dropped from 1.3×10^{-3} M to 3.2×10^{-5} M by addition of the ammonium chloride.

Note that although the salt affected the problem significantly, the salt and the base did not react with each other in the normal sense. The cation of the salt repressed the ionization of the base. *Do not write an equation with both the base and the salt on the same side of the arrow!* ☐

10.3 Water Autoionization

The **Bronsted theory** designates water as an acid in its reactions with bases and as a base in its reactions with acids. Thus it should not be too surprising that water can react with itself, acting both as an acid and a base:

$$H_2O(l) + H_2O(l) \rightleftharpoons H_3O^+(aq) + OH^-(aq)$$

It also should be no surprise that this reaction goes only to a very small extent. Its equilibrium constant expression, with its value, is

$$K_w = [H_3O^+][OH^-] = 1.0 \times 10^{-14}$$

Again, there is no concentration of water term. This equation means that in *every* dilute aqueous solution, there is at least *some* hydronium ion and *some* hydroxide ion. If the hydrogen ion concentration is greater than the hydroxide ion concentration, the solution is acidic. If the hydroxide ion concentration is greater than the hydrogen ion concentration, the solution is basic. If their concentrations are equal, the solution is neutral.

EXAMPLE 13 Calculate the hydronium ion concentration in pure water.

Solution Pure water has equal concentrations of hydronium and hydroxide ions. Let each equal x:

$$K_w = [H_3O^+][OH^-] = x^2 = 1.0 \times 10^{-14}$$
$$x = [H_3O^+] = 1.0 \times 10^{-7} \text{ M} \qquad \square$$

EXAMPLE 14 (*a*) Calculate the hydrogen ion concentration in 0.100 M NaOH. (*b*) Calculate the hydroxide ion concentration in 0.100 M HCl.

Solution (*a*) Since NaOH is a strong base, 0.100 M NaOH is 0.100 M in OH^-.

$$K_w = [H^+][OH^-] = [H^+](0.100) = 1.0 \times 10^{-14}$$
$$[H^+] = 1.0 \times 10^{-13} \text{ M}$$

(*b*) Since HCl is a strong acid, 0.100 M HCl is 0.100 M in H^+.

$$K_w = [H^+][OH^-] = (0.100)[OH^-] = 1.0 \times 10^{-14}$$
$$[OH^-] = 1.0 \times 10^{-13} \text{ M} \qquad \square$$

EXAMPLE 15 Calculate the hydronium ion concentration in 0.350 M NH_3.

Solution NH_3 is a weak base, so we have to calculate the hydroxide ion concentration using K_b. We did that for 0.350 M NH_3

in Example 11, and found $[OH^-]$ to be 2.5×10^{-3} M. Then,

$$K_w = [H_3O^+][OH^-] = [H_3O^+](2.5 \times 10^{-3}) = 1.0 \times 10^{-14}$$

$$[H_3O^+] = 4.0 \times 10^{-12} \text{ M} \qquad \square$$

What is the hydrogen ion concentration of 0.100 M NaCl? Since neither the sodium ion nor the chloride ion appears in the K_w expression, the hydrogen ion concentration and the hydroxide ion concentration are equal, and each is equal to 1.0×10^{-7} M, just as in pure water.

10.4 The pH Scale

pH is calculated with the equation

$$pH = -\log[H^+]$$

Note that pH is related to the *hydrogen* or *hydronium* ion concentration, not to the hydroxide ion concentration, the sodium ion concentration, or any other concentration. Also note that the pH, since it is a logarithm, has as many *decimal place* digits as the hydrogen ion concentration has significant digits.

EXAMPLE 16 Calculate the pH of (*a*) 0.100 M H^+; (*b*) 0.100 M HCl; (*c*) 0.100 M NaOH.

Solution

(*a*) $pH = -\log[H^+] = -\log(0.100) = 1.000$
(*b*) Since HCl is a strong acid, $[H^+] = 0.100$ and the pH is the same as in part (*a*).
(*c*) The hydronium ion concentration was calculated in Example 14(*a*) to be 1.0×10^{-13} M. The pH therefore is 13.00. $\square$

The value of the pH tells us the relative acidity of the solution:

$$[H^+] > 1 \times 10^{-7} \quad acidic \quad pH < 7$$

$$[H^+] = 1 \times 10^{-7} \quad neutral \quad pH = 7$$

$$[H^+] < 1 \times 10^{-7} \quad basic \quad pH > 7$$

EXAMPLE 17 Calculate the hydrogen ion concentration of solutions with the following pH values: (*a*) 7.50; (*b*) 2.44; (*c*) 12.70.

Solution Take the antilogarithm of the negative of each value, being careful with the significant digits. (See Section 1.3.)

(*a*) pH = 7.50; log[H$^+$] = -7.50; [H$^+$] = 3.2 × 10^{-8};

(*b*) 3.6 × 10^{-3}; (*c*) 2.0 × 10^{-13} ☐

10.5 Buffer Solutions

A **buffer solution** is a solution of an un-ionized weak acid and its conjugate base or an un-ionized weak base and its conjugate acid. We must know three things about buffer solutions: (1) their main characteristic, (2) how they are made, and (3) how they work.

1. Buffer solutions resist charges in their pH values even on addition of reasonable quantities of strong acid or strong base.
2. They are most often prepared by dissolving in the same solution a weak acid and a salt of that acid (containing the conjugate base of the acid) or a weak base and a salt of that base. They can also be prepared by carrying out a limiting quantities reaction in solution to result in one of the same combinations of reagents.

HC$_2$H$_3$O$_2$	+ NaC$_2$H$_3$O$_2$	NH$_3$	+ NH$_4$Cl
HC$_2$H$_3$O$_2$	+ NaOH in limiting quantity	NH$_3$	+ HCl in limiting quantity
NaC$_2$H$_3$O$_2$	+ HCl in limiting quantity	NH$_4$Cl	+ NaOH in limiting quantity

3. The buffer solution maintains a relatively constant pH by shifting according to LeChatelier's principle:

HC$_2$H$_3$O$_2$(aq) + H$_2$O(l)	⇌	C$_2$H$_3$O$_2^-$(aq) + H$_3$O$^+$(aq)
Large	Huge	Large Tiny
concentration	concentration	concentration concentration

If H$_3$O$^+$ is added from a strong acid, there is enough acetate ion present to cause this equilibrium to shift to the left, using up most of the added H$_3$O$^+$ and keeping the pH relatively constant. If OH$^-$ is added from a strong base, it reacts with the H$_3$O$^+$ producing water. This lowering of the H$_3$O$^+$ concentration causes the equilibrium to shift to the right, replacing H$_3$O$^+$ used up and again maintaining a relatively constant pH. If not too much base is added, there is enough un-ionized acid to replace almost all the hydronium ion used up by the base.

EXAMPLE 18 What compounds remain in solution after 0.200 mol of HC$_2$H$_3$O$_2$ is treated with 0.100 mol of NaOH?

Solution

$$HC_2H_3O_2(aq) + NaOH(aq) \rightarrow NaC_2H_3O_2(aq) + H_2O(l)$$

Since the reagents react in a $1:1$ ratio, the 0.100 mol of NaOH reacts with 0.100 mol of $HC_2H_3O_2$ leaving 0.100 mol of $HC_2H_3O_2$ and producing 0.100 mol of $NaC_2H_3O_2$. The weak acid and its salt, containing the conjugate base, $C_2H_3O_2{}^-$, are left in the solution.

□

EXAMPLE 19 (*a*) Calculate the pH of 1.00 L of a buffer solution containing 0.125 mol of NH_3 and 0.125 mol of NH_4Cl. (*b*) Recalculate the pH after 0.010 mol of HCl is added to this buffer solution. Assume no change in volume.

Solution

(*a*)

	$H_2O(l)$ +	$NH_3(aq)$ ⇌	$NH_4{}^+(aq)$ +	$OH^-(aq)$
Initial concentrations (M)		0.125	0.125	0.000
Change due to reaction (M)		x	x	x
Equilibrium concentrations (M)		$0.125 - x$	$0.125 + x$	x

Neglecting x when added to or subtracted from a larger quantity yields

$$K_b = \frac{[NH_4{}^+][OH^-]}{[NH_3]} = \frac{x(0.125)}{0.125} = 1.8 \times 10^{-5}$$

$$x = [OH^-] = 1.8 \times 10^{-5}\ M$$

$$pH = 9.26$$

(*b*) HCl reacts with NH_3 whether or not any ammonium ion is already present. The easiest way to do a problem like this is to assume that the acid and base react *completely*, and then do the equilibrium problem with the resulting concentrations as initial concentrations for that problem:

	$HCl(aq)$ +	$NH_3(aq)$ ⇌	$NH_4{}^+(aq)$ +	$Cl^-(aq)$
Beginning concentrations (M)	0.010	0.125	0.125	
Change due to reaction (M)	0.010	0.010	0.010	
End of acid-base reaction concentrations (M)	0.000	0.115	0.135	

Now the equilibrium reaction is considered:

$$H_2O(l) + NH_3(aq) \rightleftharpoons NH_4^+(aq) + OH^-(aq)$$

	NH_3	NH_4^+	OH^-
Initial concentrations (M)	0.115	0.135	0.000
Change due to reaction (M)	x	x	x
Equilibrium concentrations (M)	$0.115 - x$	$0.135 + x$	x

Neglecting x when added to or subtracted from a larger quantity yields

$$K_b = \frac{[NH_4^+][OH^-]}{[NH_3]} = \frac{x(0.135)}{0.115} = 1.8 \times 10^{-5}$$

$$x = [OH^-] = 1.5 \times 10^{-5}\ M$$

$$pH = 9.18$$

Because of the buffering action of the system, the pH drops only from 9.26 to 9.18 despite the addition of strong acid. □

10.6 Equilibrium Constants for Hydrolysis

Hydrolysis may be defined as the reaction with water of the conjugate base of a weak molecular acid or the conjugate acid of a weak molecular base. For example, the acetate ion reacts with water according to the following equilibrium:

$$C_2H_3O_2^-(aq) + H_2O(l) \rightleftharpoons HC_2H_3O_2(aq) + OH^-(aq)$$

The equilibrium constant expression for this reaction is written as usual for an ionic equilibrium:

$$K_h = \frac{[HC_2H_3O_2][OH^-]}{[C_2H_3O_2^-]}$$

where K_h is the hydrolysis constant. Note the difference between this reaction and the reverse of the ionization of $HC_2H_3O_2$:

$$C_2H_3O_2^-(aq) + H_3O^+(aq) \rightleftharpoons HC_2H_3O_2(aq) + H_2O(l)$$

The value of K for this reaction is the reciprocal of that for the ionization of $HC_2H_3O_2$, $1/K_a$, because the equation is the reverse of the ionization reaction. The K_h for the hydrolysis reaction is equal to K_w/K_a. This value may be obtained by combining the equations for the ionization and the hydrolysis, as was done in general in

Example 2:

$$HC_2H_3O_2(aq) + H_2O(l) \rightleftharpoons C_2H_3O_2^-(aq) + H_3O^+(aq)$$

$$K_a = \frac{[C_2H_3O_2][H_3O^+]}{[HC_2H_3O_2]}$$

$$C_2H_3O_2^-(aq) + H_2O(l) \rightleftharpoons HC_2H_3O_2(aq) + OH^-(aq)$$

$$K_h = \frac{[HC_2H_3O_2][OH^-]}{[C_2H_3O_2^-]}$$

When these chemical equations are **added**,

$$2 H_2O(l) \rightleftharpoons H_3O^+(aq) + OH^-(aq)$$

their equilibrium constant expressions are **multiplied** (just as in Example 2), yielding:

$$K_a K_h = [H_3O^+][OH^-] = K_w$$

Thus,

$$K_h = K_w/K_a$$

We do not need to derive this expression every time we do a hydrolysis problem; we merely must remember to use the correct value for the equilibrium constant. For the hydrolysis of the conjugate acid of a weak base,

$$K_h = K_w/K_b$$

How do we recognize a hydrolysis problem? It is a problem in which there is no molecular weak acid or weak base present initially (just a "salt"). (If any molecular weak acid or weak base is present, we may have a buffer solution problem.)

EXAMPLE 20 Calculate the hydroxide ion concentration in a solution of 0.100 M $NaC_2H_3O_2$.

Solution The sodium ion is a spectator ion. The acetate ion hydrolyzes according to the equation

	$H_2O(l) + C_2H_3O_2^-(aq) \rightleftharpoons HC_2H_3O_2(aq) + OH^-(aq)$		
Initial concentrations (M)	0.100	0.000	0.000
Change due to reaction (M)	x	x	x
Equilibrium concentration (M)	$0.100 - x$	x	x

157

$$K_h = \frac{[HC_2H_3O_2][OH^-]}{[C_2H_3O_2{}^-]} = \frac{x^2}{(0.100)} = \frac{1.0 \times 10^{-14}}{1.8 \times 10^{-5}} = 5.6 \times 10^{-10}$$

$$x^2 = 5.6 \times 10^{-11}$$

$$x = 7.5 \times 10^{-6} \text{ M} = [OH^-] \qquad \square$$

EXAMPLE 21 Calculate the pH of a solution of 0.100 M NH₄Cl.

Solution The chloride ion is a spectator ion. The ammonium ion hydrolyzes according to the equation

	$H_2O(l)$ + $NH_4{}^+$(aq)	$\rightleftharpoons$ NH_3(aq) +	H_3O^+(aq)
Initial concentrations (M)	0.100	0.000	0.000
Change due to reaction (M)	x	x	x
Equilibrium concentrations (M)	$0.100 - x$	x	x

$$K_a = \frac{[NH_3][H_3O^+]}{[NH_4{}^+]} = \frac{x^2}{(0.100)} = \frac{1.0 \times 10^{-14}}{1.8 \times 10^{-5}} = 5.6 \times 10^{-10}$$

$$x^2 = 5.6 \times 10^{-11}$$

$$x = 7.5 \times 10^{-6} \text{ M} = [H_3O^+]$$

$$pH = 5.12 \qquad \square$$

Leading Questions

1. The equilibrium constant for a certain reaction has a value of 2.5×10^{-13}. What is the value of the constant for the reverse reaction?

2. When is there a term for the concentration of water in an equilibrium constant expression?

3. For which kind of calculation do we use an algebraic variable like x—calculation of the value of K or calculation using the value of K?

4. In 0.100 M acetic acid solution, the acid is 1.3% ionized and 98.7% in the un-ionized form. Determine the percentage of products of each of the following reactions, assuming each reactant to be 0.100 M before any reaction occurs:

(a) $C_2H_3O_2^-(aq) + H^+(aq) \rightleftharpoons HC_2H_3O_2(aq)$

(b) $NaC_2H_3O_2(aq) + HCl(aq) \rightleftharpoons HC_2H_3O_2(aq) + NaCl(aq)$

5. Which of the following reactions proceeds more than 50% to completion?

(a) $HC_2H_3O_2(aq) + H_2O(l) \rightleftharpoons C_2H_3O_2^-(aq) + H_3O^+(aq)$
$HC_2H_3O_2(aq) + OH^-(aq) \rightleftharpoons C_2H_3O_2^-(aq) + H_2O(l)$

(b) $C_2H_3O_2^-(aq) + H_2O(l) \rightleftharpoons HC_2H_3O_2(aq) + OH^-(aq)$
$C_2H_3O_2^-(aq) + H_3O^+(aq) \rightleftharpoons HC_2H_3O_2(aq) + H_2O(l)$

Answers to Leading Questions

1. The value of this K is $1/(2.5 \times 10^{-13}) = 4.0 \times 10^{12}$.
2. Whenever water is involved in a reaction but is not the solvent for the reaction. For example, when the reaction is a gas-phase reaction or a reaction in another solvent, the concentration of water is included.
3. Calculation using the value of K. (Remember, we calculated values of K before we used x.)
4. (a) The ions react to form 98.7% of un-ionized acid, leaving 1.3% in the ionic form. It doesn't make any difference which way we write the equation or if we add reactants or products, the system shifts until the same equilibrium mixture is established. (b) The net ionic equation for this reaction is that given in part (a), so the answer is the same.
5. (a) The first equation represents an equilibrium reaction of a weak acid, that proceeds to the right only a tiny percentage. The second equation represents a reaction of an acid and a base that proceeds almost to completion.
   (b) The first equation represents an equilibrium reaction of the conjugate of a weak acid with water that proceeds to the right only a tiny percentage. (The reverse reaction of an acid with a strong base proceeds almost to completion.) The second equation proceeds extensively, since its reverse is the ionization of a weak acid in water, which we know proceeds only slightly.

Supplementary Problems

1. From the value of the equilibrium constant for

$$A + B \rightleftharpoons 2C \qquad K = 16.0$$

calculate the value of the equilibrium constant for each of the following equilibria:

(a) $\frac{1}{2} A + \frac{1}{2} B \rightleftharpoons C$

(b) $2 C \rightleftharpoons A + B$

(c) $C \rightleftharpoons \frac{1}{2} A + \frac{1}{2} B$

2. Write the equilibrium constant expression for the following reaction:

$$CaCO_3(s) \rightleftharpoons CaO(s) + CO_2(g)$$

3. Calculate the value of the equilibrium constant for

$$A(aq) + 2 B(aq) \rightleftharpoons C(aq) + 2 D(s)$$

if 1.20 mol of A and 1.70 mol of B are dissolved in 1.00 L of solution, whereupon 0.100 mol of C is produced at equilibrium.

4. The following system at equilibrium

$$A + 2 B \rightleftharpoons 2 C$$

had equilibrium concentrations $[A] = 0.220$ M, $[B] = 0.456$ M, and $[C] = 3.22$ M. The temperature was raised, causing the equilibrium to shift and changing the C concentration to 3.02 M. (a) Calculate the value of the original equilibrium constant. (b) Calculate the value of the new equilibrium constant. (c) Determine if the reaction is exothermic or endothermic.

5. Calculate the value of the equilibrium constant for the dissociation of formic acid ($HCHO_2$) if the hydrogen ion concentration in 0.100 M formic acid solution is 4.2×10^{-3} M.

6. Calculate the hydrogen ion concentration of a 0.250 M solution of $HC_2H_3O_2$ that also has 0.150 M $NaC_2H_3O_2$ in it. $K_a = 1.8 \times 10^{-5}$.

7. Which one of the following equilibria proceeds farthest to the right?

(a) $HC_2H_3O_2(aq) \rightleftharpoons C_2H_3O_2^-(aq) + H^+(aq)$

(b) $C_2H_3O_2^-(aq) + H^+(aq) \rightleftharpoons HC_2H_3O_2(aq)$

(c) $C_2H_3O_2^-(aq) + H_2O(l) \rightleftharpoons HC_2H_3O_2(aq) + OH^-(aq)$

8. Calculate the pH of a solution containing 0.150 M NH_3 and 0.150 M NH_4Cl. $K_b = 1.8 \times 10^{-5}$.

9. Calculate the hydrogen ion concentration of each of the following solutions: (a) pH $= 7.123$; (b) pH $= 9.90$.

10. Calculate the pH of 0.100 M boric acid, HBH_2O_3. $K_a = 7.3 \times 10^{-10}$.

11. Which ones of the following solutions would make buffer solutions?

   (a) 0.500 mol HCl + 1.00 mol $NaC_2H_3O_2$ in 1.00 L of solution
   (b) 0.500 mol HCl + 1.00 mol NaCl in 1.00 L of solution
   (c) 0.500 mol NaCl + 1.00 mol $NaC_2H_3O_2$ in 1.00 L of solution
   (d) 0.500 mol $HC_2H_3O_2$ + 1.00 mol $NaC_2H_3O_2$ in 1.00 L of solution

12. Calculate the value of the equilibrium constant for the dissociation of methyl amine, CH_3NH_2, which reacts with water just as ammonia does (but to a different extent). The hydroxide ion concentration in 0.100 M methyl amine solution is 6.6×10^{-3} M.

13. (a) State qualitatively which of the following aqueous solutions, in sufficient water to make 1.00 L of solution, has the highest pH:

   (i) 0.500 mol $HCHO_2$ and 0.250 mol $NaCHO_2$.
   (ii) 0.480 mol $HCHO_2$ and 0.270 mol $NaCHO_2$.
   (iii) 0.460 mol $HCHO_2$ and 0.290 mol $NaCHO_2$.
   (iv) 0.440 mol $HCHO_2$ and 0.310 mol $NaCHO_2$.

   (b) How much NaOH do we need to convert solution (i) to solution (ii)?   solution (ii) to solution (iii)?   solution (iii) to solution (iv)?

   (c) If that much NaOH were added to 1.00 L of solution containing 3.6×10^{-5} M HCl, what would be the final pH?

14. Calculate the value of K_b for a base (B) if a 0.100 M solution has a pH of 10.28.

15. Calculate the value of K_a for an acid if a solution of 0.100 M HA and 0.150 M NaA has a pH of 5.22.

16. Calculate the acetate ion concentration in a solution containing 0.100 M $HC_2H_3O_2$ and 0.150 M HCl. $K_a = 1.8 \times 10^{-5}$.

17. When 0.100 mol of NH_3 and 0.150 mol of NH_4Cl are dissolved in enough water to make 1.00 L of solution, (a) is a limiting quantities problem being presented? (b) What ions are present in greater than 0.010 M concentration? (c) What other ions are present? (d) What is the principal equilibrium reaction? (e) What effect does each of the ions of part (b) have on the equilibrium of part (d)? (f) What is the hydroxide ion concentration of the solution? (g) What is the pH of the solution?

18. Calculate the pH of the solution that results after 0.050 mol of NaOH is added to the buffer solution of Problem 17. Assume no change in volume.

19. Which of the following 1.00-L solutions involve the use of a hydrolysis constant for the determination of equilibrium concentrations?

(a) 0.100 mol $NaC_2H_3O_2$

(b) 0.100 mol NH_4Cl

(c) 0.100 mol $NaCl$

(d) 0.100 mol $NaOH$ + 0.100 mol $HC_2H_3O_2$

(e) 0.100 mol HCl + 0.100 mol NH_3

20. Calculate the hydroxide ion concentration of a solution prepared by adding 0.100 L of 0.200 M $NaOH$ to 0.100 L of 0.200 M $HC_2H_3O_2$.

21. Calculate the pH of a solution prepared by adding 0.100 L of 0.200 M HCl to 0.100 L of 0.200 M NH_3.

Solutions to Supplementary Problems

1. For the given reaction, the equilibrium constant expression is

$$K = \frac{[C]^2}{[A][B]} = 16.0$$

(a)
$$K = \frac{[C]}{[A]^{\frac{1}{2}}[B]^{\frac{1}{2}}}$$

Since this expression is the square root of the one given, the value of K is 4.00.

(b)
$$K = \frac{[A][B]}{[C]^2}$$

so $K = 1/(16.0) = 0.0625$.

(c)
$$K = \frac{[A]^{\frac{1}{2}}[B]^{\frac{1}{2}}}{[C]}$$

which is the square root of the value in part (b), or 0.250. (Note that the square root of a number smaller than 1 is larger than the number.)

2. $K = [CO_2]$ (Neither solid is included.)

3.

	A(aq) +	2 B(aq) $\rightleftharpoons$	C(aq) +	2 D(s)
Initial concentration (M)	1.20	1.70	0.000	
Change due to reaction (M)	0.100	0.200	0.100	
Equilibrium concentration (M)	1.10	1.50	0.100	

$$K = \frac{[C]}{[A][B]^2} = \frac{(0.100)}{(1.10)(1.50)^2} = 0.0404$$

Compare this solution to that of Example 5, and notice the great difference made by the fact that D is a solid and therefore its concentration is not included in the equilibrium constant expression.

4. (a) $K = \dfrac{[C]^2}{[A][B]^2} = \dfrac{(3.22)^2}{(0.220)(0.456)^2} = 227$

(b)

	A	+ 2 B	⇌ 2 C
Initial concentrations (M)	0.220	0.456	3.22
Change due to reaction (M)	+0.10	+0.20	−0.20
Equilibrium concentrations (M)	0.32	0.66	3.02

$$K = \frac{[C]^2}{[A][B]^2} = \frac{(3.02)^2}{(0.32)(0.66)^2} = 65$$

(c) Since the rise in temperature caused the equilibrium to shift left (the K is smaller, so the concentration of product is smaller), it is an exothermic reaction.

5.

$$HCHO_2(aq) \rightleftharpoons CHO_2^-(aq) + H^+(aq)$$

Initial concentrations (M)	0.100	0.0000	0.0000
Change due to reaction (M)	4.2×10^{-3}	4.2×10^{-3}	4.2×10^{-3}
Equilibrium concentrations (M)	0.096	4.2×10^{-3}	4.2×10^{-3}

$$K_a = \frac{[CHO_2^-][H^+]}{[HCHO_2]} = \frac{(4.2 \times 10^{-3})^2}{0.096} = 1.8 \times 10^{-4}$$

6.

$$HC_2H_3O_2(aq) \rightleftharpoons C_2H_3O_2^-(aq) + H^+(aq)$$

Initial concentrations (M)	0.250	0.150	0.000
Change due to reaction (M)	x	x	x
Equilibrium concentrations (M)	$0.250 - x$	$0.150 + x$	x

Neglecting x when added to or subtracted from a larger number, just as we did with regular equilibria, yields

$$K_a = \frac{[C_2H_3O_2{}^-][H^+]}{[HC_2H_3O_2]} = \frac{(0.150)x}{0.250} = 1.8 \times 10^{-5}$$

$$x = 3.0 \times 10^{-5} \text{ M}$$

7. Reaction (b) proceeds farthest to the right. It has a constant $(5.6 \times 10^{+3})$ equal to the reciprocal of that of reaction (a) because it is the opposite reaction. Reaction (c) proceeds much less than reaction (b) because water is much less strong an acid than H^+ is.

8. The equilibrium that we are considering is still the ionization of the ammonia.

$$H_2O(l) + NH_3(aq) \rightleftharpoons NH_4{}^+(aq) + OH^-(aq)$$

Initial concentrations (M)	0.150	0.150	0.000
Change due to reaction (M)	x	x	x
Equilibrium concentrations (M)	$0.150 - x$	$0.150 + x$	x

Neglecting x when added to or subtracted from a larger quantity yields

$$K_b = \frac{[NH_4{}^+][OH^-]}{[NH_3]} = \frac{x(0.150)}{0.150} = 1.8 \times 10^{-5}$$

$$x = [OH^-] = 1.8 \times 10^{-5} \text{ M}$$

$$[H^+] = (1.0 \times 10^{-14})/(1.8 \times 10^{-5}) = 5.6 \times 10^{-10}$$

$$pH = 9.25$$

9. (a) 7.53×10^{-8} M; (b) 1.3×10^{-10} M.

10.

$$HBH_2O_3(aq) \rightleftharpoons BH_2O_3{}^-(aq) + H^+(aq)$$

Initial concentrations (M)	0.100	0.000	0.000
Change due to reaction (M)	x	x	x
Equilibrium concentrations (M)	$0.100 - x$	x	x

$$K_a = \frac{[BH_2O_3{}^-][H^+]}{[HBH_2O_3]} = \frac{x^2}{0.100} = 7.3 \times 10^{-10}$$

$$x^2 = 7.3 \times 10^{-11}$$

$$x = 8.5 \times 10^{-6} \text{ M} = [H^+]$$

$$pH = 5.07$$

11. (a) and (d).

(a) All the HCl will react with half the $C_2H_3O_2^-$ from the sodium salt, yielding $HC_2H_3O_2$ and leaving half the $C_2H_3O_2^-$, so this is a buffer solution.

(b) A *strong* acid and its conjugate do *not* make a buffer solution.

(c) Two salts do not make a buffer solution.

(d) A weak acid, $HC_2H_3O_2$, and its conjugate, $C_2H_3O_2^-$, make a buffer solution.

12.

	$H_2O(l) +$ $CH_3NH_2(aq)$	$\rightleftharpoons$ $CH_3NH_3^+(aq) +$	$OH^-(aq)$
Initial concentrations (M)	0.100	0.000	0.000
Change due to reaction (M)	6.6×10^{-3}	6.6×10^{-3}	6.6×10^{-3}
Equilibrium concentrations (M)	0.093	6.6×10^{-3}	6.6×10^{-3}

$$K_b = \frac{[CH_3NH_3^+][OH^-]}{[CH_3NH_2]} = \frac{(6.6 \times 10^{-3})^2}{0.093} = 4.7 \times 10^{-4}$$

13. (a) Solution (iv) is the most basic. It has the lowest concentration of acid and the highest of conjugate base. (b) We convert from each solution to the next by adding 0.020 mol of NaOH. (c) That much base would completely neutralize the HCl and still be 0.020 M, with a pH of 12.30.

14. We use the pH to calculate the hydrogen ion concentration, and use that and K_w to determine the OH^- concentration:

$$[H^+] = 5.2 \times 10^{-11}$$

$$[OH^-] = (1.0 \times 10^{-14})/(5.2 \times 10^{-11}) = 1.9 \times 10^{-4}$$

	$H_2O(l) +$ $B(aq)$	$\rightleftharpoons$ $BH^+(aq) +$	$OH^-(aq)$
Initial concentration (M)	0.100	0.000	0.000
Change due to reaction (M)	1.9×10^{-4}	1.9×10^{-4}	1.9×10^{-4}
Equilibrium concentration (M)	0.100	1.9×10^{-4}	1.9×10^{-4}

$$K_b = \frac{[BH^+][OH^-]}{[B]} = \frac{(1.9 \times 10^{-4})^2}{(0.100)} = 3.6 \times 10^{-7}$$

15. $[H^+] = 6.0 \times 10^{-6}$

	HA(aq)	$\rightleftharpoons$	H^+(aq)	+	A^-(aq)
Initial					
concentration (M)	0.100		0.000		0.150
Change due					
to reaction (M)	6.0×10^{-6}		6.0×10^{-6}		6.0×10^{-6}
Equilibrium					
concentration (M)	0.100		6.0×10^{-6}		0.150

$$K_a = \frac{[H^+][A^-]}{[HA]} = \frac{(6.0 \times 10^{-6})(0.150)}{(0.100)} = 9.0 \times 10^{-6}$$

16. The H^+ from the ionization of HCl (a strong acid) represses the ionization of the acetic acid, so the concentration of H^+ is 0.150 M, entirely from the HCl.

	$HC_2H_3O_2$(aq)	$\rightleftharpoons$	$C_2H_3O_2^-$(aq)	+	H^+(aq)
Initial					
concentration (M)	0.100		0.000		0.150
Change due					
to reaction (M)	x		x		x
Equilibrium					
concentration (M)	$0.100 - x$		x		$0.150 + x$

Neglecting x when added to or subtracted from larger values yields

$$K_a = \frac{[H^+][C_2H_3O_2^-]}{[HC_2H_3O_2]} = \frac{(0.150)[C_2H_3O_2^-]}{(0.100)} = 1.8 \times 10^{-5}$$

$$[C_2H_3O_2^-] = 1.2 \times 10^{-5}$$

In 0.100 M acetic acid alone, the acetate ion concentration (equal to the hydrogen ion concentration) is 1.3×10^{-3} M. The hydrogen ion from the strong acid has lowered it to 1.2×10^{-5} M, as predicted by LeChatelier's principle. The presence of any *stronger* acid will repress the ionization of any weaker acid in the same solution.

17. (a) This is not a limiting quantities problem because the two do not react. (b) NH_4^+ and Cl^-. (c) H^+ and OH^-, as in every aqueous solution. (d) $H_2O(l) + NH_3(aq) \rightleftharpoons NH_4^+(aq) + OH^-(aq)$ (e) The

ammonium ion from ammonium chloride affects the equilibrium reaction of the ammonia with water. The chloride ion has no effect.

(f)
$$H_2O(l) + NH_3(aq) \rightleftharpoons NH_4^+(aq) + OH^-(aq)$$

Initial			
concentrations (M)	0.100	0.150	0.000
Change due			
to reaction (M)	x	x	x
Equilibrium			
concentrations (M)	$0.100 - x$	$0.150 + x$	x

Neglecting x when added to or subtracted from a larger quantity yields

$$K_b = \frac{[NH_4^+][OH^-]}{[NH_3]} = \frac{x(0.150)}{0.100} = 1.8 \times 10^{-5}$$

$$x = [OH^-] = 1.2 \times 10^{-5} \text{ M}$$

(g)   pH $= 9.08$

18.
$$OH^-(aq) + NH_4^+(aq) \rightleftharpoons NH_3(aq) + H_2O(l)$$

Beginning (mol)	0.050	0.150	0.100
Change due			
to reaction (mol)	0.050	0.050	0.050
End of acid-base			
reaction (mol)	0.000	0.100	0.150

Now the equilibrium reaction is considered:

$$H_2O(l) + NH_3(aq) \rightleftharpoons NH_4^+(aq) + OH^-(aq)$$

Initial			
concentrations (M)	0.150	0.100	0.000
Change due			
to reaction (M)	x	x	x
Equilibrium			
concentrations (M)	$0.150 - x$	$0.100 + x$	x

Neglecting x when added to or subtracted from a larger quantity yields

$$K_b = \frac{[NH_4^+][OH^-]}{[NH_3]} = \frac{x(0.100)}{0.150} = 1.8 \times 10^{-5}$$

$$x = [OH^-] = 2.7 \times 10^{-5} \text{ M}$$

$$pH = 9.43$$

The pH increased from 9.08 before the addition of NaOH to 9.43 after the addition. The small value of the increase is caused by the buffering action of the equilibrium.

19. All but (c). In (a), the acetate ion hydrolyzes. In (b), the ammonium ion hydrolyzes. In (d), the acid and base react completely to form sodium acetate, and the solution is the same as in (a). In (e), the acid and base react completely to form NH_4Cl, and the solution is the same as in (b).

20. The number of moles of each reactant is

$$0.100 \text{ L} \left(\frac{0.200 \text{ mol}}{1 \text{ L}} \right) = 0.0200 \text{ mol}$$

The total volume is 0.200 L. The acid and base react to form 0.0200 mol $NaC_2H_3O_2$, so the solution contains 0.100 M acetate ion (plus sodium ion):

$$\frac{0.0200 \text{ mol}}{0.200 \text{ L}} = 0.100 \text{ M}$$

The hydroxide ion concentration is 7.5×10^{-6} M, as shown in Example 20.

21. The number of moles of each reactant is

$$0.100 \text{ L} \left(\frac{0.200 \text{ mol}}{1 \text{ L}} \right) = 0.0200 \text{ mol}$$

The total volume is 0.200 L. The acid and base react to form 0.0200 mol NH_4Cl, so the solution contains 0.100 M ammonium ion (plus chloride ion):

$$\frac{0.0200 \text{ mol}}{0.200 \text{ L}} = 0.100 \text{ M}$$

The pH is 5.12, as shown in Example 21.

Chapter 11

Colligative Properties

Colligative properties are properties of solutions that depend on the nature of the *solvent* and the concentrations of the solute particles, but *not* on the nature of those particles. There are four such properties, and they utilize three different concentration units (Chapter 6); be sure to use the correct unit with each one. With concentrations and colligative property data, it is possible to calculate the number of moles of substance present, and once the number of moles is established, all the calculations using moles (Chapter 4) are possible.

11.1 Vapor-Pressure Lowering

The presence of a solute causes **vapor-pressure lowering** of a solvent. If the solute is **nonvolatile** (nonevaporating), the solution has a lower vapor pressure than the pure solvent does. (Review vapor pressure in Chapter 7.) From a molecular view, the solute particles at the surface of the liquid inhibit the movement of solvent molecules from going into the vapor phase, but do not inhibit solvent molecules in the vapor phase from returning to the liquid phase, so the rate of evaporation is lower than the rate of condensation until there are fewer solvent molecules in the vapor phase. For solving problems, the vapor pressure of any component (call it A) in the solution, P_A, is related to the vapor pressure of the pure substance, P_A^o, by **Raoult's law**:

$$P_A = X_A P_A^o$$

where X_A is the mole fraction of component A. Raoult's law is approximate for many solutions, and is exact only for "ideal solutions." Since X_A must be less than 1 in any solution, the vapor pressure of the component in the solution must be lower than its vapor pressure when pure—the vapor pressure has been lowered.

Solvents generally are volatile (evaporate easily) whereas solutes may be volatile or nonvolatile. In many problems, the vapor pressure of the solvent is the only one of interest.

EXAMPLE 1 (*a*) Calculate the vapor pressure of benzene in a solution of naphthalene (a nonvolatile solute) in benzene at 21.3°C in which the mole fraction of benzene is 0.900. The vapor pressure of pure benzene at that temperature is 10.7 kPa. (*b*) Calculate the vapor-pressure lowering. (*c*) What is the vapor pressure of the solution?

Solution

(*a*) $P_{solvent} = X_{solvent} P^o_{solvent} = (0.900)(10.7 \text{ kPa}) = 9.63 \text{ kPa}$
(*b*) $10.7 \text{ kPa} - 9.63 \text{ kPa} = 1.1 \text{ kPa}$
(*c*) 9.63 kPa.   (Since the solute is nonvolatile, it has no vapor pressure.) □

We can also use another form of Raoult's law for a solution of two components:

$$\Delta P_{solvent} = X_{solute} P^o_{solvent}$$

instead of

$$P_{solvent} = X_{solvent} P^o_{solvent}$$

where $\Delta P_{solvent}$ is the *vapor-pressure lowering*. These equations look very similar; do not confuse them. Note that it is the mole fraction of the *solute* in the new equation as opposed to the mole fraction of *solvent* in the first one we introduced. The new equation can give a more precise answer than the first.

EXAMPLE 2 Calculate the vapor-pressure lowering of benzene in a solution of 0.200 mol of naphthalene in 1.80 mol of benzene at 21.3°C. The vapor pressure of pure benzene at that temperature is 10.7 kPa.

Solution   First we find the mole fraction of naphthalene:

$$X_{naphthalene} = \frac{0.200 \text{ mol}}{2.00 \text{ mol total}} = 0.100$$

$$\Delta P_{benzene} = X_{naphthalene} P^o_{benzene}$$

$$= (0.100)(10.7 \text{ kPa}) = 1.07 \text{ kPa}$$

This result is the same as that for Example 1, since the mole fractions are the same, except that this answer is more precise. □

11.2 Freezing–Point Depression and Boiling-Point Elevation

The freezing point of a solvent is depressed by the presence of a solute. The **freezing-point depression** is directly proportional to the *molality* of the solute particles:

$$\Delta t_f = k_f m$$

where Δt_f is the freezing-point depression, k_f is the freezing-point-depression constant, and m is the molality of the solution. The depression of the freezing point could well be stated with a minus sign to denote the lowering, and the constant then would also have a negative value. It is customary, however, to report both as positive values. Therefore, it is necessary for us to remember that the solution has a lower freezing point than does the pure solvent. A set of freezing-point-depression constants along with freezing points is given in Table 11-1.

EXAMPLE 3 (*a*) Calculate the freezing-point depression of a 0.100 m solution of naphthalene in benzene. (*b*) Calculate the freezing point of the solution.

Solution The freezing point of benzene (the solvent) and its freezing-point constant are taken from Table 11-1.

(*a*) $\Delta t_f = k_f m = (5.12°C/m)(0.100 \text{ m}) = 0.512°C$
(*b*) $t = 5.5°C - 0.512°C = 5.0°C$

Note well the difference between freezing point and freezing-point depression! Also note that the freezing point of the solution is *below* that of the solvent. □

EXAMPLE 4 Which of the following has (*a*) the greatest freezing-point depression? (*b*) the highest freezing point?

1 m aqueous CH_3OH, 2 m aqueous CH_3OH,

or 3 m aqueous CH_3OH

Table 11-1 Freezing-Point Data

Solvent	Freezing Point (°C)	k_f(°C/m)
Benzene	5.5	5.12
Bromoform	7.8	14.4
Cyclohexane	6.5	20.0
Naphthalene	80.2	6.9
Water	0.00	1.86

Solution   (*a*) 3 m CH_3OH. The solution of highest concentration has the greatest freezing-point depression. (*b*) 1 m CH_3OH. The greater the *depression* of the freezing point, the lower is the freezing point, so the solution with smallest freezing-point depression has the highest freezing point.   □

The boiling point of a substance is the temperature at which its vapor pressure is equal to that of the surroundings. The boiling point of a solvent is elevated by the presence of a nonvolatile solute. This **boiling-point elevation**, like the freezing-point depression, is directly proportional to the *molality* of the solute particles:

$$\Delta t_b = k_b m$$

where Δt_b is the boiling-point elevation, k_b is the boiling-point-elevation constant, and m is the molality. A set of boiling-point-elevation constants, along with normal boiling points, are given in Table 11-2.

EXAMPLE 5   Determine the boiling point of a 0.100 m solution of sugar in water at 1.00 atm pressure.

Solution

$$\Delta t_b = k_b m = (0.512°C/m)(0.100\ m) = 0.0512°C$$

$$t = 100.00°C + 0.0512°C = 100.05°C$$

This problem, like the one in Example 3, must be done in two steps. Note that here the change in temperature was *added* to the normal boiling point (it is an elevation) whereas the change was subtracted in Example 3 (where a depression was observed).   □

EXAMPLE 6   Calculate the molality of a solution of a nonionic solute if its solution in naphthalene freezes at 77.7°C.

Table 11-2   Boiling-Point Data

Solvent	Normal Boiling Point (°C)	k_b (°C/m)
Benzene	80.12	2.53
Bromobenzene	155.83	6.26
Cyclohexane	80.88	2.79
Naphthalene	218	5.65
Water	100.00	0.512

Solution   Using data from Table 11-1, we calculate that the freezing-point depression is

$$80.2°C - 77.7°C = 2.5°C$$

and

$$\Delta t_f = k_f m = (6.9°C/m)(m) = 2.5°C$$

$$m = 0.36 \text{ m} \qquad \square$$

EXAMPLE 7   Calculate the value of the boiling-point-elevation constant for a solvent that boils at 53.8°C and for which a 0.359 m solution boils at 55.8°C.

Solution

$$\Delta t_b = 55.8°C - 53.8°C = 2.0°C$$

$$\Delta t_b = k_b m = (k_b)(0.359 \text{ m}) = 2.0°C$$

$$k_b = 5.6°C/m \qquad \square$$

Since these equations can get us molalities, we can use them with other data to determine molar masses.

EXAMPLE 8   Calculate the molar mass of a nonionic solute if 1.50 g of the solute in 55.2 g of benzene freezes at 4.3°C.

Solution   The freezing-point depression is 5.5°C − 4.3°C = 1.2°C. The molality of the solution is given by

$$\Delta t_f = k_f m = (5.12°C/m)(m) = 1.2°C$$

$$m = 0.23 \text{ m}$$

That means that there is 0.23 mol of solute in 1.00 kg of benzene. The data of the problem enable us to calculate the number of grams of solute in 1.00 kg of benzene:

$$\frac{1.50 \text{ g solute}}{55.2 \text{ g benzene}}\left(\frac{1000 \text{ g benzene}}{1 \text{ kg benzene}}\right) = \frac{27.2 \text{ g solute}}{1 \text{ kg benzene}}$$

That means that 0.23 mol is 27.2 g, and the molar mass is

$$(27.2 \text{ g})/(0.23 \text{ mol}) = 120 \text{ g/mol} = 1.2 \times 10^2 \text{ g/mol} \qquad \square$$

11.3 Osmotic Pressure

When a solution is separated from a sample of its pure solvent by a semipermeable membrane (Fig. 11-1), an **osmotic pressure**

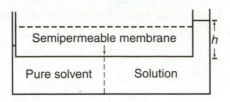

Fig. 11-1 Osmotic Pressure.

develops. This pressure stems from the fact that the solvent can pass through the membrane, but solute particles cannot. The solute particles partially block passage of solvent molecules from the solution into the pure solvent, but not the other way. The passage of more solvent into the solution tends to dilute the solution, even if it has to raise the level of the solution with respect to that of the solvent. An external piston can be used to keep the levels the same and prevent dilution of the solution (Fig. 11-2). This added pressure is the osmotic pressure of the solution. Osmotic pressure may be calculated with an equation very similar to the ideal gas equation (Chapter 7):

$$\pi V = nRT$$

where π is the osmotic pressure of the solution, and the other symbols have the same meanings they had earlier.

EXAMPLE 9   Calculate the osmotic pressure of a 0.100 M solution of a nonionic solute at 25°C.

Solution

$$\pi V = nRT$$

Dividing both sides of this equation by V yields an equation with *molarity* as one of the variables:

$$\pi = \left(\frac{n}{V}\right)(RT) = (0.100 \text{ M})(8.31 \text{ L·kPa/mol·K})(298 \text{ K}) = 248 \text{ kPa}$$

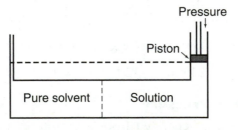

Fig. 11-2   Measurement of Osmotic Pressure.

This is a very large pressure indeed! Compared to other colligative properties, osmotic pressure measurements allow very precise determinations of molar masses. □

EXAMPLE 10 Determine the molar mass of a solute if 2.00 g in 100.0 mL of solution at 25°C has an osmotic pressure of 5.77 kPa.

Solution

$$\pi V = nRT$$

$$\frac{\pi}{RT} = \frac{n}{V} = M = \frac{5.77 \text{ kPa}}{(8.31 \text{ L·kPa/mol·K})(298 \text{ K})} = 0.00233 \text{ M}$$

There is 0.00233 mol per liter and 20.0 g per liter:

$$\frac{2.00 \text{ g solute}}{100.0 \text{ mL solution}} \left(\frac{1000 \text{ mL}}{1 \text{ L}} \right) = \frac{20.0 \text{ g}}{1 \text{ L}}$$

so the molar mass is

$$\frac{20.0 \text{ g}}{0.00233 \text{ mol}} = 8580 \text{ g/mol} = 8.58 \times 10^3 \text{ g/mol}$$

It would be impossible to determine the molar mass of this solute with a freezing-point depression experiment. (See Supplementary Problems 11 and 19.) □

11.4 Ionic Solutes

Ionic solutes are dissociated in solution into cations and anions. Thus a 1 m aqueous solution of NaCl contains 1 mol of Na^+ ions and 1 mol of Cl^- ions per kilogram of solvent. There are 2 mol of particles per kilogram of solvent, and therefore the colligative properties of the solution are greater than those of a 1 m solution of nonionic solute. In very dilute solutions, the colligative properties of solutions of ionic solutes are a multiple of the analogous properties of nonionic solutes. For example,

Compound	Constitution	No. of Particles Formula Unit
CH_3OH	1 molecule/formula unit	1
NaCl	2 ions/formula unit	2
$MgCl_2$	3 ions/formula unit	3
$AlCl_3$	4 ions/formula unit	4
$MgSO_4$	2 ions/formula unit	2

EXAMPLE 11 Which of the following 0.00100 m solutions has the greatest freezing-point depression?

$$NaCl \quad MgCl_2 \quad AlCl_3 \quad MgSO_4 \quad CH_3OH$$

Solution The 0.00100 m $AlCl_3$, which has four ions per formula unit, has the greatest freezing-point depression. It is 0.00400 m in particles. ☐

A solution of 0.00100 m NaCl has about twice the colligative properties as a solution of 0.00100 m CH_3OH, because there are twice the number of particles per kilogram of solvent. However, as the concentration of the ionic solution increases, the interionic attractions increase markedly, and the particles become less independent of each other. The solutions of ionic solutes still have greater colligative properties than solutions of equal concentrations of non-ionic solutes, but not as great a factor as the factor of the number of ions per formula unit. Thus NaCl might have 1.7 times the effect as CH_3OH (instead of 2 times the effect) in a certain more concentrated solution.

Leading Questions

1. Add the subscript "solvent" or "solute" to each term in each of the following equations for a two-component solution:
   (a) $P = (X \quad)(P^\circ \quad)$
   (b) $\Delta P = (X \quad)(P^\circ \quad)$
2. State the difference between each pair:
   (a) Vapor pressure and vapor-pressure lowering
   (b) Freezing point and freezing-point depression
   (c) Boiling point and boiling-point elevation
3. Does the liquid phase extend over a wider temperature range for a solution or for its pure solvent?

Answers to Leading Questions

1.
$$P_{solvent} = X_{solvent} P^\circ_{solvent}$$

$$\Delta P_{solvent} = X_{solute} P^\circ_{solvent}$$

2. The first item in each part is a property of a substance or a solution; the second is the colligative property of the solution—the difference between the property of the pure substance and that in the solution.

3. Since the freezing point is depressed and the boiling point is raised by the presence of a solute, the solution has a wider liquid range. (This fact might be useful to remind us which phase change is lowered and which is raised.)

Supplementary Problems

1. (a) Calculate the vapor pressure of ethyl alcohol containing glucose (a sugar) at 25°C in which the mole fraction of glucose is 0.0500. The vapor pressure of pure ethyl alcohol at 25°C is 59.0 torr. (b) Calculate the vapor-pressure lowering.

2. (a) Calculate the freezing-point depression of a 0.150 m solution of sucrose (table sugar) in water. (b) Calculate the freezing point of the solution.

3. Calculate the molality of a solution of a nonionic solute if its solution in cyclohexane freezes at 3.3°C.

4. Calculate the osmotic pressure of a solution of 0.225 mol of sucrose (sugar) in 1550 mL of aqueous solution at 25°C.

5. Determine the molar mass of a solute if 1.12 g in 157 mL of solution at 25°C has an osmotic pressure of 0.145 atm.

6. Calculate the freezing point of an aqueous solution of a nonvolatile solute with a boiling point of 101.55°C at 1.000 atm pressure.

7. Calculate the molar mass of a nonionic solute if 4.31 g of the solute in 155 g of cyclohexane freezes at 2.7°C.

8. Calculate the molar mass of a nonvolatile solute if a solution of 1.44 g of the solute in 55.0 g of cyclohexane, C_6H_{12}, has a vapor pressure of 0.103 atm at 20.7°C. The vapor pressure of pure cyclohexane at that temperature is 0.106 atm.

9. Calculate the freezing point of a solution of glucose (a simple sugar) in water with mole fraction of glucose equal to 0.0555.

10. Calculate the vapor-pressure lowering in a solution of 2.00 m aqueous sucrose (table sugar) at 25°C. The vapor pressure of pure water at that temperature is 3.20 kPa.

11. Calculate the freezing point of a solution of sucrose ($C_{12}H_{22}O_{11}$) in water if the density of the solution is 1.01 g/mL and its osmotic pressure at 25°C is 55.5 kPa.

12. Calculate the vapor pressure of a solution of sucrose (table sugar) in 1550 mL of aqueous solution at 25°C if its freezing point could be measured to be 0.00010°C. The vapor pressure of pure water at that temperature is 24.0 torr. (Assume that the density of the solution is 1.00 g/mL.)

13. Calculate the osmotic pressure of a solution of 0.00200 mol of NaCl in 345 mL of aqueous solution at 25°C.

14. Calculate the osmotic pressure of a solution of 0.00200 mol of $AlCl_3$ in 0.550 L of aqueous solution at 25°C.

15. Calculate the freezing point of a solution of 0.100 mol of KNO_3 in 0.500 kg of water at 25°C.

16. A solution of 4.31 g of solute in 149 g of cyclohexane freezes at 2.7°C. The solute contains 40.0% carbon, 6.67% hydrogen, and 53.3% oxygen. (a) What can we calculate from the change in freezing point and tabulated data? (b) What can we calculate from the masses and the answer to part (a)? (c) What can we calculate from the percent composition data? (d) What can we calculate from the answers to parts (b) and (c)?

17. A solution of 4.31 g of solute in 149 g of cyclohexane freezes at 2.7°C. The solute contains 40.0% carbon, 6.67% hydrogen, and 53.3% oxygen. (a) Calculate the molality of the solute. (b) Calculate the molar mass of the sample. (c) Calculate the empirical formula of the sample. (d) Calculate the molecular formula of the sample.

18. Calculate the molecular formula of 5.02 g of solute in 165 g of cyclohexane that freezes at 3.1°C. The solute contains 40.0% carbon, 6.67% hydrogen, and 53.3% oxygen.

19. Calculate the freezing-point depression of a solution containing 2.00 g of a solute (MM = 8580 g/mol) in 100.0 g (a) of water; (b) of bromoform (Table 11-1).

20. Calculate the molality of 0.00224 M aqueous sucrose. (Assume that the density of the solution is 1.01 g/mL.)

Solutions to Supplementary Problems

1. (a) The mole fraction of solvent is $1.0000 - 0.0500 = 0.9500$.

$$P_{solvent} = X_{solvent}P_{solvent}^{\circ}$$
$$= (0.9500)(59.0 \text{ torr}) = 56.1 \text{ torr}$$

(b) 59.0 torr − 56.1 torr = 2.9 torr
or
$$\Delta P_{solvent} = X_{solute}P_{solvent}^{\circ} = 0.0500(59.0 \text{ torr}) = 2.95 \text{ torr}$$

2. (a) $\Delta t_f = k_f m = (1.86°C/m)(0.150 \text{ m}) = 0.279°C$

(b) $t = 0.000°C - 0.279°C = -0.279°C$
Be careful. The freezing point of the solution is equal in magnitude to the freezing-point depression, because the freezing

point of water is 0.000°C. No other solvent has a freezing point of zero, so don't expect the magnitude of the freezing point to be equal to the magnitude of the freezing-point depression in general.

3. Using data from Table 11-1, we find that the freezing-point depression is

$$\Delta t_f = 6.5°C - 3.3°C = 3.2°C$$

$$= k_f m = (20.0°C/m)(m) = 3.2°C$$

$$m = 0.16\ m$$

4. $\pi V = nRT$

$$\pi = \frac{nRT}{V} = \frac{(0.225\ mol)(0.0821\ L\cdot atm/mol\cdot K)(298\ K)}{1.55\ L} = 3.55\ atm$$

5. $\pi V = nRT$

$$\frac{\pi}{RT} = \frac{n}{V} = M = \frac{0.145\ atm}{(0.0821\ L\cdot atm/mol\cdot K)(298\ K)} = 0.00593\ M$$

$$\frac{1.12\ g\ solute}{157\ mL\ solution}\left(\frac{1000\ mL}{1\ L}\right) = \frac{7.13\ g}{1\ L}$$

There is 0.00593 mol of solute per liter and 7.13 g per liter, so the molar mass is

$$\frac{7.13\ g}{0.00593\ mol} = 1200\ g/mol = 1.20 \times 10^3\ g/mol$$

6. First we calculate the molality from the Δt_b:

$$\Delta t_b = k_b m = 1.55°C = (0.512°C/m)(m)$$

$$m = 3.03\ m$$

Then we calculate the Δt_f from the molality:

$$\Delta t_f = k_f m = (1.86°C/m)(3.03\ m) = 5.64°C$$

The freezing point is $0.00°C - 5.64°C = -5.64°C$

7. $\Delta t_f = k_f m = (20.0°C/m)(m) = 6.5°C - 2.7°C = 3.8°C$

$$= m(20.0°C/m)$$

$$m = 0.19\ m$$

The number of grams of solute per kilogram of solvent is

$$\frac{4.31 \text{ g solute}}{155 \text{ g solvent}}\left(\frac{1000 \text{ g solvent}}{1 \text{ kg solvent}}\right) = \frac{27.8 \text{ g solute}}{1 \text{ kg solvent}}$$

$$\frac{27.8 \text{ g}}{0.19 \text{ mol}} = 150 \text{ g/mol} = 1.5 \times 10^2 \text{ g/mol}$$

8. $55.0 \text{ g } C_6H_{12}\left(\dfrac{1 \text{ mol } C_6H_{12}}{84.0 \text{ g } C_6H_{12}}\right) = 0.655 \text{ mol } C_6H_{12}$

$$P_{\text{solvent}} = X_{\text{solvent}} P^{\circ}_{\text{solvent}}$$

$$0.103 \text{ atm} = (X_{\text{solvent}})(0.106 \text{ atm})$$

$$X_{\text{solvent}} = 0.972 = \frac{0.655 \text{ mol}}{0.655 \text{ mol} + y \text{ mol}}$$

$$0.637 + 0.972y = 0.655$$

$$0.972y = 0.018$$

$$y = 0.019 \text{ mol solute}$$

$$MM = (1.44 \text{ g})/(0.019 \text{ mol}) = 76 \text{ g/mol}$$

9. Freezing-point depression is directly proportional to *molality*, so we first change the mole fraction of glucose to molality of glucose. Assuming that we have 1.0000 mol total, there are present 0.0555 mol of glucose and

$$0.9445 \text{ mol } H_2O\left(\frac{18.0 \text{ g } H_2O}{1 \text{ mol } H_2O}\right)\left(\frac{1 \text{ kg } H_2O}{1000 \text{ g } H_2O}\right) = 0.0170 \text{ kg } H_2O$$

The molality of glucose is then
$(0.0555 \text{ mol})/(0.0170 \text{ kg } H_2O) = 3.26 \text{ m}.$

$$\Delta t_f = k_f m = (1.86°C/m)(3.26 \text{ m}) = 6.06°C$$

$$t = -6.06°C$$

10. Vapor-pressure lowering is directly proportional to *mole fraction of solute*, so we first change the molality of the sucrose to mole fraction of sucrose:

Assuming that we have 1.00 kg of water, we have 2.00 mol of sucrose and

$$1000 \text{ g } H_2O\left(\frac{1 \text{ mol } H_2O}{18.0 \text{ g } H_2O}\right) = 55.6 \text{ mol } H_2O$$

The mole fraction of sucrose is then $(2.00 \text{ mol})/(57.6 \text{ mol total}) = 0.0347$.

$$\Delta P_{solvent} = X_{solute} P^{\circ}_{solvent} = (0.0347)(3.20 \text{ kPa}) = 0.111 \text{ kPa}$$

11. The osmotic pressure can get us the molarity:

$$\pi V = nRT$$

$$M = \frac{\pi}{RT} = \frac{n}{V} = \frac{55.5 \text{ kPa}}{(8.31 \text{ L·kPa/mol·K})(298 \text{ K})} = 0.0224 \text{ M}$$

Assume that we have 1.00 L, that is 1.01 kg of solution and 0.0224 mol sucrose.

$$0.0224 \text{ mol } C_{12}H_{22}O_{11} \left(\frac{344 \text{ g } C_{12}H_{22}O_{11}}{1 \text{ mol } C_{12}H_{22}O_{11}} \right) = 7.71 \text{ g } C_{12}H_{22}O_{11}$$

The mass of water then is $1.01 \text{ kg} - 0.00771 \text{ kg} = 1.00 \text{ kg}$
The molality of the sucrose is 0.0224 m, and its freezing-point depression is

$$\Delta t_f = k_f m = (1.86°C/m)(0.0224 \text{ m}) = 0.0417°C$$

$$t = -0.0417°C$$

Notice how a solution with a significant osmotic pressure has an extremely tiny freezing-point depression. Osmotic pressure is much more sensitive a measure of solute concentration than freezing-point depression is.

12. $\Delta t_f = k_f m = (1.86°C/m)(m) = 0.00010°C$
$m = 5.4 \times 10^{-5} \text{ m}$
If we assume that we have 1.00 kg of water, we have 55.6 mol of water and 5.4×10^{-5} mol of sucrose. The mole fraction of sucrose is

$$(5.4 \times 10^{-5} \text{ mol})/(55.6 \text{ mol total}) = 9.7 \times 10^{-7}$$

and the vapor-pressure depression is

$$\Delta P_{solvent} = X_{solute} P^{\circ}_{solvent} = (9.7 \times 10^{-7})(24.0 \text{ torr}) = 2.3 \times 10^{-5} \text{ torr}$$

Vapor-pressure lowering is not significantly more precise than freezing-point depression is.

13. $\pi V = nRT$

In such a dilute solution, the ions act almost independently. There are 0.00200 mol of sodium ions and 0.00200 mol of chloride ions in the solution, for a total of 0.00400 mol of solute particles:

$$\pi = \frac{nRT}{V} = \frac{(0.00400 \text{ mol})(0.0821 \text{ L·atm/mol·K})(298 \text{ K})}{0.345 \text{ L}}$$

$$= 0.284 \text{ atm}$$

14. The $AlCl_3$ solution is dilute enough to expect four moles of completely independent ions (1 mol of Al^{3+} and 3 mol of Cl^-) in each mole of $AlCl_3$. Therefore, there are 0.00800 mol of ions.

$$\pi V = nRT$$

$$\pi = \frac{nRT}{V} = \frac{(0.00800 \text{ mol})(0.0821 \text{ L·atm/mol·K})(298 \text{ K})}{0.550 \text{ L}}$$

$$= 0.356 \text{ atm}$$

15. The KNO_3 dissociates into 2 mol of ions (1 mol K^+ and 1 mol NO_3^-) for each mole of salt. The molality of particles is $(0.200 \text{ mol})/(0.500 \text{ kg}) = 0.400 \text{ m}$. Neglecting the interionic attractions,

$$\Delta t_f = k_f m = (1.86°\text{C/m})(0.400 \text{ m}) = 0.744°\text{C}$$

The freezing point is $-0.744°\text{C}$ (or perhaps a little higher due to interionic attractions).

16. (a) The molality of the solute.

(b) The molar mass of the solute.

(c) The empirical formula.

(d) The molecular formula. (See the next two problems.)

17. (a) $\Delta t_f = k_f m = (20.0°\text{C/m})(m) = 6.5°\text{C} - 2.7°\text{C} = 3.8°\text{C}$

$$= m(20.0°\text{C/m})$$

$$m = 0.19 \text{ m}$$

(b) The number of grams of solute per kilogram of solvent is

$$\frac{4.31 \text{ g solute}}{149 \text{ g solvent}} \left(\frac{1000 \text{ g solvent}}{1 \text{ kg solvent}} \right) = \frac{28.9 \text{ g solute}}{1 \text{ kg solvent}}$$

$$MM = \frac{28.9 \text{ g/kg solvent}}{0.19 \text{ mol/kg solvent}} = 150 \text{ g/mol} = 1.5 \times 10^2 \text{ g/mol}$$

(c) $\quad 40.0 \text{ g C}\left(\dfrac{1 \text{ mol C}}{12.0 \text{ g C}}\right) = 3.33 \text{ mol C}$

$\quad 6.67 \text{ g H}\left(\dfrac{1 \text{ mol H}}{1.008 \text{ g H}}\right) = 6.62 \text{ mol H}$

$\quad 53.3 \text{ g O}\left(\dfrac{1 \text{ mol O}}{16.0 \text{ g O}}\right) = 3.33 \text{ mol O}$

The mole ratio is 1 mol C : 2 mol H : 1 mol O.
The empirical formula is CH_2O.

(d) The empirical formula mass is 30.0 g/mol, the molar mass is 150 g/mol, so there are five empirical formula units per molecule, and the molecular formula is $C_5H_{10}O_5$.

18. This problem is similar to Problem 17, but it is not stated in parts. The molecular formula is $C_6H_{12}O_6$.

19. The number of moles of solute is

$2.00 \text{ g}\left(\dfrac{1 \text{ mol}}{8580 \text{ g}}\right) = 2.33 \times 10^{-4} \text{ mol}$

The molality is $(2.33 \times 10^{-4} \text{ mol})/(0.1000 \text{ kg}) = 2.33 \times 10^{-3} \text{ m}$

(a) $\Delta t_f = k_f m = (1.86°\text{C/m})(2.33 \times 10^{-3} \text{ m}) = (4.33 \times 10^{-3})°\text{C}$

(b) $\Delta t_f = k_f m = (14.4°\text{C/m})(2.33 \times 10^{-3} \text{ m}) = (3.36 \times 10^{-2})°\text{C}$

These changes in temperature would be very difficult to measure.

20. Assume that we have 1.00 L, that is 1.01 kg of solution and 0.00224 mol sucrose.

$0.00224 \text{ mol } C_{12}H_{22}O_{11}\left(\dfrac{344 \text{ g } C_{12}H_{22}O_{11}}{1 \text{ mol } C_{12}H_{22}O_{11}}\right) = 7.71 \text{ g } C_{12}H_{22}O_{11}$

The mass of water then is $1.01 \text{ kg} - 0.00771 \text{ kg} = 1.00 \text{ kg}$
The molality of the sucrose is 0.0224 m.

Chapter 12

Thermodynamics

Before studying this chapter, review the measurement of enthalpy change (Chapter 8), potential (Chapter 9), and equilibrium (Chapter 10). As usual with quantities of energy, we must be very careful with both units and signs. For example, Tables 12-1 and 12-2 include entropy in units including *joules* and free energy change in units including *kilojoules*.

12.1 Entropy

Entropy, denoted S, is a quantitative measure of randomness. (Be careful with this word; it sounds very much like enthalpy, introduced in Chapter 8.) In order to confirm that our answers to problems are reasonable, we must know (1) that greater numbers of moles, especially of gases, have greater randomness than smaller numbers of moles (other factors being equal), (2) that gases have much greater randomness than liquids, which have greater randomness than solids, (3) that greater volumes of gases have greater randomness than smaller volumes (other factors being equal), and (4) similarly, higher temperatures imply greater randomness. Unlike enthalpy change (Chapter 8), entropy is *not* a relative quantity. Absolute entropy, is a measure of the actual randomness of a substance or a system. The **standard absolute entropies**, $S°$, of selected substances are presented in Table 12-1. *Standard* means the substance is at unit activity, where the activity of a pure solid or liquid is defined as 1, the activity of a solute is equal to its molarity, and that of a gas is equal to its pressure in atmospheres or its number of moles per liter. The entropy of a pure, crystalline solid at 0 K is zero. Warming the substance to room temperature gives it an entropy above zero. No substance can have a negative randomness, so none can have a negative absolute entropy (but *entropy changes*

Table 12-1 Absolute Entropies of Selected Substances at 298 K

Substance	State	$S°$ (J/mol·K)	Substance	State	$S°$ (J/mol·K)
C	s	5.69	NO	g	210.62
CO	g	197.9	NO_2	g	240.45
CO_2	g	213.6	H_2O	g	188.83
Cl_2	g	222.96	H_2O	l	69.91
Ca	s	41.4	H_2O_2	l	109.6
H_2	g	130.58	Na	s	51.45
HCl	g	186.69	NaCl	s	72.33
O_2	g	205.0	N_2	g	191.50

can be negative). Note especially that the entropies of elements are *not* zero at room temperature, as are their enthalpies of formation by definition.

For a chemical reaction, we calculate the entropy change by subtracting the total absolute entropy of the reactants from the total absolute entropy of the products:

$$\Delta S° = S°(\text{products}) - S°(\text{reactants})$$

The units of ΔS for a given equation are J/K since the units *mole* cancel out.

EXAMPLE I   Calculate the standard entropy change for the reaction of a mole of carbon monoxide with oxygen to produce carbon dioxide at 25°C.

Solution   The absolute entropies are taken from Table 12-1. Note the units.

$$CO(g) + \tfrac{1}{2} O_2(g) \rightarrow CO_2(g)$$

$$\Delta S° = S°(\text{products}) - S°(\text{reactants})$$

$$= (1 \text{ mol } CO_2)(213.6 \text{ J/mol·K}) - (1 \text{ mol } CO)(197.9 \text{ J/mol·K})$$

$$- \left(\tfrac{1}{2} \text{ mol } O_2 \right)(205.0 \text{ J/mol·K}) = -86.8 \text{ J/K}$$

The negative value signifies that there is a lowering of the randomness (because the reaction has reduced the number of moles of gas). Note that the units include kelvins. Note also that the element in its standard state has a finite (nonzero) entropy, unlike its enthalpy of formation (Chapter 8). □

12.2 Gibbs Free Energy Change

The **free energy change**, ΔG, is equal to the enthalpy change minus the product of the absolute temperature times the entropy change. Its value enables us to predict in which direction an equation will proceed, or if the system is at equilibrium. It is defined as

$$\Delta G = \Delta H - T\Delta S$$

We will use this equation extensively.

EXAMPLE 2 Calculate the free energy change for a reaction at 25°C in which the enthalpy change is 24.4 kJ and the entropy change is 35.1 J/K.

Solution

$$\Delta G = \Delta H - T\Delta S$$
$$= 24.4\,\text{kJ} - (298\,\text{K})(0.0351\,\text{kJ/K}) = 13.9\,\text{kJ}$$

Note that it was necessary to convert joules to kilojoules (or vice versa) and also that the kelvins in the second term canceled. □

The free energy of a substance, like its enthalpy, is a relative quantity. **Standard free energy of formation**, ΔG_f°, of a substance is the free energy change of the reaction of the elements in their standard states to produce the substance in its standard state, quite analogous to the enthalpy of formation. Also analogous is the fact that the free energy of formation of an *element* in its standard state is zero by definition. Standard free energy changes of selected substances are presented in Table 12-2. The equation given above for ΔG, with all quantities in their standard states, becomes:

$$\Delta G^\circ = \Delta H^\circ - T\Delta S^\circ$$

We must be very careful to use the degree sign where and only where it is supposed to be used; that sign on the thermodynamic functions means that all substances are in their standard states (Chapter 8). Any equation that is true for ΔG in general is also true for ΔG° (under the special conditions of unit activities for all reactants and products). The reverse is *not* true.

Table 12-2 Standard Free Energies of Formation of Selected
Substances at 298 K

Substance	State	ΔG_f° (kJ/mol)	Substance	State	ΔG_f° (kJ/mol)
CO	g	−137.2	NO	g	86.71
CO_2	g	−394.4	NO_2	g	51.84
HCl	g	−95.27	H_2O	g	−228.57
NaCl	s	−384.0	H_2O	l	−237.13
Na_2CO_3	s	−1048	H_2O_2	l	−120.4
CH_4	g	−50.8			

EXAMPLE 3 Calculate the standard enthalpy of formation of NO(g)
at 298 K from data in Tables 12-1 and 12-2.

Solution

$$\tfrac{1}{2} N_2(g) + \tfrac{1}{2} O_2(g) \rightarrow NO(g)$$

$$\Delta S^\circ = (1 \text{ mol NO})(210.62 \text{ J/mol·K}) - (\tfrac{1}{2} \text{ mol } N_2)(191.50 \text{ J/mol·K})$$

$$- (\tfrac{1}{2} \text{ mol } O_2)(205.0 \text{ J/mol·K}) = 12.4 \text{ J/K}$$

Since this reaction represents the formation of a compound from its
elements in their standard states,

$$\Delta G^\circ = \Delta G_f^\circ(NO) = 86.71 \text{ kJ}$$

$$\Delta G^\circ = \Delta H^\circ - T\Delta S^\circ = \Delta H^\circ - (298 \text{ K})(12.4 \text{ J/K})$$

$$= \Delta H^\circ - (298 \text{ K})(0.0124 \text{ kJ/K})$$

$$\Delta H^\circ = 86.71 \text{ kJ} + 3.70 \text{ kJ} = 90.41 \text{ kJ}$$

Note that $S^\circ(NO)$ is not ΔS_f, and cannot be used directly in the
equation for ΔG. □

We can determine the free energy change of any reaction if
we have the free energies of formation of all the substances in the
reaction, analogous to ΔH°:

$$\Delta G^\circ = \Delta G_f^\circ(\text{products}) - \Delta G_f^\circ(\text{reactants})$$

The principles of Hess's law (Chapter 8) also apply to free energy
change calculations.

EXAMPLE 4 Calculate the value of $\Delta G°$ at 25°C for the reaction of 125 g of NO with O_2 to produce NO_2.

Solution

$$NO(g) + \tfrac{1}{2}O_2(g) \rightarrow NO_2(g)$$

For 1 mol of NO(g):

$$\Delta G° = \Delta G_f°(\text{products}) - \Delta G_f°(\text{reactants})$$

$$= \Delta G_f°(NO_2) - \Delta G_f°(NO)$$

$$= 51.84\,\text{kJ} - (86.71\,\text{kJ}) = -34.87\,\text{kJ}$$

For 125 g of NO:

$$125\,\text{g NO} \left(\frac{1\text{ mol NO}}{30.0\text{ g NO}} \right) \left(\frac{-34.87\,\text{kJ}}{1\text{ mol NO}} \right) = -145\,\text{kJ}$$

Note that $\Delta G_f°$ of O_2 is zero, because O_2 is an element in its standard state. ☐

The sign of the free energy change enables us to predict if a reaction (or other process) proceeds as written, goes in the opposite direction, or neither (because the system is at equilibrium).

ΔG	Direction of Spontaneous Reaction
Negative	Spontaneous as written
Zero	At equilibrium
Positive	Spontaneous in the opposite direction

There are two tendencies that tend to make a process spontaneous: (1) change to a lower energy and (2) change to a greater randomness. In a given process, if the energy of a system decreases (ΔH is negative) and its randomness increases (ΔS is positive), the process is spontaneous as written at all temperatures (because ΔG is always negative).

$$\Delta G \quad = \quad \Delta H \quad - \quad T\Delta S$$

negative   negative minus (positive × positive)

If the energy of a system increases and its randomness decreases, the process is spontaneous in the opposite direction at all temperatures (ΔG is always positive). If both ΔH and ΔS increase or both decrease, the term with the larger magnitude determines in which direction the process is spontaneous, and that depends on the temperature. For example, consider ice and water at 0°C.

$$H_2O(s) \rightarrow H_2O(l)$$

The randomness increases as the solid melts, but the energy increases also. At 0°C, the two balance each other and the system is at equilibrium. ΔG is 0. If we raise the temperature slightly,

$$\Delta G = \Delta H - T\Delta S$$

since T increases, the randomness term $(T\Delta S)$ becomes greater in magnitude, ΔG becomes negative, the process becomes spontaneous, and the ice melts. In contrast, if we decrease the temperature from 0°C slightly, the randomness term decreases, making the energy term more important, ΔG becomes positive, and the equilibrium shifts to the left (toward lower energy). The liquid water freezes.

Neither ΔH nor ΔS change much with temperature. We can use that fact to estimate values of ΔG at temperatures other than 25°C with the data from Table 12-2.

EXAMPLE 5 Given the following values for a certain reaction at 25°C: $\Delta H = -10.00$ kJ and $\Delta S = -25.0$ J/K. Calculate the value of ΔG for the reaction at (a) 25°C; (b) 125°C.

Solution

(a) $\Delta G = \Delta H - T\Delta S = -10.00$ kJ $- (298$ K$)(-25.0$ J/K$)$

$\qquad = -10.00$ kJ $- (298$ K$)(-0.0250$ kJ/K$)$

$\qquad = -10.00$ kJ $+ 7.45$ kJ $= -2.55$ kJ

(Note the conversion of joules to kilojoules.)

(b) $\Delta G = \Delta H - T\Delta S = -10.00$ kJ $- (398$ K$)(-25.0$ J/K$)$

$\qquad = -10.00$ kJ $+ 9.95$ kJ $= -0.05$ kJ

The same values of ΔH and ΔS were used at the higher temperature, but a very different value of ΔG was obtained. ☐

12.3 Relationship of $\Delta G°$ to K

The free energy change of a chemical reaction is dependent on the activities of the substances in the chemical equation (Section 12-1 and Chapter 9). The relationship is

$$\Delta G = \Delta G° + RT \ln Q$$

where R and T have their usual meanings and Q is the concentration ratio as described in Chapter 9.

EXAMPLE 6 Determine the value of ΔG at 25°C for the general reaction

$$A(aq) + 2\,B(aq) \rightarrow 2\,C(aq)$$

for which $\Delta G° = -11.0\,kJ$, if the A concentration is 0.500 M, the B concentration is 0.150 M, and the C concentration is 2.00 M.

Solution

$$\Delta G = \Delta G° + RT\ln Q$$

$$= \Delta G° + (8.31\,J/K)(298\,K)\ln \frac{[C]^2}{[A][B]^2}$$

$$= -11.0\,kJ + (8.31\,J/K)(298\,K)\ln \frac{(2.00)^2}{(0.500)(0.150)^2} = 3.5\,kJ \quad \square$$

EXAMPLE 7 Determine if the following reaction is spontaneous at 25°C:

$$CH_4(g) + 2\,O_2(g) \rightarrow CO_2(g) + 2\,H_2O(l)$$

Solution We can determine the value of $\Delta G°$ from the data of Table 12-2:

$$\Delta G° = \Delta G_f°(\text{products}) - \Delta G_f°(\text{reactants})$$

$$= \Delta G_f°(CO_2) + 2\Delta G_f°(H_2O) - \Delta G_f°(CH_4) - 2\Delta G_f°(O_2)$$

$$= (-394.4\,kJ) + 2\,mol(-237.13\,kJ/mol) - (-50.8\,kJ)$$

$$-2\,mol(0\,kJ/mol) = -817.9\,kJ$$

Since the value of $\Delta G°$ is so highly negative, ΔG must also be negative, and the reaction is spontaneous as written. $\quad \square$

We can derive another useful relationship if we solve the equation for ΔG for the special case of a reaction at equilibrium. At that point, the value of ΔG (but not $\Delta G°$) is zero, and the value of Q is K:

In general: $\qquad\qquad \Delta G = \Delta G° + RT\ln Q$
At equilibrium: $\qquad\quad 0 = \Delta G° + RT\ln K$
or $\qquad\qquad\qquad \Delta G° = -RT\ln K$

This equation relates the free energy change *under standard conditions* to the molarity ratio *at equilibrium*! If ΔG° is positive, $\ln K$ is negative, and K is less than 1.

EXAMPLE 8 Calculate the value of the equilibrium constant for a reaction with ΔG° equal to 255 J at 25°C. Comment on the magnitude of the constant.

Solution

$$\Delta G^\circ = -RT \ln K = 255\,J = -(8.31\,J/K)(298\,K) \ln K$$

$$\ln K = -0.103$$

$$K = 0.902$$

The positive value of ΔG° means that the equilibrium constant has a value less than 1 since it suggests that the equation would spontaneously shift left from its concentrations at unit activity (all 1). □

12.4 Relationship of ΔG to Potential

We have seen that a negative value of ΔG means that a reaction may proceed spontaneously in the direction of the equation as written and, in Chapter 9, that an electrochemical reaction will proceed as written if the potential is positive. We may wonder if there is any connection between free energy change and potential, and indeed there is:

$$\Delta G = -\epsilon nF$$

where ϵ is the potential, n is the number of moles of electrons, and F is the Faraday constant, 96,500 C/mol e⁻. The minus sign is easy to remember, since the potential is positive and the free energy change is negative for spontaneous reactions.

EXAMPLE 9 Calculate the free energy change for a two-electron reaction in which the potential is −5.00 V.

Solution

$$\Delta G = -\epsilon nF = -(-5.00\,V)(2\,mol\ e^-)(96,500\,C/mol\ e^-)$$

$$= 965,000\,J = 965\,kJ$$

Note that 1 C times 1 V equals 1 J (and that the answer has been converted to kilojoules for significant digit purposes). A negative potential has produced a positive free energy change, both indicating that the reverse reaction is spontaneous. □

Leading Questions

1. Simplify the following equation for standard conditions:

$$\Delta G = \Delta G^\circ + RT \ln Q$$

2. In the equation $\Delta G = \Delta G^\circ + RT \ln Q$ (Section 12.3), substitute $-\epsilon nF$ and $-\epsilon^\circ nF$ for ΔG and ΔG°, respectively. What equation results?

Answers to Leading Questions

1. At standard conditions, the value of Q is 1, its natural log (ln) is 0, and $\Delta G = \Delta G^\circ$, as expected, leading to the identity $\Delta G^\circ = \Delta G^\circ$.

2. $\Delta G = \Delta G^\circ + RT \ln Q$

   $-\epsilon nF = -\epsilon^\circ nF + RT \ln Q$

   Dividing each side by $-nF$ yields

   $$\epsilon = \epsilon^\circ - \frac{RT}{nF} \ln Q$$

   which is the Nernst equation (in the form of its natural logarithm instead of its common logarithm).

Supplementary Problems

1. (a) Calculate the value of ΔS° for the reaction of carbon with oxygen to produce carbon dioxide. (b) Explain why this ΔS° has a lower magnitude than does the ΔS° calculated in Example 1 for carbon monoxide and oxygen.

2. Calculate the ΔG° of vaporization of a mole of water at 25°C.

3. Calculate the free energy change for a reaction at 80°C in which the enthalpy change is 14.88 kJ and the entropy change is 7.44 J/K.

4. Calculate the enthalpy of combustion of $NO(g)$ to $NO_2(g)$ at 298 K from data in Tables 12-1 and 12-2.

5. Calculate the value of ΔG° for the reaction at 25°C of 2.65 g of CH_4 with O_2 to produce $CO_2(g)$ and $H_2O(l)$.

6. Given the following values for a certain reaction at 25°C: $\Delta H = 4.22$ kJ and $\Delta S = -6.10$ J/K. Calculate the value of ΔG for the reaction at 125°C.

7. Determine the value of ΔG at 25°C for the general reaction

$$2\,A(aq) + B(aq) \rightarrow C(aq)$$

for which $\Delta G° = -877$ J, if the A concentration is 0.750 M, the B concentration is 1.75 M, and the C concentration is 0.330 M.

8. Calculate the potential for a three-electron reaction in which the free energy change is -12.7 kJ.

9. Calculate the value of Q at which a reaction with $\Delta G° = -1.000$ kJ would not be spontaneous at 25°C.

10. Calculate the value of T at which a reaction with $\Delta H = -5.01$ kJ and $\Delta S = -10.0$ J/K would not be spontaneous.

11. A two-electron reaction in a voltaic cell has a standard potential at 25°C of 0.130 V. Calculate the value of the equilibrium constant for the reaction.

12. A voltaic cell

$$3\,M(s) + 2\,AuCl_4^{-}(aq) \rightarrow 8\,Cl^{-}(aq) + 3\,M^{2+}(aq) + 2\,Au(s)$$

operating at 25°C has a potential of -0.250 V when $[AuCl_4^{-}] = 0.110$ M, $[Cl^{-}] = 1.00$ M, and $[M^{2+}] = 0.500$ M.
(a) How many electrons are involved in the reaction?
(b) Calculate the value of $\epsilon°$. (c) Calculate the value of $\Delta G°$.
(d) Calculate the value of K.

13. A voltaic cell

$$3\,M(s) + 2\,AuCl_4^{-}(aq) \rightarrow 8\,Cl^{-}(aq) + 3\,M^{2+}(aq) + 2\,Au(s)$$

operating at 25°C has a potential of -0.25 V when $[AuCl_4^{-}] = 0.110$ M, $[Cl^{-}] = 1.00$ M, and $[M^{2+}] = 0.500$ M. Calculate the value of K.

14. Derive one equation relating the variables of the voltaic cell of the prior problem to its equilibrium constant.

15. Calculate the value of K for the following reaction at 25°C:

$$CH_4(g) + 2\,O_2(g) \rightarrow CO_2(g) + 2\,H_2O(l)$$

16. Calculate the value of K for a two-electron electrochemical reaction at 25°C in which

$$\epsilon° = -0.00100\ V$$

17. Calculate the value of K for each of the following reactions at 25°C:

(a) $2\,CH_4(g) + 3\,O_2(g) \rightarrow 2\,CO(g) + 4\,H_2O(l)$
(b) $CH_4(g) + 1.5\,O_2(g) \rightarrow CO(g) + 2\,H_2O(l)$

18. Compare the values of K in the two parts of Problem 17, and explain the results.

Solutions to Supplementary Problems

1. (a) $C(s) + O_2(g) \rightarrow CO_2(g)$

$$\Delta S° = S°(\text{products}) - S°(\text{reactants})$$

$$= (1 \text{ mol } CO_2)(213.6 \text{ J/mol·K}) - (1 \text{ mol } C)(5.69 \text{ J/mol·K}) -$$

$$(1 \text{ mol } O_2)(205.0 \text{ J/mol·K}) = 2.9 \text{ J/K}$$

(b) The number of moles of *gas* is the same on each side of the equation (and the total number of moles decreases).

2. $H_2O(l) \rightarrow H_2O(g)$

$$\Delta G° = \Delta G_f°(\text{products}) - \Delta G_f°(\text{reactants})$$

$$= \Delta G_f°\{H_2O(g)\} - \Delta G_f°\{H_2O(l)\}$$

$$= (-228.57 \text{ kJ}) - (-237.13 \text{ kJ}) = +8.56 \text{ kJ}$$

3. $\Delta G = \Delta H - T\Delta S = 14.88 \text{ kJ} - (353 \text{ K})(0.00744 \text{ kJ/K}) = 12.25 \text{ kJ}$

4. $NO(g) + \frac{1}{2} O_2(g) \rightarrow NO_2(g)$
First we calculate $\Delta S°$, then $\Delta G°$, and finally $\Delta H°$:

$$\Delta S° = (1 \text{ mol } NO_2)(240.45 \text{ J/mol·K}) - (1 \text{ mol } NO)(210.62 \text{ J/mol·K}) -$$

$$\left(\tfrac{1}{2} \text{ mol } O_2\right)(205.0 \text{ J/mol·K}) = -72.7 \text{ J/K}$$

$$\Delta G° = \Delta G_f°(\text{products}) - \Delta G_f°(\text{reactants})$$

$$= \Delta G_f°(NO_2) - \Delta G_f°(NO) - \tfrac{1}{2}\Delta G_f°(O_2)$$

$$= (51.84 \text{ kJ}) - (86.71 \text{ kJ}) - 0 \text{ kJ} = -34.87 \text{ kJ}$$

$$\Delta G° = \Delta H° - T\Delta S° = \Delta H° - (298 \text{ K})(-72.7 \text{ J/K}) = -34.87 \text{ kJ}$$

$$\Delta H° = (-34.87 \text{ kJ}) - 21.7 \text{ kJ} = -56.6 \text{ kJ}$$

5. For 1 mol of $CH_4(g)$:

$$CH_4(g) + 2 O_2(g) \rightarrow CO_2(g) + 2 H_2O(l)$$

$$\Delta G^\circ = \Delta G_f^\circ(\text{products}) - \Delta G_f^\circ(\text{reactants})$$
$$= \Delta G_f^\circ(CO_2) + 2\Delta G_f^\circ(H_2O) - \Delta G_f^\circ(CH_4) - 2\Delta G_f^\circ(O_2)$$
$$= (-394.4\,kJ) + 2\,mol(-237.13\,kJ/mol) - (-50.8\,kJ) -$$
$$2\,mol(0\,kJ/mol) = -817.9\,kJ$$

For 2.65 g of CH_4:

$$2.65\,g\;CH_4\left(\frac{1\,mol\;CH_4}{16.0\,g\;CH_4}\right)\left(\frac{-817.9\,kJ}{1\,mol\;CH_4}\right) = -135\,kJ$$

6. Because ΔH and ΔS do not change much with temperature, we can use their 25°C values at 125°C:

$$\Delta G = \Delta H - T\Delta S = 4.22\,kJ - (398\,K)(-6.10\,J/K)$$
$$= 4.22\,kJ + 2.43\,kJ = 6.65\,kJ$$

7. $\Delta G = \Delta G^\circ + RT \ln Q$

$$= \Delta G^\circ + (8.31\,J/K)(298\,K)\ln\frac{[C]}{[A]^2[B]}$$

$$= (-877\,J) + (8.31\,J/K)(298\,K)\ln\frac{(0.330)}{(0.750)^2(1.75)} = -3580\,J$$

8.
$$\Delta G = -\epsilon nF$$
$$-12,700\,J = -(\epsilon)(3\,mol\;e^-)(96,500\,C/mol\;e^-)$$
$$\epsilon = +0.0439\,V$$

Note that 1 J divided by 1 C equals 1 V.

9. For the reaction to be nonspontaneous, ΔG must be zero (or positive).

$$\Delta G = 0 = \Delta G^\circ + RT \ln Q$$
$$0 = -1000\,J + (8.31\,J/K)(298\,K)\ln Q$$
$$\ln Q = 0.404$$
$$Q = 1.50$$

10. For the reaction to be nonspontaneous, ΔG must be zero (or positive).

$$\Delta G = \Delta H - T\Delta S$$
$$0 = (-5010\,J) - T(-10.0\,J/K)$$
$$T = 501\,K$$

11. $\Delta G° = -\epsilon°nF = -(0.130\,V)(2\,mol\,e^-)(96,500\,C/mol\,e^-)$

$= -25,100\,J$

$\Delta G° = -RT\,\ln K = -25,100\,J = -(8.31\,J/K)(298\,K)\,\ln K$

$\ln K = 10.1$

$K = 2 \times 10^4$

12. (a) 6 (equal to the total change in oxidation number of M or Au)

(b) $$\epsilon = \epsilon° - \frac{0.0592}{n}\,\log\,\frac{[Cl^-]^8[M^{2+}]^3}{[AuCl_4^-]^2}$$

$$-0.250 = \epsilon° - \frac{0.0592}{6}\,\log\,\frac{(1.00)^8(0.500)^3}{(0.110)^2}$$

$$= \epsilon° - (0.00987)(1.01)$$

$$\epsilon° = -0.240\,V$$

(c) $\Delta G° = -\epsilon°nF$

$$= +(0.240\,V)(6\,mol\,e^-)(96,500\,C/mol\,e^-) = 139\,kJ$$

(d) $\Delta G° = -RT\,\ln K$

$\ln K = -\Delta G°/RT$

$$= -(139,000\,J)/(8.31\,J/mol\cdot K)(298\,K) = -56.1$$

$K = 4 \times 10^{-25}$

13. This is the same problem as the prior problem, but not stated in parts.

14.
$$\epsilon = \epsilon° - \frac{RT}{nF}\,\ln Q$$

$$\epsilon = \frac{-\Delta G°}{nF} - \frac{RT}{nF}\,\ln Q$$

$$\epsilon = \frac{+RT}{nF}\,\ln K - \frac{RT}{nF}\,\ln Q = \frac{RT}{nF}\,\ln\frac{K}{Q}$$

$$\ln(K/Q) = \epsilon nF/RT$$

15. $\Delta G° = -817.9\,kJ$, as calculated in Supplementary Problem 5.

196

$$\Delta G^\circ = -RT \ln K$$

$$\ln K = -\frac{(-817,900\,J)}{(8.31\,J/K)(298\,K)} = 330$$

$$\log K = (\ln K)/(\ln 10) = 330/(2.303) = 143$$

$$K = 10^{143}$$

This huge value of K corresponds to the very large magnitude of ΔG°.

16. $\Delta G^\circ = -RT \ln K = -\epsilon^\circ n F$

$$\ln K = \frac{\epsilon^\circ n F}{RT} = \frac{(-0.00100\,V)(2)(96,500\,C)}{(8.31\,J/K)(298\,K)} = -0.0779$$

$$K = 0.925$$

17. (a) For 2 mol of $CH_4(g)$:

$$2\,CH_4(g) + 3\,O_2(g) \rightarrow 2\,CO(g) + 4\,H_2O(l)$$

$$\Delta G^\circ = \Delta G_f^\circ(\text{products}) - \Delta G_f^\circ(\text{reactants})$$

$$= 2\Delta G_f^\circ(CO) + 4\Delta G_f^\circ(H_2O) - 2\Delta G_f^\circ(CH_4) + 3\Delta G_f^\circ(O_2)$$

$$= 2(-137.2\,kJ) + 4(-237.13\,kJ) - 2(-50.8\,kJ) - 3(0\,kJ)$$

$$= -1121.3\,kJ$$

$$\Delta G^\circ = -RT \ln K$$

$$\ln K = \frac{1,121,300\,J}{(8.31\,J/K)(298\,K)} = 453$$

$$\log K = (\ln K)/(\ln 10) = 453/2.303 = 197$$

$$K = 10^{197}$$

(b) For 1 mol of $CH_4(g)$:

$$CH_4(g) + 1.5\,O_2(g) \rightarrow CO(g) + 2\,H_2O(l)$$

$$\Delta G^\circ = \Delta G_f^\circ(\text{products}) - \Delta G_f^\circ(\text{reactants})$$

$$= \Delta G_f^\circ(CO) + 2\Delta G_f^\circ(H_2O) - \Delta G_f^\circ(CH_4) + 1.5\Delta G_f^\circ(O_2)$$

$$= (-137.2\,kJ) + 2(-237.13\,kJ) - (-50.8\,kJ) - 1.5(0\,kJ)$$

$$= -560.7\,kJ$$

$$\Delta G° = -RT \ln K$$

$$\ln K = \frac{560{,}700\,J}{(8.31\,J/K)(298\,K)} = 226$$

$$\log K = (\ln K)/(\ln 10) = 226/2.303 = 98.1$$

$$K = 1 \times 10^{98}$$

18. Within rounding error, the answer of part (b) is the square root of that in part (a), as predictable from the equilibrium constant expressions:

(a) $\quad K = \dfrac{[CO]^2}{[CH_4]^2[O_2]^3}$ $\qquad$ (b) $K = \dfrac{[CO]}{[CH_4][O_2]^{1.5}}$

Chapter 13

Miscellaneous Problems

Use the Periodic Table When Necessary.

1. The key to dimensional analysis is knowing the units associated with each quantity or constant. What are the units of (*a*) molar mass? (*b*) density? (*c*) molarity? (*d*) specific heat? (*e*) mole fraction? (*f*) vapor pressure of water? (*g*) entropy? (*h*) freezing-point lowering constant? (*i*) *R*, the ideal gas law constant?

2. What can we calculate from each of the following sets of data? Tell the law or principle that we would use.

   (*a*) Density of a gas at a given temperature and pressure
   (*b*) Molarity of a solution and its volume
   (*c*) Mass of each reactant in a reaction and mass of all but one product
   (*d*) Density of a solution and its mass
   (*e*) Mass and volume of a sample
   (*f*) Formula of a compound and the atomic masses of its elements
   (*g*) Percent composition of a compound and the atomic masses of its elements
   (*h*) Empirical formula of a compound and its molar mass
   (*i*) Concentration and volume of one reactant in a titration and volume of the other
   (*j*) Concentration and volume of both reactants in a reaction

3. Tell how we can calculate each of the following:

   (*a*) Molar mass from a formula
   (*b*) Molar mass from experimental data (several methods)
   (*c*) Molecular formula from empirical formula and molar mass
   (*d*) Density of a sample of liquid
   (*e*) Density of a particular gas at known pressure and temperature

4. Calculate the density of ammonia gas at 373 K and 1.00 atm.
5. Calculate the freezing point of a solution containing 1.76 g of a solute (MM = 133 g/mol) in 50.0 g of cyclohexane ($k_f = 20.0°C/m$, f.p. = 6.5°C).
6. Calculate the molar mass of an acid, HA, if 4.30 g neutralizes 25.72 mL of 4.000 M NaOH.
7. (a) Calculate the number of grams of magnesium in 14.0 g of $Mg(ClO_3)_2$. (b) Calculate the percentage of magnesium in $Mg(ClO_3)_2$.
8. Calculate the number of liters in 2.50 m^3.
9. Write the balanced chemical equation for the reaction of 50.00 mL of 2.110 M H_3PO_4 with 43.00 mL of 2.453 M NaOH.
10. Calculate the freezing point of a solution of 0.0200 mol of K_2SO_4 in 0.350 kg of water.
11. Calculate the volume of oxygen collected over water at 25°C and 110.0 kPa barometric pressure prepared by thermal decomposition of 1.70 g of HgO. ($P_{H_2O} = 3.2$ kPa)
12. Calculate the volume of 12.5 g of H_2O at 25°C and 1.00 atm pressure.
13. Calculate the mass of $KClO_3$ that must be decomposed to produce 3.00 L of oxygen at STP.
14. Calculate the molar mass of a 21.1-g sample of a gas that occupies 10.7 L at 25°C and 121 kPa.
15. Two light sources emit energy. The first emits 2.0×10^6 photons of energy 1.0×10^{-14} J/photon, and the second 1.0×10^6 photons of energy 2.0×10^{-14} J/photon. (a) Which source, if either, emits more energy? (b) Which source, if either, emits photons with lower wavelength?
16. Calculate the mass of K_2SO_4 that will be produced by the reaction of 156 g of (aqueous) KOH and 262 mL of 3.00 M H_2SO_4.
17. Calculate, to the proper number of significant digits, the density of a liquid if a beaker plus 25.00 mL of the liquid has a mass of 107.4 g, and the beaker itself has a mass of 52.00 g.
18. Calculate the mass of Li_2CO_3 that will be produced by the reaction of 38.8 mL of 5.00 M LiOH and 1.46 L of CO_2 at 25°C and 1.00 atm pressure.
19. Calculate the mass of copper metal produced from $CuCl_4^{2-}$ solution by passage of a 4.15-A current for 12.0 hours.

$$CuCl_4^{2-}(aq) + Fe(s) \rightarrow Cu(s) + 4\,Cl^-(aq) + Fe^{2+}(aq)$$

20. State in another way the fact that red light consists of photons

having less energy than photons of violet light. Use the word "wavelength," but do not use the word "energy."

21. Can all light be detected by the human eye? Explain.

22. Consider the general reaction: $A + 2 B \rightleftharpoons 2 C$, with $K = 1.00 \times 10^{-6}$. Calculate the equilibrium concentrations of A, B, and C after 1.20 mol of A and 2.30 mol of B are dissolved in 1.00 L of solution and allowed to come to equilibrium.

23. Calculate the enthalpy change for the reaction of 19.6 g of CO with oxygen to yield carbon dioxide: $\Delta H_f(CO) = -110$ kJ/mol; $\Delta H_f(CO_2) = -393$ kJ/mol

24. Calculate the molar mass of ammonia at 373 K and 1.00 atm.

25. Determine the new volume of a 1.000-L sample of gas if the pressure was increased at constant temperature (a) 13.0%. (b) 100%.

26. Calculate the final temperature after 43.9 g of a metal alloy ($c = 0.451$ J/g·°C) at 59.3°C is immersed in 242 g of water at 14.5°C.

27. Calculate the standard potential of the cell produced when the copper(II)/copper half-cell ($\epsilon° = 0.34$ V) is combined with the iron(III)/iron(II) half-cell ($\epsilon° = 0.77$ V).

28. Calculate the number of mercury atoms in 1.50 L of mercury, (density $= 13.6$ g/mL).

29. Calculate the heat involved in the conversion of 51.7 g of liquid water at 50.3°C to ice at -5.4°C : $c_{liquid} = 4.184$ J/g·°C; $c_{ice} = 2.089$ J/g·°C; $\Delta H_{fusion} = 335$ J/g.

30. Calculate the value of $\Delta G°$ for a reaction with the equilibrium constant equal to 4.44 at 25°C.

31. Calculate the value of ϵ for the reduction of permanganate ion to manganese(II) ion in a solution of 0.100 M H^+, 0.750 M Mn^{2+}, and 1.11 M MnO_4^- ($\epsilon° = 1.51$ V).

32. Calculate the pH of 1.00 L of a buffer solution containing 0.175 mol of $HC_2H_3O_2$ and 0.175 mol of $KC_2H_3O_2$ after 0.010 mol of HCl is added to the solution. Assume no change in volume.

33. A 1.00-L solution contains 0.0200 mol of a weak acid, HA. The solution has an osmotic pressure of 0.528 atm at 25°C. Calculate the value of K_a for the acid.

34. Calculate the free energy change for a reaction at 80°C in which the enthalpy change is 14.88 kJ and the entropy change is 7.44 J/K.

35. Calculate the hydrogen ion concentration of solutions with the following pH values: (a) 3.96; (b) 13.31; (c) 1.55.

36. Calculate the concentration of nitrate ions in a solution produced by diluting 15.00 mL of 2.000 M $Al(NO_3)_3$ to 50.00 mL.

37. Show that the following data are in accord with the law of multiple proportions:

	Compound A	Compound B
Element 1	40.0%	52.2%
Element 2	6.67%	13.0%
Element 3	53.3%	34.8%

38. Calculate the molecular formula of a compound consisting of 40.0% carbon, 6.67% hydrogen, and 53.3% oxygen if 10.00 g of the compound in 100.0 g of water freezes at $-1.24°C$.

39. Calculate the time it takes ammonia to diffuse across a room if it takes sulfur trioxide 4.20 minutes to diffuse there under the same conditions.

40. Calculate the osmotic pressure at $25°C$ of an aqueous solution of a nonionic solute with molar mass 80.0 g/mol that freezes at $-4.11°C$. The density of the solution is 1.11 g/mL.

41. Calculate the value of K for the reaction $A + B \rightleftharpoons C$, in which ΔG is -25.3 kJ when $[A] = 2.00$ M, $[B] = 4.00$ M, and $[C] = 0.100$ M.

42. Which of the following solutions require the use of a hydrolysis constant to calculate its pH? (a) 0.100 mol NaOH + 0.100 mol $HC_2H_3O_2$. (b) 0.100 mol HCl + 0.100 mol $NaC_2H_3O_2$. (c) 0.100 mol HCl + 0.100 mol NH_3. (d) 0.100 mol NaOH + 0.200 mol $HC_2H_3O_2$. (e) 0.100 mol HCl + 0.200 mol $NaC_2H_3O_2$. (f) 0.100 mol HCl + 0.200 mol NH_3.

43. (a) When 4.03 g of element A and 11.8 g of element B completely react with each other to produce the only compound of A and B, what mass of the compound is produced? (b) What law allows calculation of this quantity? (c) When 4.03 g of element A and 15.5 g of element B are treated with each other, what mass of the compound is produced? (d) What law allows calculation of this quantity?

44. Calculate the mass of magnesium chloride produced and the mass of excess reactant left unreacted after 92.4 g of magnesium carbonate is treated with 86.1 g of hydrochloric acid (in water).

45. Calculate the mole fraction of 1.62 M sucrose ($C_{12}H_{22}O_{11}$) in water if the density of the solution is 1.21 g/mL.

46. After a 2.50 m solution containing 0.500 mol of solute was added to a 1.40 m solution of the same two substances, a 1.95 m solution was produced. Calculate the mass of solvent in the second solution. (*Hint*: Let x equal the mass of solvent in the final solution.)

47. Calculate the average kinetic energy of a gas molecule in a sample at $25°C$.

48. Calculate the root mean square speed (u) of the nitrogen molecules in a sample of the gas at 298 K.

49. Calculate the freezing point of 0.0100 m aqueous NaCl.

50. Determine the number of moles of nitrogen atoms in 146 g of ammonium nitrate.

51. Calculate the potential of a one-electron electrochemical reaction with a value of $\Delta G° = -15.2$ kJ and a value of $\Delta G = -16.6$ kJ.

Solutions to Miscellaneous Problems

1. (a) grams/mole; (b) grams/milliliter, kilograms/liter, and others; (c) moles/liter; (d) joules/gram·degree; (e) no units; (f) torr, atmospheres, or kilopascals; (g) joules/kelvin or joules/mol·kelvin; (h) degrees/molal; (i) L·atm/mol·K, L·kPa/mol·K, or other equivalent sets of units.

2. (a) The molar mass. Assume a volume, calculate the number of moles of the gas (with the ideal gas law, for example), and divide that into the number of grams in the selected volume of gas.

(b) The number of moles of solute. Definition of molarity.

(c) The mass of the last product. The law of conservation of mass.

(d) The volume of the solution. Definition of density.

(e) Density. Definition of density.

(f) The molecular mass (molar mass) and also the percent composition. Multiply the numbers of atoms of each element in a formula unit by the atomic mass, sum these values to get the molecular mass. Divide the mass of each *element* (not each atom) by the total mass and multiply by 100% to get the percent composition.

(g) The empirical formula. Convert percentages to masses and then to moles; calculate the simplest mole ratio.

(h) The molecular formula. Divide the molecular mass (the molar mass in amu) by the empirical formula mass to get the number of empirical formula units in a molecule, then multiply the subscripts in the empirical formula by that value.

(i) The concentration of the other reactant, assuming that a balanced chemical equation is available.

(j) The mole ratio, and thus the balanced equation. For example, it might be necessary to do this type of calculation to determine if one or two hydrogen atoms in H_2SO_4 have been replaced in its reaction with NaOH:

$$H_2SO_4(aq) + NaOH(aq) \rightarrow NaHSO_4(aq) + H_2O(l)$$

$$H_2SO_4(aq) + 2\,NaOH(aq) \rightarrow Na_2SO_4(aq) + 2\,H_2O(l)$$

3. (a) Add the atomic masses for each atom (not merely each element), and report the sum in grams per mole.
   (b) Divide the mass by the number of moles. The number of moles may be calculated with the ideal gas law, colligative properties data, titration data, or other methods.
   (c) Add the atomic masses for each atom in the empirical formula and divide the sum into the molecular mass. That yields the number of empirical formula units per molecule. Multiply each subscript in the empirical formula (including the assumed values of one) by that number to get the molecular formula.
   (d) Divide the mass of the sample by the volume.
   (e) Assume a volume (like 1.00 L), calculate the number of moles in that sample, and divide the number of grams in the sample by that number of moles.

4. Assume 1.00 L of gas. The number of moles of ammonia is

$$n = \frac{PV}{RT} = \frac{(1.00\ \text{atm})(1.00\ \text{L})}{(0.0821\ \text{L·atm/mol·K})(373K\,)} = 0.0327\ \text{mol}$$

The mass of that quantity of ammonia is

$$0.0327\ \text{mol}\left(\frac{17.0\ \text{g}}{1\ \text{mol}}\right) = 0.556\ \text{g}$$

The density of ammonia under these conditions is therefore 0.556 g/L.

5. The number of moles of solute is

$$1.76\ \text{g}\left(\frac{1\ \text{mol}}{133\ \text{g}}\right) = 0.0132\ \text{mol}$$

The molality is $(0.0132\ \text{mol})/(0.0500\ \text{kg}) = 0.264\ m$

$$\Delta t_f = k_f m = (20.0°C/m)(0.264\ m) = 5.28°C$$

Freezing point $= 6.5°C - 5.28°C = 1.2°C$

6. We can immediately calculate the number of millimoles of NaOH:

$$25.72 \text{ mL}\left(\frac{4.000 \text{ mmol}}{1 \text{ mL}}\right) = 102.9 \text{ mmol}$$

Since they react in a 1 : 1 mol ratio, that is also the number of millimoles of HA. Its molar mass is

$$(4.30 \text{ g})/(0.1029 \text{ mol}) = 41.8 \text{ g/mol}$$

7. *(a)* $14.0 \text{ g Mg(ClO}_3)_2\left(\dfrac{1 \text{ mol Mg(ClO}_3)_2}{191 \text{ g Mg(ClO}_3)_2}\right)\left(\dfrac{1 \text{ mol Mg}}{1 \text{ mol Mg(ClO}_3)_2}\right) \times$

$$\left(\frac{24.3 \text{ g Mg}}{1 \text{ mol Mg}}\right) = 1.78 \text{ g Mg}$$

(b) $\dfrac{1.78 \text{ g Mg}}{14.0 \text{ g Mg(ClO}_3)_2} \times 100\% = 12.7\%$

8. $2.50 \text{ m}^3\left(\dfrac{1000 \text{ L}}{1 \text{ m}^3}\right) = 2500 \text{ L} = 2.50 \times 10^3 \text{ L}$

9. The numbers of millimoles of each reactant can easily be calculated:

$$50.00 \text{ mL}\left(\frac{2.110 \text{ mmol}}{1 \text{ mL}}\right) = 105.5 \text{ mmol H}_3\text{PO}_4$$

$$43.00 \text{ mL}\left(\frac{2.453 \text{ mmol}}{1 \text{ mL}}\right) = 105.5 \text{ mmol NaOH}$$

Since there is a 1 : 1 mole ratio, the equation is

$$\text{H}_3\text{PO}_4(aq) + \text{NaOH}(aq) \rightarrow \text{NaH}_2\text{PO}_4(aq) + \text{H}_2\text{O}(l)$$

10. The K_2SO_4 dissociates into three moles of ions (2 mol K^+ and 1 mol SO_4^{2-}) for each mole of salt. The molality of the ions is $(0.0600 \text{ mol})/(0.350 \text{ kg}) = 0.171 \text{ m}$. Neglecting the interionic attractions,

$$\Delta t_f = k_f m = (1.86°\text{C/m})(0.171 \text{ m}) = 0.318°\text{C}$$

The freezing point is $-0.318°\text{C}$ (or perhaps a little higher due to interionic attractions).

11. The pressure of oxygen is

$$P_{\text{O}_2} = P_{\text{barometric}} - P_{\text{H}_2\text{O}} = 110.0 \text{ kPa} - 3.2 \text{ kPa} = 106.8 \text{ kPa}$$

The number of moles of oxygen gas is determined:

$$2\,HgO(s) \rightarrow 2\,Hg(l) + O_2(g)$$

$$1.70\,g\,HgO\left(\frac{1\,mol\,HgO}{216.6\,g\,HgO}\right)\left(\frac{1\,mol\,O_2}{2\,mol\,HgO}\right) = 0.00392\,mol\,O_2$$

The volume of oxygen is then given by the ideal gas law:

$$V = \frac{nRT}{P} = \frac{(0.00392\,mol)(8.31\,L\cdot kPa/mol\cdot K)(298\,K)}{106.8\,kPa} = 0.0909\,L$$

12. Be careful not to use a gas law for water at 25°C and 1.00 atm, where it is a liquid. The volume is found from the mass and density! (We must not only know the rules, but when to use each one!)

$$V = 12.5\,g\left(\frac{1\,mL}{1.00\,g}\right) = 12.5\,mL$$

(The actual density is 0.997 g/mL, but 1.00 g/mL is sufficiently close for most purposes.)

13. $2\,KClO_3(s) \rightarrow 2\,KCl(s) + 3\,O_2(g)$

$$3.00\,L\,O_2\left(\frac{1\,mol\,O_2\,(at\,STP)}{22.4\,L\,O_2}\right)\left(\frac{2\,mol\,KClO_3}{3\,mol\,O_2}\right)\left(\frac{122\,g\,KClO_3}{1\,mol\,KClO_3}\right)$$

$$= 10.9\,g\,KClO_3$$

14. Use the ideal gas law (or the molar mass and the combined gas law) to determine the number of moles of gas. Then divide the mass by that number of moles.

$$n = \frac{PV}{RT} = \frac{(121\,kPa)(10.7\,L)}{(8.31\,L\cdot kPa/mol\cdot K)(298\,K)} = 0.523\,mol$$

$$MM = (21.1\,g)/(0.523\,mol) = 40.3\,g/mol$$

15. (a) The total energy of each source is the product of the number of photons times the energy of each:
First source: $E_1 = (2.0 \times 10^6\,photons)(1.0 \times 10^{-14}\,J/photon)$
$$= 2.0 \times 10^{-8}\,J$$
Second source: $E_2 = (1.0 \times 10^6\,photons)(2.0 \times 10^{-14}\,J/photon)$
$$= 2.0 \times 10^{-8}\,J$$

Both sources emit the same *total* energy.

(b) The wavelength is inversely proportional to the energy of *each* photon, so the second source (with higher-energy photons) has the shorter wavelength.

16. $2 KOH(aq) + H_2SO_4(aq) \rightarrow K_2SO_4(aq) + 2 H_2O(l)$

$$156\,g\ KOH\left(\frac{1\ mol\ KOH}{56.0\,g\ KOH}\right) = 2.79\ mol\ KOH$$

$$0.262\,L\ H_2SO_4\left(\frac{3.00\ mol\ H_2SO_4}{1\,L\ H_2SO_4}\right) = 0.786\ mol\ H_2SO_4$$

Less than 1 mol of H_2SO_4 will react with less than 2 mol of KOH, but there is more than 2 mol of KOH present, so the H_2SO_4 is limiting.

$$0.786\ mol\ H_2SO_4\left(\frac{1\ mol\ K_2SO_4}{1\ mol\ H_2SO_4}\right)\left(\frac{174\,g\ K_2SO_4}{1\ mol\ K_2SO_4}\right) = 137\,g\ K_2SO_4$$

17. The mass of the liquid is $107.4\,g - 52.00\,g = 55.4\,g$. The density is therefore $(55.4\,g)/(25.00\ mL) = 2.22\ g/mL$.

   If you do this problem in one step, the subtraction still yields a value with three significant digits, so the density has only three significant digits.

18. $2\ LiOH(aq) + CO_2(g) \rightarrow Li_2CO_3(aq) + H_2O(l)$

$$0.0388\,L\ LiOH\left(\frac{5.00\ mol\ LiOH}{1\,L\ LiOH}\right) = 0.194\ mol\ LiOH$$

$$n = \frac{PV}{RT} = \frac{(1.00\ atm)(1.46\ L)}{(0.0821\ L\cdot atm/mol\cdot K)(298\ K)} = 0.0597\ mol\ CO_2$$

There is more than twice as much LiOH present as CO_2, so the CO_2 is limiting:

$$0.0597\ mol\ CO_2\left(\frac{1\ mol\ Li_2CO_3}{1\ mol\ CO_2}\right)\left(\frac{74.0\,g\ Li_2CO_3}{1\ mol\ Li_2CO_3}\right) = 4.42\,g\ Li_2CO_3$$

19. $12.0\,hours\left(\frac{3600\ s}{1\ hour}\right)\left(\frac{4.15\ C}{1\ s}\right)\left(\frac{1\ mol\ e^-}{96,500\ C}\right)\left(\frac{1\ mol\ Cu}{2\ mol\ e^-}\right) \times$

$$\left(\frac{63.5\,g\ Cu}{1\ mol\ Cu}\right) = 59.0\,g\ Cu$$

20. "Red light has a longer wavelength than violet light does."

21. Only "visible light" can be detected by the human eye. The word "light" is often used to mean the entire electromagnetic spectrum, so not all light can be detected by the human eye.

22.

	A	+	2 B	⇌	2 C
Initial concentration (M)	1.20		2.30		0.000
Change due to reaction (M)	x		$2x$		$2x$
Equilibrium concentrations (M)	$1.20 - x$		$2.30 - 2x$		$2x$

$$K = \frac{[C]^2}{[A][B]^2} = \frac{(2x)^2}{(1.20)(2.30)^2} = 1.00 \times 10^{-6}$$

$$4x^2 = 6.35 \times 10^{-6}$$

$$x = 1.26 \times 10^{-3}$$

$$[C] = 2x = 2.52 \times 10^{-3} \text{ M}$$

$$[A] = 1.20 - 1.26 \times 10^{-3} = 1.20 \text{ M}$$

$$[B] = 2.30 - 2(1.26 \times 10^{-3}) = 2.30 \text{ M}$$

The approximations are valid.

23. $2\,CO(g) + O_2(g) \rightarrow 2\,CO_2(g)$

The number of kilojoules is calculated for reaction of 2 mol of CO:

$$\Delta H = 2\Delta H_f(CO_2) - 2\Delta H_f(CO) = 2(-393 \text{ kJ}) - 2(-110 \text{ kJ})$$

$$= -566 \text{ kJ}$$

For 19.6 g of CO:

$$\Delta H = 19.6 \text{ g CO} \left(\frac{1 \text{ mol CO}}{28.0 \text{ g CO}}\right)\left(\frac{-566 \text{ kJ}}{2 \text{ mol CO}}\right) = -198 \text{ kJ}$$

24. The molar mass of ammonia is 17.0 g/mol (the sum of the atomic masses of all four atoms), no matter what the conditions.

25.

(a)

	P	V
1	$1.00P_1$	1.000 L
2	$P_2 = 1.13P_1$	V_2

$$V_2 = \frac{P_1V_1}{P_2} = \frac{(1.00P_1)(1.000 \text{ L})}{1.13P_1} = 0.885 \text{ L}$$

Note that the increase in pressure of 13.0% did *not* decrease the volume 13.0%, but only 11.5%. The ratio 1.00/1.13 is not equal to 87.0/100.

(b) In the same manner,

$$V_2 = \frac{(1.00P_1)(1.00 \text{ L})}{2.00P_1} = 0.500 \text{ L}$$

Note that the increase in pressure of 100.0% did *not* decrease the volume 100.0%.

26. $q = 0 = m_{water}\, c_{water}\, \Delta t_{water} + m_{metal}\, c_{metal}\, \Delta t_{metal}$

$0 = (242\ g)(4.184\ J/g \cdot °C)(t - 14.5°C) +$

$$(43.9\ g)(0.451\ J/g \cdot °C)(t - 59.3°C)$$

$t = 15.4°C$

27. The two reduction half-cells are

$$Cu^{2+}(aq) + 2\ e^- \rightarrow Cu(s) \qquad\qquad 0.34\ V$$
$$Fe^{3+}(aq) + e^- \rightarrow Fe^{2+}(aq) \qquad\qquad 0.77\ V$$

We reverse the equation with the lower potential, and change the sign of the potential:

$$Cu(s) \rightarrow Cu^{2+}(aq) + 2\ e^- \qquad\qquad -0.34\ V$$

We multiply the other equation by 2 to get equal numbers of electrons, without changing the potential:

$$2\ Fe^{3+}(aq) + 2\ e^- \rightarrow 2\ Fe^{2+}(aq) \qquad\qquad 0.77\ V$$

All that is left to do is to add these equations, and add the corresponding potentials:

$$Cu(s) + 2\ Fe^{3+}(aq) \rightarrow Cu^{2+}(aq) + 2\ Fe^{2+}(aq) \qquad 0.43\ V$$

28. $1.50\ L\left(\dfrac{1000\ mL}{1\ L}\right)\left(\dfrac{13.6\ g}{1\ mL}\right)\left(\dfrac{1\ mol\ Hg}{200.6\ g}\right)\left(\dfrac{6.02 \times 10^{23}\ atoms}{1\ mol}\right)$

$$= 6.12 \times 10^{25}\ atoms$$

29. The total heat involved is the sum of the heats of three steps:

$$q = mc\,\Delta t = (51.7\ g)(4.184\ J/g \cdot °C)(-50.3°C) = -10.9\ \ kJ$$

$$51.7\ g\left(\dfrac{-335\ J}{1\ g}\right) = -17.3\ \ kJ$$

$$q = mc\,\Delta t = (51.7\ g)(2.089\ J/g \cdot °C)(-5.4°C) = -0.58\ kJ$$

The total heat required is
$(-10.9\ kJ) + (-17.3\ kJ) + (-0.58\ kJ) = -28.8\ kJ$

30. $\Delta G° = -RT\ \ln K$
$= -(8.31\ J/K)(298\ K)\ \ln(4.44) = -3.69 \times 10^3\ J = -3.69\ kJ$

31. $MnO_4^-(aq) + 8 H^+(aq) + 5 e^- \rightarrow Mn^{2+}(aq) + 4 H_2O(l)$

$$\epsilon = \epsilon^\circ - \frac{0.0592}{5} \log \frac{[Mn^{2+}]}{[H^+]^8[MnO_4^-]}$$

$$= 1.51 - \frac{0.0592}{5} \log \frac{(0.750)}{(0.100)^8(1.11)} = 1.51 - 0.0927 = 1.42 \, V$$

32. HCl reacts with $C_2H_3O_2^-$ to give $HC_2H_3O_2$ (in addition to that already present). If the acid and base react completely:

	$HCl(aq)$	+	$C_2H_3O_2^-(aq)$	$\rightarrow$	$HC_2H_3O_2(aq)$	+ $Cl^-(aq)$
Beginning number of moles	0.010		0.175		0.175	
Change due to reaction (mol)	0.010		0.010		0.010	
End of acid-base reaction (mol)	0.000		0.165		0.185	

Now the equilibrium reaction is considered:

	$H_2O(l)$ +	$HC_2H_3O_2(aq)$	$\rightleftharpoons$	$C_2H_3O_2^-(aq)$	+ $H_3O^+(aq)$
Initial concentrations (M)		0.185		0.165	0.000
Change due to reaction (M)		x		x	x
Equilibrium concentrations (M)		0.185 − x		0.165 + x	x

Neglecting x when added to or subtracted from a larger quantity yields

$$K_a = \frac{[C_2H_3O_2^-][H_3O^+]}{[HC_2H_3O_2]} = \frac{(0.165)x}{0.185} = 1.8 \times 10^{-5}$$

$$x = [H_3O^+] = 2.0 \times 10^{-5} \, M$$

$$pH = 4.70$$

33. The osmotic pressure gives the total concentration of solute particles—molecules plus ions:

$$\pi V = nRT$$

$$n = \frac{(0.528 \text{ atm})(1.00 \text{ L})}{(0.0821 \text{ L·atm/mol·K})(298 \text{ K})} = 0.0216 \text{ mol of particles}$$

With 0.0200 mol of acid and 0.0216 mol of particles (un-ionized acid molecules, hydronium ions, and anions), the increase in concentration corresponds to the number of each type of ion produced, since two ions are produced from each molecule. There is 0.0016 mol/L of HA ionized, as seen in the following table:

	HA	= H$^+$	+ A$^-$	Total solute particles
Initial concentrations (M)	0.0200	0.0000	0.0000	0.0200
Change due to reaction (M)	−0.0016	+0.0016	+0.0016	+0.0016
Final concentrations (M)	0.0184	0.0016	0.0016	0.0216

$$K_a = \frac{(0.0016)^2}{0.0184} = 1.4 \times 10^{-4}$$

It does not matter that H_2O is not included in the equation, since the H_2O molecules are solvent particles, not solute particles.

34. $\Delta G = \Delta H - T\Delta S = 14.88 \text{ kJ} - (353 \text{ K})(0.00744 \text{ kJ/K}) = 12.25 \text{ kJ}$

35. (a) 1.1×10^{-4} M   (b) 4.9×10^{-14} M   (c) 2.8×10^{-2} M

36. Number of millimoles of nitrate ion in initial solution:

$$15.00 \text{ mL} \left(\frac{2.000 \text{ mmol Al(NO}_3)_3}{1 \text{ mL}} \right) \left(\frac{3 \text{ mmol NO}_3{}^-}{1 \text{ mmol Al (NO}_3)_3} \right)$$

$$= 90.00 \text{ mmol NO}_3{}^-$$

In final solution:

$$\frac{90.00 \text{ mmol NO}_3{}^-}{50.00 \text{ mL}} = 1.800 \text{ M NO}_3{}^-$$

37. Changing each percentage to grams and dividing each by the magnitude of the mass of element 2 yields:

	Compound A	Compound B
Element 1	6.00 g	4.02 g
Element 2	1.00 g	1.00 g
Element 3	7.99 g	2.68 g

The ratio of masses of element 1 is $3:2$, and that of element 3 is $3:1$.

38. $40.0 \text{ g C}\left(\dfrac{1 \text{ mol C}}{12.0 \text{ g C}}\right) = 3.33 \text{ mol C}$

$6.67 \text{ g H}\left(\dfrac{1 \text{ mol H}}{1.008 \text{ g H}}\right) = 6.62 \text{ mol H}$

$53.3 \text{ g O}\left(\dfrac{1 \text{ mol O}}{16.0 \text{ g O}}\right) = 3.33 \text{ mol O}$

The mole ratio is $1:2:1$, and the empirical formula is CH_2O.

$$\Delta t_f = mk_f = 1.24°C = m(1.86°C/m)$$

$$m = 0.667 \text{ m}$$

In 1.000 kg of solvent, there are 0.667 mol of solute and 100.0 g of solute, so the molar mass is $(100.0 \text{ g})/(0.667 \text{ mol}) = 150 \text{ g/mol}$, and the molecular mass is 150 amu. The empirical formula mass is 30.0 amu, so the molecular formula is $C_5H_{10}O_5$.

39.

$$\frac{r_{SO_3}}{r_{NH_3}} = \sqrt{\frac{MM_{NH_3}}{MM_{SO_3}}} = \sqrt{\frac{17.0 \text{ g/mol}}{80.0 \text{ g/mol}}} = 0.461$$

$$r_{SO_3} = (0.461)r_{NH_3}$$

The *rate* of diffusion of SO_3 is less than that of NH_3, so it takes the NH_3 *less time*:

$$(0.461)(4.20 \text{ minutes}) = 1.94 \text{ minutes}$$

40. $m = \Delta t_f/k_f = (4.11°C)/(1.86°C/m) = 2.21 \text{ m}$
Assuming that we have 1.000 kg of solvent, we then have 2.21 mol of solute.

$$2.21 \text{ mol}\left(\frac{80.0 \text{ g}}{1 \text{ mol}}\right) = 177 \text{ g solute} = 0.177 \text{ kg solute}$$

There is 1.177 kg of solution, and

$$1.177 \text{ kg}\left(\frac{1 \text{ L}}{1.11 \text{ kg}}\right) = 1.06 \text{ L of solution}$$

The osmotic pressure is thus

$$\pi = \frac{nRT}{V} = \frac{(2.21 \text{ mol})(0.0821 \text{ L·atm/mol·K})(298 \text{ K})}{1.06 \text{ L}} = 51.0 \text{ atm}$$

41. We must find $\Delta G°$ first, because that is related to K:

$$\Delta G = \Delta G° + RT \ \ln \frac{[C]}{[A][B]}$$

$$= \Delta G° + (8.31 \text{ J/K})(298 \text{ K}) \ \ln \frac{0.100}{(2.00)(4.00)}$$

$$-25.3 \text{ kJ} = \Delta G° - 10.9 \text{ kJ}$$

$$\Delta G° = -14.4 \text{ kJ}$$

$$\ln K = \frac{-\Delta G°}{RT} = \frac{+14,400 \text{ J}}{(8.31 \text{ J/K})(298 \text{ K})} = 5.81$$

$$K = 3.3 \times 10^2$$

42. (a) 0.100 mol NaOH + 0.100 mol $HC_2H_3O_2$ produces 0.100 mol $NaC_2H_3O_2$, which requires a hydrolysis constant.

(b) 0.100 mol HCl + 0.100 mol NaC_2H_3O produces (NaCl plus) 0.100 mol $HC_2H_3O_2$, a weak acid problem which does not require a hydrolysis constant.

(c) 0.100 mol HCl + 0.100 mol NH_3 produces 0.100 mol NH_4Cl, which requires a hydrolysis constant.

(d) 0.100 mol NaOH + 0.200 mol $HC_2H_3O_2$ produces 0.100 mol $NaC_2H_3O_2$ and leaves 0.100 mol $HC_2H_3O_2$ in excess, a buffer solution problem.

(e) 0.100 mol HCl + 0.200 mol $NaC_2H_3O_2$ produces 0.100 mol $HC_2H_3O_2$ and leaves 0.100 mol $NaC_2H_3O_2$ in excess, a buffer solution problem.

(f) 0.100 mol HCl + 0.200 mol NH_3 produces 0.100 mol NH_4Cl and leaves 0.100 mol NH_3 in excess, a buffer solution problem.

43. (a) 15.8 g. (b) The law of conservation of mass. (All of the reactants combine to form the product.) (c) 15.8 g. (d) The law of definite proportions. (The same ratio of elements must be present in the compound. Some of the B is left unreacted.)

44. $MgCO_3 + 2 \ HCl \rightarrow MgCl_2 + CO_2 + H_2O$

$$92.4 \text{ g } MgCO_3\left(\frac{1 \text{ mol } MgCO_3}{84.3 \text{ g } MgCO_3}\right) = 1.10 \text{ mol } MgCO_3$$

$$86.1 \text{ g HCl} \left(\frac{1 \text{ mol HCl}}{36.5 \text{ g HCl}} \right) = 2.36 \text{ mol HCl}$$

The quantity of HCl required to react with 1.10 mol $MgCO_3$ is

$$1.10 \text{ mol } MgCO_3 \left(\frac{2 \text{ mol HCl}}{1 \text{ mol } MgCO_3} \right) = 2.20 \text{ mol HCl}$$

Since there is more HCl than that present, the $MgCO_3$ is limiting.

$$1.10 \text{ mol } MgCO_3 \left(\frac{1 \text{ mol } MgCl_2}{1 \text{ mol } MgCO_3} \right) \left(\frac{95.2 \text{ g } MgCl_2}{1 \text{ mol } MgCl_2} \right) = 105 \text{ g } MgCl_2$$

2.36 mol HCl present $-$ 2.20 mol reacting $= 0.16$ mol excess HCl

$$0.16 \text{ mol HCl} \left(\frac{36.5 \text{ g HCl}}{1 \text{ mol HCl}} \right) = 5.8 \text{ g HCl excess}$$

45. Assume 1.00 L of solution. There are thus 1.62 mol of sucrose and 1210 g of solution. The mass of the sucrose is

$$1.62 \text{ mol } C_{12}H_{22}O_{11} \left(\frac{342 \text{ g } C_{12}H_{22}O_{11}}{1 \text{ mol } C_{12}H_{22}O_{11}} \right) = 554 \text{ g } C_{12}H_{22}O_{11}$$

The mass of the water is 1210 g $-$ 554 g $= 660$ g $= 0.66$ kg.
The molality of the sucrose is (1.62 mol)/(0.66 kg) $= 2.5$ m

46. The first solution contained 0.500 mol of solute and

$$0.500 \text{ mol solute} \left(\frac{1 \text{ kg solvent}}{2.50 \text{ mol solute}} \right) = 0.200 \text{ kg solvent}$$

The final solution contains x kg of solvent and

$$x \text{ kg solvent} \left(\frac{1.95 \text{ mol solute}}{1 \text{ kg solvent}} \right) = 1.95x \text{ mol solute}$$

The second solution thus contained $(x - 0.200)$ kg solvent and $(1.95x - 0.500)$ mol solute. Its molality is

$$1.40 \text{ m} = \frac{(1.95x - 0.500) \text{ mol solute}}{(x - 0.200) \text{ kg solvent}}$$

$$1.95x - 0.500 = 1.40(x - 0.200)$$

$$x = 0.40 \text{ kg}$$

The mass of solvent in the second solution is thus
0.40 kg − 0.200 kg = 0.20 kg.

47. $\overline{KE} = \dfrac{3RT}{2N} = \dfrac{3(8.31 \text{ J/K})(298 \text{ K})}{2(6.02 \times 10^{23})} = 6.17 \times 10^{-21} \text{ J}$

48. The average kinetic energy is obtained from the prior problem. The value of u is obtained from $\overline{KE} = \frac{1}{2}mu^2$

$$u = \sqrt{\dfrac{2\overline{KE}}{m}} = \sqrt{\dfrac{2(6.17 \times 10^{-21} \text{ J})}{(28.0 \text{ amu})}\left(\dfrac{6.02 \times 10^{26} \text{ amu}}{1 \text{ kg}}\right)} = 515 \text{ m/s}$$

49. Since NaCl is ionic, the solution is 0.0200 m in ions. Since the solution is dilute, the ions act more or less independently.

$$\Delta t_f = k_f m = (1.86°\text{C/m})(0.0200 \text{ m}) = 0.0372°\text{C}$$

$$t_f = -0.0372°\text{C}$$

50. $146 \text{ g NH}_4\text{NO}_3\left(\dfrac{1 \text{ mol NH}_4\text{NO}_3}{80.0 \text{ g NH}_4\text{NO}_3}\right)\left(\dfrac{2 \text{ mol N atoms}}{1 \text{ mol NH}_4\text{NO}_3}\right) = 3.65 \text{ mol N}$

51.

$$\Delta G = -\epsilon n F \qquad \text{(The value of } \Delta G° \text{ does not matter.)}$$

$$\Delta G = -16,600 \text{ J} = -\epsilon(1 \text{ mol e}^-)(96,500 \text{ C/mol e}^-)$$

$$\epsilon = 0.172 \text{ V}$$

List of Important Equations

The student must know the conditions, if any, under which each equation is applicable.

Chapter 2

$$d = m/V$$

$$t = (F - 32°)/1.8$$

$$T = t + 273°$$

$$\text{KE} = \tfrac{1}{2} mv^2$$

Chapter 6

$$M = \text{(moles of solute)/(liter of solution)}$$

$$m = \text{(moles of solute)/(kilogram of solvent)}$$

$$X_A = \text{(moles of A)/(total number of moles)}$$

Chapter 7

$$P_1 V_1 = P_2 V_2 \qquad \text{(constant } T)$$

$$V_1/T_1 = V_2/T_2 \qquad \text{(constant } P)$$

$$P_1 V_1/T_1 = P_2 V_2/T_2$$

$$PV = nRT$$

$$\frac{P_i}{P_{\text{total}}} = \frac{n_i}{n_{\text{total}}} \qquad \text{(constant } V \text{ and } T)$$

$$\frac{V_i}{V_{\text{total}}} = \frac{n_i}{n_{\text{total}}} \qquad \text{(constant } P \text{ and } T)$$

$$\frac{r_1}{r_2} = \sqrt{\frac{MM_2}{MM_1}}$$

$$\overline{KE} = 3RT/2N$$

Chapter 8

$$q = \Delta H = mc\Delta t$$

$$\Delta H = \Delta H_f(\text{products}) - \Delta H_f(\text{reactants})$$

Chapter 9

$$\epsilon = \epsilon^\circ - \frac{0.0592}{n} \log \frac{[C]^c[D]^d}{[A]^a[B]^b}$$

Chapter 10

$$K = \frac{[C]^c[D]^d}{[A]^a[B]^b}$$

$$K_a = \frac{[A^-][H_3O^+]}{[HA]} \qquad \text{or} \qquad K_a = \frac{[A^-][H^+]}{[HA]}$$

$$K_b = \frac{[BH^+][OH^-]}{[B]}$$

$$K_w = [H_3O^+][OH^-] = 1.0 \times 10^{-14}$$

$$pH = -\log[H_3O^+] \qquad \text{or} \qquad pH = -\log[H^+]$$

Chapter 11

$$P_A = X_A P_A^\circ$$

$$\Delta P_A = X_B P_A^\circ \quad \text{(two components)}$$

$$\Delta t_f = k_f m$$

$$\Delta t_b = k_b m$$

$$\pi V = nRT$$

Chapter 12

$$\Delta S^o = S^o(\text{products}) - S^o(\text{reactants})$$

$$\Delta G = \Delta H - T\Delta S$$

$$\Delta G = \Delta G_f(\text{products}) - \Delta G_f(\text{reactants})$$

$$\Delta G = \Delta G^o + RT \ln Q$$

$$\Delta G^o = -RT \ln K$$

$$\Delta G = -\epsilon nF$$

Constants with Values That Must Be Remembered

Constant	Identification	Value	Chapter Introduced
d_{H_2O}	density of water (4°C)	1.00 g/mL	2
	mass of ^{12}C atom	12.0000 amu	4
N	Avogadro's number	6.02×10^{23}	4
R	ideal gas law constant	0.0821 L·atm/mol·K	7
R	ideal gas law constant	8.31 L·kPa/mol·K	7
R	ideal gas law constant	8.31 J/K	12
	standard temperature	0°C = 273 K	7
	standard pressure	1 atm, 101.3 kPa, 760 torr	7
c_{H_2O}	specific heat of water	4.184 J/g·°C	8
$\epsilon^o_{H_2}$	potential of standard hydrogen electrode	0.000 V	9
	Nernst equation constant	0.0592 V	9
K_w	water ionization constant	1.0×10^{-14}	10
pH_{H_2O}	pH of pure water	7.00	10

Glossary

Absolute temperature. A temperature on the Kelvin temperature scale (with zero equal to $-273°C$).

Acid dissociation constant. The equilibrium constant for the reaction of a weak acid with water to form its anion and hydronium (hydrogen) ion.

Activity. Tendency to react chemically.

Ampere. The unit of electric current, equal to 1 coulomb per second.

amu. Atomic mass unit.

Atomic mass. The weighted average of the masses of the naturally occurring mixture of isotopes of an element.

Atomic mass unit. The unit of atomic, molecular, and formula masses.

Atomic weight. Atomic mass.

Avogadro's number. The number of carbon-12 atoms in exactly 12 g of carbon-12: 6.02×10^{23}.

Base dissociation constant. The equilibrium constant for the reaction of a weak base with water to form its cation and hydroxide ion.

Boiling-point elevation. The rise of the boiling point of a solution (compared to the pure solvent) due to the presence of a solute.

Boyle's law. At constant temperature, the volume of a given sample of gas is inversely proportional to its pressure.

Bronsted theory. A theory that defines acids as proton donors and bases as proton acceptors.

Buffer solution. A solution of a weak acid or base plus its conjugate; it resists change in its pH even on addition of strong acid or base.

Charles' law. The volume of a given sample of gas at constant pressure is directly proportional to its *absolute* temperature.

Colligative properties. Properties of a solution that depend on the nature of the solvent and the concentration of solute particles.

Combined gas law. The volume of a given sample of gas is directly proportional to its *absolute* temperature and inversely proportional to its pressure.

Concentration. The quantity of solute per unit quantity of solution or solvent. (See molarity, molality, mole fraction.)

Condensation. The conversion of a gas to a liquid or solid.

Coulomb. The unit of electric charge.

Cubic meter. The unit of volume in SI.

Dalton's law of partial pressures. The sum of the partial pressures of the gases in a mixture is equal to the total pressure of the mixture.

Δ **(Greek delta).** Change in.

ΔG. Free energy change.

ΔG_f°. Standard free energy of formation.

ΔH. Enthalpy change.

ΔH_f°. Standard enthalpy of formation.

Density. The mass per unit volume of a sample.

Diffusion. The passage of gas molecules of one substance through the molecules of other gaseous substances in a mixture of gases.

Dimensional analysis. A system to solve problems using the units to determine whether to multiply or divide to convert a quantity to an equal or equivalent quantity.

Effusion. The passage of gas molecules through the pores of a porous container.

Electrode. (1) The electrical conductor (usually a metal or graphite) at which the electric current in a circuit is changed from a movement of electrons to or from a movement of ions. (2) A half-cell.

Electrolysis cell. A cell in which electric current is used to cause chemical reaction.

Empirical formula. The simplest formula for a compound, in which the subscripts are at their lowest integral ratios.

End point. The point in a titration at which the indicator signals an end to the process (at a point as close to the stoichiometric ratio of reactants as possible to that in the balanced equation).

Enthalpy change. The heat of a process carried out at constant pressure with no work other than expansion against the atmosphere.

Entropy. A measure of the randomness of a system.

ϵ. The symbol for the potential of a cell.

Equilibrium. A state in which two exactly opposite processes occur at equal rates, resulting in no *net* change.

Equilibrium constant expression. The mathematical equation including the constant ratio of concentrations of products to concentrations of reactants, all raised to the appropriate powers, at equilibrium.

Excess quantity. The quantity of one reagent greater than required by the balanced chemical equation to react with all of another reagent.

Factor label method. Dimensional analysis.

Formula mass. The sum of the atomic masses of each *atom* in a formula.

Formula unit. The collection of bonded atoms represented by the formula of a substance. For example, the formula unit of SCl_2 contains one sulfur atom and two chlorine atoms.

Free energy change. The free energy of the products of a process minus that of the reactants, equal to the enthalpy change minus the product of the absolute temperature times the entropy change.

Free energy of formation. The free energy change in a process of forming a substance in its standard state from its elements in their standard states.

Freezing-point depression. The lowering of the freezing point of a solution (compared to that of the pure solvent) due to the presence of a solute.

Fusion. Melting.

Galvanic cell. A cell in which a chemical reaction can produce an electric current; a voltaic cell.

Graham's law. The rate of effusion or diffusion of a gas is inversely proportional to the square root of its molar mass.

Gram. The basic unit of mass in the metric system.

Half-cell. The combination of oxidizing and reducing agents that make half a galvanic cell.

Heat capacity. The heat required to raise a specified quantity (usually one gram or one mole) of a substance $1°C$.

Heat of sublimation. The heat required to change a specified quantity (one gram or one mole) of a substance from solid to gas.

Hess's law. When chemical reactions or physical processes are combined, their enthalpy changes can be added to yield the enthalpy change of the total process.

Hydrogen electrode. The half-cell consisting of hydrogen gas and hydrogen ions with an inert electrode such as platinum.

Hydronium ion. H_3O^+.

Ideal gas law. $PV = nRT$.

Indicator (acid-base). A compound that is one color in acid solution and a different color in base solution, used to signal the end point of an acid-base titration.

Joule. The SI unit of energy.

Kelvin. The unit of the absolute (Kelvin) temperature scale.

Kinetic molecular theory. The theory that explains the behavior of gases (and other phases) in terms of the properties of their molecules.

KMT. Kinetic molecular theory.

Law of combining volumes. The ratio of the volumes of gases in a given chemical reaction, all measured at the same temperature and pressure, are in the ratio of the coefficients of the balanced chemical equation.

Law of conservation of mass. In any chemical reaction (or physical change), mass cannot be created or destroyed.

Law of definite proportions. Each (pure) compound is composed of the same percentage by mass of its elements. For example, every sample of pure water is 88.8% oxygen and 11.2% hydrogen by mass.

Law of multiple proportions. For two or more compounds consisting of the same elements, for a given mass of one of the elements, the masses of the other element(s) are in a small, integral ratio.

LeChatelier's principle. If a stress is applied to a system at equilibrium, the equilibrium will tend to shift in an effort to reduce the stress.

Limiting quantity. The quantity of one reactant in a chemical reaction that is not sufficient to react with all the other reactant(s) present.

Liter. The unit of volume in the (older) metric system.

Meter. The basic unit of length in the metric system.

Metric system. The system of units used by scientists in which multiples or subdivisions of units are powers of 10 times the unit, and all such multiples or subdivisions are designated by the same prefix no matter what unit is involved.

Millimole. One-thousandth of a mole.

Molal. The unit of molality.

Molality. The number of moles of solute per kilogram of solvent in a solution.

Molar. The unit of molarity.

Molar mass. The formula mass of any substance, expressed in grams per mole.

Molar volume. The volume of one mole of a gas measured at standard temperature and pressure: 22.4 L.

Molarity. The number of moles of solute per liter of solution.

Mole. The unit of chemical quantity; Avogadro's number of formula units.

Mole fraction. The number of moles of a substance in a solution divided by the total number of moles in the solution.

Molecular formula. The formula for a molecule of a substance, telling the ratio of the number of moles of each element to the number of moles of the substance.

Molecular mass. The sum of the atomic masses of the atoms in a molecule.

Nernst equation. The mathematical equation relating the potential of a cell or half-cell to its standard potential.

Nonvolatile. Not (easily) convertible to the gaseous state.

Of. Multiplied by. (For example, "20 is one-half *of* 40" means $20 = \frac{1}{2} \times 40$.)

Osmotic pressure. The pressure exerted by a solution because of the presence of a solute.

Per. Divided by.

pH. $-\log [H^+]$.

Phase. The solid, liquid, or gaseous state.

Physical equilibrium. A state in which two opposite physical processes occur at equal rates, resulting in no *net* change.

π. The symbol for osmotic pressure.

Potential. The "driving force" of an electrochemical reaction.

Precedence. The required order of operations in a mathematical expression or equation. Operations with higher precedence are done before operations with lower precedence.

Proton acceptor. A compound that accepts hydrogen ions from another substance (a Bronsted base).

Proton donor. A compound that provides hydrogen ions to another substance (a Bronsted acid).

Raoult's law. The vapor pressure of a component in a solution is equal to the mole fraction of that component times the vapor pressure of the pure substance.

S. Entropy.

$S°$. Standard absolute entropy.

Scientific notation. The form of a number stated as a coefficient of 1 or more but less than 10, times 10 to an integral power.

SI, system internationale. The modern version of the metric system. (Differences from the older metric system include the cubic meter as the unit of volume rather than the liter, and pascals used for pressure.)

Significant digit. A digit in a properly reported value that indicates the precision with which a measurement was made.

Significant figure. Significant digit.

Specific heat. The heat required to raise one gram of a substance 1°C.

Standard. The defined quantity against which all other quantities are compared. For example, the *standard* of mass (in SI as well as legally in the United States) is the kilogram, whereas the gram is the *unit* of mass.

Standard absolute entropy. The entropy of a substance compared to its entropy when crystalline and at 0 K.

Standard enthalpy of formation. The enthalpy change in a process of forming a substance in its standard state from its elements in their standard states.

Standard exponential notation. Scientific notation.

Standard free energy of formation. Free energy of formation when each substance is at unit activity.

Standard half-cell. A half-cell in which each substance is at unit activity.

Standard reduction potential. The reduction potential of a half-cell in which each substance is at unit activity.

Standard state. A state in which each substance is at unit activity.

Standard temperature and pressure. 0°C and 1 atm pressure.

Stoichiometry. The study of the quantitative relationships among substances in a chemical reaction.

STP. Standard temperature and pressure.

Sublimation. The passage of a substance from the solid state directly to the gaseous state.

System internationale. SI—the modern version of the metric system.

Titration. The technique in which a measured volume of one solution is treated with a measured volume of another, in which the known molarity of one solution allows the calculation of the molarity of the other.

Unit activity. Pure solids and liquid, 1 M solute, and/or gas at 1 atm pressure.

Vaporization. Passage of a liquid into the gas phase.

Vapor-pressure lowering. The reduction of the vapor pressure of a solution (compared to the pure solvent) due to the presence of the solute.

Volt. The unit of potential.

Voltaic cell. A galvanic cell.

Water dissociation constant. K_w, the equilibrium constant for the reaction of water with itself to produce hydronium and hydroxide ions.

Weighted average. The average of several sets of values taking into account the number of items in each set. For example, the atomic mass of an element is a weighted average of the masses of its isotopes, taking into account the relative abundance of each isotope.

Index

The items in this index that have (t) attached refer to tables, those with (f) refer to figures, and those with (g) refer to the glossary.

About the Author

David Goldberg, Ph. D., is Professor of Chemistry at Brooklyn College. He is author or coauthor of 15 books, over 30 journal articles, and numerous bookelets for student use.